The Five Disciplines of Intelligence Collection

Mark M. Lowenthal
Robert M. Clark

EDITORS

SAGE | CQPRESS

Los Angeles | London | New Delhi
Singapore | Washington DC | Boston

Los Angeles | London | New Delhi
Singapore | Washington DC | Boston

FOR INFORMATION:

CQ Press

An Imprint of SAGE Publications, Inc.

2455 Teller Road

Thousand Oaks, California 91320

E-mail: order@sagepub.com

SAGE Publications Ltd.

1 Oliver's Yard

55 City Road

London, EC1Y 1SP

United Kingdom

SAGE Publications India Pvt. Ltd.

B 1/I 1 Mohan Cooperative Industrial Area

Mathura Road, New Delhi 110 044

India

SAGE Publications Asia-Pacific Pte. Ltd.

3 Church Street

#10-04 Samsung Hub

Singapore 049483

Acquisitions Editor: Suzanne Flinchbaugh

Editorial Assistant: Davia Grant

Production Editor: David. C. Felts

Typesetter: Hurix Systems Pvt. Ltd.

Copy Editor: Megan Markanich

Proofreader: Annie Lubinsky

Indexer: Joan Shapiro

Cover Designer: Karine Hovsepian

Marketing Manager: Amy Whitaker

Printed in the United States of America

A catalog record of this book is available from the Library of Congress.

ISBN 978-1-4522-1763-5 (pbk.)

This book is printed on acid-free paper.

MIX
Paper from
responsible sources
FSC® C014174

15 16 17 18 19 10 9 8 7 6 5 4 3 2 1

The Five Disciplines of Intelligence Collection

CQ Press, *an imprint of SAGE, is the leading publisher of books, periodicals, and electronic products on American government and international affairs. CQ Press consistently ranks among the top commercial publishers in terms of quality, as evidenced by the numerous awards its products have won over the years. CQ Press owes its existence to Nelson Poynter, former publisher of the St. Petersburg Times, and his wife Henrietta, with whom he founded Congressional Quarterly in 1945. Poynter established CQ with the mission of promoting democracy through education and in 1975 founded the Modern Media Institute, renamed The Poynter Institute for Media Studies after his death. The Poynter Institute (www.poynter. org) is a nonprofit organization dedicated to training journalists and media leaders.*

In 2008, CQ Press was acquired by SAGE, a leading international publisher of journals, books, and electronic media for academic, educational, and professional markets. Since 1965, SAGE has helped inform and educate a global community of scholars, practitioners, researchers, and students spanning a wide range of subject areas, including business, humanities, social sciences, and science, technology, and medicine. A privately owned corporation, SAGE has offices in Los Angeles, London, New Delhi, Singapore, and Boston, in addition to the Washington, D.C., office of CQ Press.

To the men and women of the U.S. Intelligence Community

SAGE was founded in 1965 by Sara Miller McCune to support the dissemination of usable knowledge by publishing innovative and high-quality research and teaching content. Today, we publish more than 750 journals, including those of more than 300 learned societies, more than 800 new books per year, and a growing range of library products including archives, data, case studies, reports, conference highlights, and video. SAGE remains majority-owned by our founder, and after Sara's lifetime will become owned by a charitable trust that secures our continued independence.

Los Angeles | London | Washington DC | New Delhi | Singapore | Boston

Brief Contents

Detailed Contents

Preface

Collection is one of the bedrock activities in the intelligence business. We both have written about the subject in other books. Mark Lowenthal devotes a chapter to collection in his book *Intelligence: From Secrets to Policy*. Robert Clark has written *The Technical Collection of Intelligence* and *Intelligence Collection*, a systems approach to the intelligence collection disciplines (INTs). But what has been missing from intelligence literature is a text that addresses intelligence collection in toto—one that fully characterizes, in accessible language, the five INTs that are recognized within the U.S. Intelligence Community (IC): Open Source Intelligence (OSINT), Human Intelligence (HUMINT), Signals Intelligence (SIGINT), Geospatial Intelligence (GEOINT), and Measurement and Signature Intelligence (MASINT). In this book, we describe, in nontechnical terms, the definition, history, process, management, and future trends of each collection source. A major advantage for our readers is that the chapter authors are past or current senior practitioners of the INT they discuss. Therefore, each chapter is more than an academic description of the INT; it is a rich assessment from a professional who understands how his particular type of collection fits within the larger context of the U.S. IC.

The Five Disciplines of Intelligence Collection will be of value to professors who teach undergraduate- and graduate-level collegiate courses in intelligence, national security, or political science. It will benefit collection practitioners and managers who must work cooperatively across collection "stovepipes." It will provide a full picture for all-source analysts who need to better understand how to task and collaborate with their collection partners, as well as collectors who want to understand what happens beyond their stovepipe. Finally, customers of intelligence who read the text will be more aware of the capabilities and limitations of collection when the results are cited to support intelligence conclusions.

Acknowledgments

There are several people to whom we wish to express our gratitude. Darryl Murdock, one of the coauthors of the Geospatial Intelligence (GEOINT) chapter, first came up with the idea of writing this book. All chapter authors were selected on the basis of their exceptional careers and their breadth of knowledge about intelligence collection. The product bears out those choices, and we appreciate their dedication to the project.

A number of people in the U.S. Intelligence Community (IC) and academia have provided wisdom that we have incorporated. Our special thanks go to Bill Huntington, former director of the Defense Human Intelligence (HUMINT) Service, who provided extensive guidance on the HUMINT chapter. We both appreciate the untiring efforts of Robert Clark's wife, Abigail, who lent her skilled hand to the editing process. We are especially grateful to reviewers within and outside the U.S. IC who have contributed their time to improving the text. We especially want to thank Charisse Kiino at CQ Press for her unstinting support and the staff at SAGE and CQ Press for shaping the finished product.

All statements of fact, opinion, or analysis expressed are those of the chapter authors and do not reflect the official positions or view of the Central Intelligence Agency (CIA) or any other U.S. government agency. Nothing in the contents should be construed as asserting or implying U.S. government authentication of information or agency endorsement of the authors' views. This material has been reviewed by the CIA and other IC agencies to prevent the disclosure of classified information.

Mark M. Lowenthal
Reston, Virginia

Robert M. Clark
Wilmington, North Carolina

About the Editors

Mark M. Lowenthal has over thirty-nine years experience in U.S. intelligence. Dr. Lowenthal has served as the Assistant Director of Central Intelligence for Analysis and Production, Vice Chairman for Evaluation on the National Intelligence Council, staff director of the House Permanent Select Committee on Intelligence, office director and as a Deputy Assistant Secretary of State in the State Department's Bureau of Intelligence and Research (INR), and Senior Specialist in U.S. Foreign Policy at the Congressional Research Service, Library of Congress. Dr. Lowenthal has written extensively on intelligence and national security issues, including five books and over 100 articles or studies. His book *Intelligence: From Secrets to Policy* (6th ed., 2014) is the standard college and graduate school text on the topic. Dr. Lowenthal received his BA from Brooklyn College and his PhD in history from Harvard University. He is an adjunct professor at the Johns Hopkins University; he was an adjunct at Columbia University from 1993–2007. Currently, Dr. Lowenthal is President and CEO of the Intelligence & Security Academy, an education and consulting firm.

Robert M. Clark currently is an independent consultant performing threat analyses for the U.S. Intelligence Community (IC). He is also a faculty member of the Intelligence and Security Academy and a professor of intelligence studies at the University of Maryland University College. He previously was a faculty member of the director of National Intelligence (DNI) *Intelligence Community Officers' Course* and course director of the DNI *Introduction to the Intelligence Community* course. Dr. Clark served as a U.S. Air Force electronics warfare officer and intelligence officer, reaching the rank of lieutenant colonel. At the Central Intelligence Agency (CIA), he was a senior analyst and group chief responsible for managing analytic methodologies. Clark holds an SB from MIT, a PhD in electrical engineering from the University of Illinois, and a JD from George Washington University. He has previously authored three books: *Intelligence Analysis: A Target-Centric Approach* (4th edition, 2013), *The Technical Collection of Intelligence* (2010), and *Intelligence Collection* (2014).

About the Contributors

Michael Althoff served nearly three decades as a collection management officer, analyst, supervisor, and executive manager at the Central Intelligence Agency (CIA), focused primarily on managing the collection and dissemination of intelligence on Russia, the states of the former Soviet Union and both Eastern and Western Europe. This breadth of experience provided him with extensive knowledge of the intelligence process, from the generation of requirements to their assignment to relevant collectors and ultimately to the dissemination of the product to appropriate consumers within the U.S. Intelligence Community (IC). He also acquired considerable insight into IC collection priorities, intelligence sharing, and their associated problems by dealing with IC members and foreign partners during both domestic and overseas assignments. Such experience further heightened his appreciation of the significance of counterintelligence to the Human Intelligence (HUMINT) discipline. Mr. Althoff earned a BA in history from LaSalle University and an MA in history from Penn State University. He also served in the U.S. Navy as a Russian linguist.

Eliot A. Jardines is senior director for cyber, analytics, and social media consulting at one of the largest software firms in the world. In 2005, Mr. Jardines was appointed as the inaugural assistant deputy director of National Intelligence for Open Source (ADDNI/OS), in response to recommendations from the 9-11 and WMD Commissions. As the U.S. Intelligence Community (IC) senior Open Source Intelligence (OSINT) official, Mr. Jardines was responsible for developing a strategic direction, establishing policy, and overseeing fiscal resources for OSINT across sixteen intelligence agencies. In addition, he served as the IC senior document and media exploitation officer, as well as provided oversight to the Open Source Center (OSC), the National Media Exploitation Center, and the National Virtual Translation Center. Mr. Jardines has testified before the U.S. Congress on intelligence and homeland security issues and has done numerous media appearances to include C-SPAN and the CBS Evening News.

John L. Morris was functional manager of Measurement and Signature Intelligence (MASINT) for the U.S. Intelligence Community (IC), where he became widely known as "Mr. MASINT" by successfully advocating MASINT as a major intelligence source. His persistence, strong advocacy, and technical leadership were key to MASINT becoming operationally relevant to

U.S. forces in combat in the late 1990s. After honing his tradecraft at the National Air and Space Intelligence Center (NASIC) in Dayton, Ohio, for over twenty-five years, Mr. Morris attained a leadership role in every nonnuclear MASINT discipline—even developing new ones, such as laser intelligence (LASINT)—and directed energy weapons intelligence. He was called to Washington, DC, in late 1995 to organize, equip, and lead the fledgling U.S. MASINT community as the director of the Central MASINT Office (CMO). With over forty years of specialized experience at various IC agencies (U.S. Air Force, Defense Intelligence Agency [DIA], Central Intelligence Agency [CIA], and National Geospatial-Intelligence Agency [NGA]), Mr. Morris is viewed today as the definitive community expert in Advanced Geospatial Intelligence (AGI), overhead persistent infrared (OPIR), MASINT, technical intelligence, activity-based intelligence (ABI), and intelligence integration. A native of Louisiana and graduate of Louisiana Tech University and SMU, Mr. Morris continues to mentor young specialists and advise many senior leaders.

Darryl Murdock is vice president of professional development at the United States Geospatial Intelligence Foundation. A twenty-year geosciences business professional and remote sensing scientist, Mr. Murdock began his career as a U.S. Army aviation officer, serving as platoon leader and battalion flight operations officer. After his service, Mr. Murdock cofounded Highland Geographic, a geographic information systems (GIS) and remote sensing applications development company. He later served as a Light Detection and Ranging (LiDAR) project manager and image scientist at Eastman Kodak and as an account manager at Esri, where he oversaw imagery-related geospatial software programs, business development, and client management within the U.S. Intelligence Community (IC). Mr. Murdock earned his BS in human factors from the U.S. Military Academy, and his MS and PhD in environmental resources engineering from the State University of New York College of Environmental Science and Forestry. He is a member of the American Society for Photogrammetry and Remote Sensing and the American Society of Civil Engineers and is also a commercial pilot.

William M. Nolte is research professor at the School of Public Policy, University of Maryland. He also serves on the university's national security advisory committee. He completed a thirty-year career with the federal government in early 2006, as the first chancellor of the National Intelligence University system. He previously served in analytic and executive positions with the National Security Agency (NSA), the National Intelligence Council, and the Office of the Director of National Intelligence (ODNI) Council. He has been a research fellow at the Hoover Institution and lectures regularly at the Naval Postgraduate School, the Army War College, and at other colleges and universities. Mr. Nolte is a member of the Council on Foreign Relations, former chair of the intelligence committee of the Armed Forces Communications Electronics Association, and a member of the executive committee of the Intelligence and National Security Alliance. He serves on the editorial boards of the *International Journal of Intelligence and Counterintelligence* and *Intelligence and National Security.* He holds an AB from La Salle University and a PhD from the University of Maryland, both in history.

Abbreviations and Acronyms

ABI	Activity-based intelligence
ABM	Anti-ballistic missile
ACIC	U.S. Air Force Aeronautical Chart and Information Center
ACINT/ ACOUSTINT	Acoustic intelligence
ACSI	Assistant chief of staff of intelligence (now the A2)
ADC	Air Defense Command
ADDNI/OS	Assistant Deputy Director of National Intelligence for Open Source
AFIT	Air Force Institute of Technology
AFSC	Air Force Systems Command
AGI	Advanced geospatial intelligence
ARPA	Advanced Research Projects Agency
BBC	British Broadcasting Corporation
CBR	Chemical, biological, and radiological
CBRNE	Chemical, biological, radiological, nuclear, and explosive
C4ISR	Command, control, communications, computers, intelligence, surveillance, and reconnaissance
CI	Counterintelligence
CIA	Central Intelligence Agency
CIO	Central Imagery Office
CMO	Central MASINT Office
CMTCO	Central MASINT Technology Coordination Office
CNN	Cable News Network
COCOMs	Combatant commands
COMINT	Communications intelligence
COMIREX	Committee on Imagery Requirements and Exploitation
COMSEC	Communications security
CONOP	Concept of operations
COSPO	Community Open Source Program Office
CPB	Charged particle beam
D&D	Denial and deception

DCI	Director of Central Intelligence
DCID	DCI Directive
DCRI	*Direction Centrale du Renseignement Interieur*
DDII	Deputy director of National Intelligence for Intelligence Integration
DDO	Directorate of Operations
DDP	Directorate of Plans
DEA	U.S. Drug Enforcement Administration
DEFSMAC	Defense Special Missile and Astronautics Center
DEW	Directed energy weapons
DGSE	*Directoire Generale de la Securite Exterieure*
DHS	U.S. Department of Homeland Security
DIA	Defense Intelligence Agency
DIGO	Defence Imagery and Geospatial Organization
DIJE	Defence Intelligence Joint Environment
DMA	Defense Mapping Agency
DNI	Director of National Intelligence
DoD	U.S. Department of Defense
DoDD	Department of Defense Directive
DOE	U.S. Department of Energy
DSP	Defense Support Program
DST	*Direction de la Surveillance du Territoire*
EEI	Essential element of information
ELINT	Electronic intelligence
EMP	Electromagnetic pulse
EO	Electro-optical
EO	Executive Order
EUCOM	U.S. European Command
FBI	Federal Bureau of Investigation
FBIS	Foreign Broadcast Information Service
FBMS	Foreign Broadcast Monitoring Service
FCC	Federal Communications Commission
FISINT	Foreign instrumentation signals intelligence
FMV	Full motion video
FSB	Federal Security Service of the Russian Federation
FTD	Foreign Technology Division
GCHQ	Government Communications Headquarters
GDIP	General Defense Intelligence Program
GEOINT	Geospatial Intelligence

GIS	Geographic information systems
GPS	Global Positioning System
GRU	*Glavnoe Razvedyvatelnoye Upravleniye*, or Main Intelligence Administration
HPMW	High-powered microwave
HUMINT	Human Intelligence
IA	Information assurance
I&W	Indications and warning
IC	U.S. Intelligence Community
ICBM	Intercontinental ballistic missiles
ICD	Intelligence Community Directive
IDF	Israeli Defense Forces
IED	Improvised explosive device
IMINT	Imagery Intelligence
IMS	International Monitoring System
INR	Bureau of Intelligence and Research (State Department)
INT	Intelligence collection discipline
IOSWG	International Open Source Working Group
IPB	Intelligence Preparation of the Battlefield
IRBM	intermediate-range ballistic missiles
IRINT	Infrared intelligence
IRTPA	Intelligence Reform and Terrorism Prevention Act of 2004
ISO	International Organization for Standardization
IT	Information technology
IUSS	Integrated Undersea Surveillance System
JARIC	Joint Air Reconnaissance Intelligence Centre
KGB	*Komitet Gosudarstvennoi Bezopasnosti*
LASINT	Laser intelligence
LiDAR	Light Detection And Ranging
MASCOM	MASINT Committee
MASDRs	Measurement and Signature Data Requirements
MASINT	Measurement and Signature Intelligence
MCIA	Marine Corps Intelligence Activity
MI5	Military Intelligence, Section 5
MOVEINT	Movement intelligence
MSIC	Missile and Space Intelligence Center
MSS	Ministry of State Security China
NASA	National Aeronautics and Space Administration
NASIC	National Air and Space Intelligence Center

NATO	North Atlantic Treaty Organization
NBC	Nuclear, biological, and chemical
NCMI	National Center for Medical Intelligence
NCS	National Clandestine Service
NCTC	National Counterterrorism Center
NFIP	National Foreign Intelligence Program
NGA	National Geospatial-Intelligence Agency
NHCD	National HUMINT Collection Directive
NHRTC	National HUMINT Requirements Tasking Center
NIIRS	National Imagery Interpretability Rating Scale
NIM	National intelligence manager
NIMA	National Imagery and Mapping Agency
NIPF	National Intelligence Priorities Framework
NIR	Near infrared
NMICC	National Military Intelligence Collection Center
NMO	National MASINT Office
NOSE	National Open Source Enterprise (now the OSE)
NPIC	National Photographic Interpretation Center
NRO	National Reconnaissance Office
NSA	National Security Agency
NSC	National Security Council
NSG	National System for Geospatial Intelligence
NTM	National technical means
NUCINT	Nuclear intelligence
NVTC	National Virtual Translation Center
ODNI	Office of the Director of National Intelligence
OGC	Open Geospatial Consortium
ONI	Office of Naval Intelligence
OPIR	Overhead persistent infrared
OPSEC	Operational security
OPTINT	Optical intelligence
ORCON	Originator control
OSC	Open Source Center
OSCAR-MS	Open Source Collection Acquisition Requirements Management System
OSE	Open Source Enterprise (formerly the NOSE)
OSINT	Open Source Intelligence
OSIS	Open Source Information System
OSO	Open source officer

OSS	Office of Strategic Services
OSW	Open Source Works
OTH	Over the horizon
P&E	Processing and exploitation
PDB	President's Daily Brief
PLA	People's Liberation Army
POWs	Prisoners of war
RADINT	Radar intelligence
R&D	Research and development
RCS	Radar cross section
RDT&E	Research, development, test, and evaluation
RF	Radio frequency
RFI	Request for information
RINT	Unintentional radiation intelligence
ROWG	RADINT and OPTINT Working Group
SALT	Strategic Arms Limitations Talks
S&T	Science and Technology
S&TI	Scientific and technical intelligence
SAR	Synthetic Aperture Radar
SBIRS	Space-Based Infrared System
SIGINT	Signals Intelligence
SIS	Signal Intelligence Service (U.S.); British Secret Intelligence Service or Military Intelligence, Section 6 (MI6)
SMO	Support to military operations
SNA	Social network analysis
SOI	Space object identification
START	Strategic Arms Reduction Treaty
SVR	*Sluzhba Vneshnei Razvedki*/Foreign Intelligence Service (Russian)
TCPED	Tasking, collection, processing, exploitation, and dissemination
TIARA	Tactical Intelligence and Related Activities
TIRA	Tracking and imaging radar
TPED	Tasking, processing, exploitation, and dissemination
UAS	Unmanned Aircraft Systems (same as UAV)
UAV	Unmanned aerial vehicle
USA PATRIOT Act	Uniting and Strengthening America by Providing Appropriate Tools Required to Intercept and Obstruct Terrorism
USCENTCOM	U.S. Central Command

USCIB	U.S. Communications Intelligence Board
USGS	U.S. Geological Survey
USIB	U.S. Intelligence Board
USPACOM	U.S. Pacific Command
USSOCOM	U.S. Special Operations Command
USTRANSCOM	U.S. Transportation Command
UV	Ultraviolet
WARP	Web Access and Retrieval Portal
WBIL	World Basic Information Library
WMD	Weapon of mass destruction

1

Introduction

Intelligence collection is one of the earliest recorded organized human activities, along with war. The earliest writing about intelligence collection dates from the seventh and sixth centuries BCE: Caleb the spy in the Book of Numbers and *The Art of War* by Sun Tzu. It is striking that two cultures, ancient Hebrew and Chinese, geographically remote from one another and undoubtedly unknown to one another, should both discuss the importance of intelligence collection at roughly the same time in an early part of human history. But the precept is elementary at its core—information confers power. Whoever is best at gathering (and exploiting) relevant information tends to win. In the twenty-first century, the U.S. Intelligence Community (IC) is premier in its capabilities for doing both.

Collection in the IC generally refers to five disciplines (or sources): Open Source Intelligence (OSINT), Human Intelligence (HUMINT), Signals Intelligence (SIGINT), Geospatial Intelligence (GEOINT), and Measurement and Signature Intelligence (MASINT). A great deal of mystery and myth surrounds the subject of those sources and the capabilities and uses implied. And many popular perceptions are far afield from reality. That is why we have written this book. Our intention is to give readers an approachable but detailed picture of U.S. intelligence collection capabilities. To that end, each chapter follows a similar construct. We discuss the unique origin and history of the INT, or intelligence collection discipline, which is important to understand in terms of both its development and how it is used today. We discuss the types of intelligence issues that each INT is best suited for and those for which it is of little help. We also discuss issues involved in managing each INT, introducing what is sometimes called the TPED or TCPED process: tasking, collection, processing, exploitation, and dissemination. Each INT, no matter the sources it targets or whether it is a technical or non-technical INT, must go through the TPED process in order to produce intelligence that can be used by analysts and policymakers.

We would also note that although this book is U.S. centric, the United States is not the only nation to use these techniques. Many nations now collect GEOINT from space; many also have SIGINT and some MASINT capabilities. HUMINT and OSINT are the most "democratic" intelligence disciplines, as they require no advanced technology. It is difficult to imagine a state that does not conduct HUMINT and pay attention to OSINT.

A note about this book's organization: we have chosen to address the INTs within their traditional "stovepipes"—meaning in parallel but separated activities, INT by INT. It is the best way to provide a detailed and coherent discussion of core capabilities. It is also important to understand that this is the collectors' view. Let us put some context into how these silos, or specialty organizations, evolved.

Properly speaking, the IC should not be described as an organization. Though it has a titular head (the director of National Intelligence [DNI]), it has many independent components with different organizational structures, roles and missions. The current IC was not planned. It developed into its present form over time as a result of laws, executive decisions, experience, and new capabilities.

The IC developed after World War II and the enactment of the National Security Act of 1947, which created the director of Central Intelligence and the Central Intelligence Agency (CIA). In the following decades, specific organizations were created to collect and process different types of intelligence. For example, the National Security Agency (NSA) focused on SIGINT—especially the collecting, processing, decrypting, and analyzing of adversaries' communications. The CIA Directorate of Operations developed expertise in spotting, recruiting, vetting, tasking, and running clandestine human sources. The National Photographic Interpretation Center (NPIC) became the technical experts in the interpretation of imagery—first from aircraft and then from satellites as well. Again, these specialty organizations operated as information silos and thus became known as stovepipes. Each managed the TPED process of raw intelligence, essentially without interference from the others. At the time, it was an efficient and effective approach to conducting challenging and diverse collection tasks. However, as intelligence collection grew in size and complexity, multiple agencies became involved in each INT. NSA and CIA both collected SIGINT. CIA, the Defense Intelligence Agency (DIA), and the military services all collected HUMINT. And every agency collected OSINT. The result was duplicative efforts, wasted resources, and often budget competition that promoted information hoarding rather than information sharing. Cross-INT management became a major issue, and we discuss this in the closing chapter of the book.

Throughout the chapters of this book, we urge the reader to keep in mind that there are individuals who are responsible for creating strategies and managing overall collection so that the INTs perform in a more integrated manner. The goals are to identify and close gaps in collection and to use the different INTs either to support or to raise questions about one another's collected intelligence—both of which are important analytically. Collectors would be the first to acknowledge that they must understand the overall objectives of the collection effort in order to respond most effectively to the intelligence requirements. Analysts have a role to play here. Without analysis to detail what is missing, to assess the collection and to give it context, collection is much less useful. So analysts need to understand the capabilities of collection systems to be able to apply those to their intelligence issues effectively. The analysts often have the best understanding of the target and therefore can help develop a collection strategy to get the desired intelligence. We need both collection and analysis, as DNI James Clapper has urged in his emphasis on intelligence integration.

Some Important Definitions

All intelligence collection disciplines have their specialized jargon, or short-hand for communicating concepts. Some of these terms are explained in the appropriate chapters of this book. A few terms are common to almost all collection, and their definitions are given next.[1]

> **Clandestine versus covert:** These two terms are often confused by the layman. They tend to be used interchangeably, but they have distinct meanings in intelligence. *Clandestine* refers to something that is secret but attributable; *covert* is secret but not attributable. So, for example, if a case officer is caught trying to recruit a spy, his home country will likely acknowledge their relationship, as they want him returned. That makes him clandestine. But they will never admit what he was doing. That is covert.

> **Collateral:** This term has a very specific meaning in all collection organizations. It refers to material or information that is extrinsic to the organization—usually reporting or intelligence that is produced by another INT. A communications intelligence (COMINT) organization that used imagery to supplement a COMINT report would refer to the imagery as *collateral*. Conversely, a GEOINT organization would refer to any COMINT used in its reporting as collateral.

> **Collection:** This term has two meanings in practice, and both meanings are used in this book. It can mean the entire process, from the planning stage to the dissemination of raw intelligence—which is the meaning that is applied in this book's title. Or it can mean one step in the process where information or something else of intelligence value is physically acquired. The context usually suggests which meaning is relevant.

> **INTs:** Collection disciplines are often called "INTs" as shorthand because they have a common suffix—for example, SIGINT, MASINT, and HUMINT.

> **Multi-INT versus all-source analysis:** The difference between these two terms is a controversial issue. Some authors argue that there is no difference. Others distinguish multi-INT analysis (often called multi-INT fusion) as being the merging, or fusion, of raw intelligence from different collection sources—usually GEOINT and SIGINT—as opposed to all-source, which will involve other INTs as well. The controversy usually arises from the analysis added to the report, with the chief complainants being the all-source analysts or managers who argue that

multi-INT fusion is less nuanced and less able to provide political context and that multi-INT can be confusing to policymakers who cannot discern the difference between the two types of intelligence and analysis. Multi-INT supporters argue that their product is a useful fusion and do not worry about these other issues.

Raw versus finished intelligence: The end product of intelligence collection is referred to as raw intelligence. *Finished intelligence* is the term customarily applied to the product of all-source analysis (described next).

Single-source versus all-source analysis: All-source analysts, as the name implies, make use of all relevant sources of intelligence in producing what is described as *finished intelligence*. But collection organizations also have analysts who specialize in exploiting, analyzing, and reporting the collection product, for example, COMINT analysts, OSINT analysts, and GEOINT analysts. The functions performed by these single-source analysts are described in this book.

Reference

1. Robert M. Clark, *Intelligence Collection* (Washington, DC: CQ Press, 2013).

2

Open Source Intelligence

Eliot A. Jardines

Defining Open Source Intelligence

Open source intelligence (OSINT) is frequently described within intelligence circles as "the source of first resort" due to its ubiquitous nature and its ability to be shared broadly. The use of open sources of information for intelligence purposes dates back to the advent of the printing press, if not earlier. Even in the age of kings, proclamations, decrees, laws, ennoblements, trials, and arrests of retainers, etc., all served as OSINT. Therefore, OSINT can be defined as information that is publicly available to anyone through legal means, including request, observation, or purchase, that is subsequently acquired, vetted, and analyzed in order to fulfill an intelligence requirement.[1]

This definition establishes the bounds within which intelligence activities can be considered to be based on open sources. Although there tends to be some degree of overlap between the various intelligence collection disciplines (INTs), a clear understanding of the bounds of OSINT will aid the reader in understanding not only where it starts and stops but also where it can serve as an enabler of other INTs. The first requirement of the definition is that of being publicly available or, in other words, that any member of the general public would be able to gain access to the information openly through a request, observation or by purchasing the information.

The second requirement is that the intelligence activity be lawful. Any activity that requires an individual to commit trespass, theft, or computer hacking or to engage in social engineering falls outside the scope of OSINT and is illegal. Any of the previously mentioned unlawful activities fall outside the scope of OSINT as the information gleaned from these unlawful acts cannot be considered "publicly available." The concept of public availability is critical to a clear understanding of the bounds of OSINT. In some instances, the distinction can be subtle. For example, an individual's Facebook profile can be considered publicly available if it is wide open. However, should the individual choose to restrict their profile to "friends only," then the profile is no longer publicly available. Any actions then to obtain access, such as sending the individual a friend request or attempting to hack their Facebook account, falls outside the scope of OSINT.

The third key requirement is that the information be properly vetted. Vetting is of critical importance with all INTs but particularly so with OSINT as the information acquired is publicly available and not collected firsthand. That is not to say OSINT is less reliable than other INTs. Indeed, given the plethora of OSINT reporting sources, individuals and organizations who wish to censor or to provide misinformation or disinformation through public channels are increasingly finding that such efforts are futile. A clear example of the difficulty in manipulating open sources can be seen in the failed attempts of Arab governments to suppress or manipulate open sources of information during the Arab Spring in 2011.

A key point is that open sources of information are acquired secondhand. In order for the information to be open source, it must be obtained, organized, and published by an individual (or organization) who has a particular motivation for doing so and publishes with his or her own inherent bias. Open source professionals make a distinction between the concept of traditional intelligence collection and the open source equivalent they term *open source acquisition*. This difference is not merely one of semantics; rather, it is intended to draw a distinction between the other INTs that engage in firsthand collection of intelligence and OSINT where the information is acquired secondhand. In other words, in order for the information to be open source, someone else had to obtain the information firsthand, edit, and publish the information that is subsequently acquired secondhand by the OSINT practitioner.

The final definitional requirement for OSINT is that it be produced to satisfy an intelligence requirement. This focus on the customer's intelligence requirement differentiates OSINT from investigative journalism, academic research, or commercial research. OSINT exploitation is done by intelligence agencies, law enforcement, and competitive intelligence elements of corporations. Other organizations such as political campaigns, labor unions, and personal security (bodyguard) firms have been known to engage in OSINT activities to answer key intelligence questions for their leadership.

What Is Collected with Open Source Intelligence

Officially, the U.S. government defines OSINT by both U.S. public law and Intelligence Community Directive (ICD) 301, which governs U.S. Intelligence Community (IC) OSINT activities. These are defined as intelligence "produced from publicly available information that is collected, exploited, and disseminated in a timely manner to an appropriate audience for the purpose of addressing a specific intelligence requirement."[2] In this instance, the term *collection* was added because of the legal connotation of *acquisition,* which is commonly viewed in law as synonymous with procurement. ICD 301, under Definitions, states the following:

Open source acquisition: The act of gaining possession of, or access to, open source information synonymous with "open source collection." The preferred term is acquisition because by definition open sources are collected and disseminated by others—open source exploiters acquire previously collected and publicly available information second-hand.[3]

At first glance, it would seem counterintuitive that an INT would be built around publicly available information. However, the value of intelligence is not determined by how hard it is to acquire but rather how well it answers an intelligence consumer's request for information (RFI). Indeed, OSINT is the most ubiquitous of the INTs, given the availability of massive amounts of information that are readily available in the Information Age.

However, OSINT is not simply relegated to the confines of cyberspace but rather constitutes a wide variety of media. Beyond the Internet and social media, open sources range from television and radio broadcasts to the more traditional books and magazines, as well as a broad range of public documents that virtually all governments publish. Beyond these common sources are the more exotic but frequently rewarding sources, such as pirate radio broadcasts, pamphlets, and even graffiti. An important, yet frequently overlooked component of OSINT is gray literature, which is defined as materials that are of limited distribution, typically not through mass marketing channels. Examples of gray literature include the following:

Product brochures and case studies	Tracts and pamphlets	Patent documentation and technical reports
Symposia presentations and proceedings	Professional newsletters and reports	Underground newspapers

An illustrative example of the value of gray literature comes from the Defense Intelligence Agency (DIA) relating to the original U.S. invasion of Iraq in 1991. Prior to launching Operation Desert Shield/Storm, the commander of U.S. Central Command (USCENTCOM) requested of his intelligence section a soil composition and trafficability analysis to support General Norman Schwarzkopf's vaunted "left hook" maneuver that required moving an unprecedented number of personnel and equipment through vast stretches of the southern Iraq desert. Given that the United States had been focused on the Cold War, little priority had been given to collecting this type of data on Iraq.

The USCENTCOM planners, lacking the essential data, requested the information from DIA. After an exhaustive search, no such data were found in the agency's holdings. Plans were being developed to drop Special Forces troops deep behind enemy lines to collect the data when a DIA intelligence officer suggested exploring Library of Congress holdings. With the aid of the library's Federal Research Division, DIA was able to find detailed soil composition and trafficability data.

The requisite data was found in a nearly century-old report from an American archaeological expedition that traveled through Iraq on camelback. The archaeologists, being convinced they would find a highly significant site where they could retrieve large artifacts, had taken copious notes on the terrain so as to establish a route for extracting their finds that would support the great size and weight of the anticipated artifacts.

Ultimately, the expedition was not successful, but the team dutifully filed their expedition report with the Library of Congress where it sat largely unused for almost a century.

It was this very detailed data that DIA was able to use as a basis for providing the USCENTCOM planners with viable transportation corridors for the invasion. The soil composition and trafficability data, so critical to mission planning, was ultimately acquired at no risk to either life or operational security (OPSEC). The congressional after-action report on Desert Shield/Storm cited this example, stating, "There is a popular notion that intelligence comes exclusively from listening in on communications, purloining documents and the like. But often intelligence information comes from unlikely sources right under one's nose."[4]

This particular example is instructive in two ways: first, it demonstrates the value of thinking outside the box with regard to gray literature. Frequently, the data one seeks are available through open sources and can be discovered by considering who might have needed such data in the past and contemplating where they would have likely saved that data. Second, it highlights that the value of data changes over time—and does not necessarily decline. Data that have little value today may be an essential element of information (EEI) tomorrow. The implication here is twofold: the open source practitioner should not forsake or undervalue archival research, and the OSINT practitioner should not discard previously acquired data as these may prove useful in the future.

The modern ability to store massive amounts of data cheaply and retrieve that data quickly makes old concerns about storage limitations largely irrelevant. OSINT professionals speak of "recycling" information, as they frequently are able to reuse information previously acquired to meet current RFIs. In an article on lessons learned from the Swedish military's OSINT operations, Mats Björe, a then–senior analyst in the Swedish Armed Forces Headquarters, observed that an effective storage and retrieval system was critical to enable the recycling of open source data that results in time and cost savings. An added benefit of recycling previously acquired OSINT is that it minimizes OPSEC considerations as there is no need to acquire the information for a second time.[5]

The Role of Open Source Intelligence Vis-à-Vis the Other Intelligence Collection Disciplines

OSINT is considered the source of first resort—and in that sense it is a precursor and enabler to the other INTs. One frequently cited metaphor describes OSINT as the outer pieces of a jigsaw puzzle. Dr. Joseph Nye, a Harvard professor and former chairman of the National Intelligence Council employed the metaphor in this manner:

Open source intelligence provides the outer pieces of the jigsaw puzzle, without which one can neither begin nor complete the puzzle. But they are not sufficient of themselves. The precious inner pieces of the puzzle, often the most difficult and most expensive to obtain, come from the traditional intelligence disciplines. Open source intelligence is the critical foundation for the all-source intelligence product, but it cannot ever replace the totality of the all-source effort.[6]

By focusing initial efforts on OSINT exploitation, intelligence professionals can frame the problem set and quickly establish what is known via open sources as well as what intelligence gaps exist. This approach allows collection managers to give better focus to collection requirements while at the same time saving our more limited clandestine collection capabilities for hard targets. In addition, an in-depth OSINT exploitation operation can then specifically queue other INTs.

Examples of OSINT queuing other INTs include the following:

- Human Intelligence (HUMINT)—OSINT frequently assists with identifying targets for recruitment and can provide a detailed dossier on the potential target to aid with the recruitment pitch.
- Signals Intelligence (SIGINT)—OSINT can provide detailed technical data to enable the identification and characterization of an adversary's telecommunications infrastructure.
- Geospatial Intelligence (GEOINT)—Open source geospatial data in the form of commercial imagery (private sector satellite imagery and commercial aerial photography) and handheld photography can frequently provide the needed information in a manner that is readily shareable with uncleared or coalition partners. OSINT has frequently played a role in facilitating the job of imagery analysts by identifying the activities in surrounding structures. Much of the terrain data used in GEOINT comes from open sources, as in the example of Iraq's terrain trafficability cited earlier.
- Measurement and Signature Intelligence (MASINT)—OSINT has played a frequent role in assisting with identification and characterization of underground detonations through exploitation of worldwide seismic data as reported in open sources.

Although OSINT can provide a great deal of support to other INTs, it should not be perceived as a replacement for the other disciplines. Some OSINT proponents advocate the notion that OSINT is the be-all and end-all of intelligence. The argument is based on the view that if OSINT can provide much of the baseline information the national security apparatus requires, then a relatively modest increase in OSINT funding could enable a dramatic reduction in funding of the other INTs. Although it is true that OSINT activities are underfunded in the IC, such an argument assumes that the information acquired through additional OSINT funding would be the same as that which is collected through the other INTs.

United States Bombs Chinese Embassy

During the North Atlantic Treaty Organization (NATO) bombardment of Belgrade, Yugoslavia, the United States inadvertently bombed the Chinese Embassy on May 7, 1999. Having been the only target nominated by the Central Intelligence Agency (CIA), the blunder was heavily criticized—particularly when it came to light that the embassy's address was listed in the Belgrade phone book. Subsequently, the Department of Defense (DoD) No-Strike Database has relied heavily on Open Source Intelligence (OSINT) to ensure such a mistake is never repeated.

To be of most value, finished intelligence products should be the result of an all-source collection and analysis process. In this manner, the full spectrum of intelligence is made available to the decision maker. Although a robust use of OSINT is advantageous as stated previously, it cannot supplant the all-source process, as no single INT is more valuable than another. Much like academic disciplines, each INT provides an in-depth view of the target from a particular perspective. To claim that only OSINT is needed is akin to proposing that only chemistry is needed to understand the universe.

An important distinction between OSINT and other INTs is the notion that OSINT is a passive collection activity. Unlike the other INTs in which the collectors own the means of collection, such as sensors and satellites, or control the means of collection as with HUMINT sources, OSINT collectors neither own nor control the means of collection. OSINT collectors must rely on others to collect, edit, and publish information, which is then subsequently acquired, vetted, and analyzed.

Much like the notion of collection versus acquisition, active versus passive collection is a subtle but important distinction. To that end, a hypothetical example of where OSINT ends and HUMINT begins is instructive:

Country A is keenly interested in the military technological advances of Country B, a neighboring adversary. Intelligence operatives from Country A are dispatched to the Paris Air Show where Country B is displaying its latest fighter jets and unmanned aerial vehicles (UAVs). Country A's spies openly acquire Country B's sales literature, technical specifications, and video their public product demonstrations—all of which falls well within the realm of OSINT. Should Country A's agents decide to ask questions at the product demonstrations and thus elicit new or additional information in public, it is still OSINT. However, should Country A's agents ask these questions of the Country B salesmen in a local bar, they have now crossed into the HUMINT tradecraft of elicitation.

Legal Restrictions

Like any INT, OSINT is subject to legal, regulatory, and policy restrictions. OSINT professionals, whether within the IC, law enforcement, or the private sector, must abide by these restrictions in order to conduct lawful OSINT exploitation that protects the civil rights and civil liberties of U.S. persons. Such rules may vary from country to country, but a look at the constraints on OSINT in the United States presents a valid exemplar.

At the highest level, the U.S. Constitution's Bill of Rights guarantees certain civil rights such as the freedom of speech and limitations on search and seizure. These civil rights could be affected by OSINT exploitation. As a result, most OSINT activities in the IC operate under a strict set of rules and regulations. At first blush, it may seem counterintuitive that the acquisition of publicly available information could potentially violate civil rights and liberties, and so we will address each in greater detail.

The First Amendment provides in part the freedom of speech, freedom of the press, and "the right of the people peaceably to assemble, and to petition the government for a redress of grievances." In order to protect these rights, governmental OSINT activities must ensure that their activities take place in accordance with applicable laws and U.S. Department of Justice guidelines and are consistent with their agency's mission. For example, an IC member such as the Office of Naval Intelligence may not engage in OSINT exploitation efforts against a suspected radical militia group in Wyoming, as such an operation falls outside of its national defense mission. Additionally, such OSINT exploitation against the press, U.S. persons, or groups without just and legal cause by an element of the government could be said to have a chilling or intimidating effect that is a violation of First Amendment protections.

The Fourth Amendment provides for the protection against unreasonable searches and seizures. In the OSINT exploitation context, this protection means that although the information may be publicly available, it does not mean that intelligence or law enforcement entities should acquire it. In this instance, OSINT exploitation must have a nexus to the mission of the agency and a direct and well-documented rationale for collection. Otherwise, the OSINT effort will violate the reasonable expectation of privacy that has been supported in several court decisions.

The Posse Comitatus Act of 1878 is enshrined in Title 18 of the U.S. Code. Posse comitatus is in essence a prohibition from using the U.S. military for law enforcement activities. The concept has been expanded further by law, executive order and practice to include a prohibition for Intelligence Community elements which focus on external threats such as the military intelligence services, the CIA, and NSA from engaging in domestic collection.

A multitude of federal, state, and local laws may apply to OSINT exploitation, and such a discussion is beyond the scope of this book. However, it may prove instructive to cover two important rule sets. The first is Executive Order (EO) 12333, which covers intelligence activities by the IC and other executive branch agencies.

Signed by President Ronald Reagan in 1981, EO 12333 has been amended three times, the most recent being in 2008 to incorporate the role and authority of the Director of National Intelligence (DNI). EO 12333 in its current form has provisions that relate specifically to OSINT. The order states that all appropriate sources of information including open sources of information should be used by the IC to meet the intelligence requirements of decision makers and subsequently specifically authorizes the IC to collect "information that is publicly available."

The EO goes a step further and enumerates a list of agencies that are given the primary responsibility to engage in overt and OSINT collection—according to their mission and authorities. Specifically, these agencies include the office of the Director of National Intelligence (ODNI); the National Counterterrorism Center (NCTC); and the intelligence elements of the Departments of State, Treasury, Homeland Security, and Energy, as well as the Drug Enforcement Administration (DEA). For many of these agencies, OSINT and overt collection activities represent the primary means of intelligence collection as they are not authorized to conduct clandestine collection.

Lastly, the order requires agencies to disseminate actionable and timely intelligence to decision makers and all those who lawfully require such information for national security purposes to include state, local, and tribal government as critical infrastructure owners. Given the significant obstacles to dissemination of classified reporting to those outside the federal government, this provision provides the impetus for many of the IC OSINT production efforts. In particular, the Defense HUMINT Service relies heavily on OSINT products to meet the standing information needs of the department's constituents. Frequently, time-sensitive OSINT can be disseminated at the Unclassified or For Official Use Only level via a simple e-mail.

Another legal restriction that applies, in this instance, to the dissemination of OSINT are the copyright provisions of Title 17 of the U.S. Code. A detailed examination of the various legal principles are beyond the scope of this text, but a few general guidelines are important to keep in mind. First, as open sources are acquired secondhand from information that has already been published or disseminated, any further dissemination may be a violation of the intellectual property owner's rights. U.S. courts have frequently held that the lack of a copyright notice on intellectual property does not provide license for further unauthorized distribution, so the OSINT practitioner should treat all open sources as if they were copyrighted. A common source of copyright violations is the incorporation of photographs, graphics, or multimedia into OSINT products.

However, the OSINT practitioner should bear in mind that the specific facts concerning an event that appear in open sources are not copyrightable. What is copyrightable is the manner in which the author chooses to portray those facts. A frequent means of dealing with these restrictions is the use of gisting of articles or media reports where the factual content of the original source is distilled and thereby not subject to copyright restrictions. However, care must be taken to ensure very little (if any) of the original wording is used.

All of these legal restrictions from civil rights protections to copyright restrictions are applicable not only to the organizations that engage in OSINT exploitation but also any of their representatives or agents. A common misperception is that these legal restrictions can be worked around by simply outsourcing the activity. No agency or organization may task or contract out any OSINT exploitation activity that it is not already empowered by charter, regulation, or law to do itself. Along these lines, EO 12333 section 2.12 states, "No element of the Intelligence Community shall participate in or request any person to undertake activities forbidden by this Order." In all instances, a clear understanding and delineation of the legal boundaries of the proposed OSINT exploitation efforts should be acquired from competent (and generally highly specialized) legal counsel, prior to engaging in such activities.

Why Open Source Intelligence Matters

Although open sources of information have always been important to intelligence activities throughout the ages, there are a number of technological drivers that have now greatly expanded the utility, availability, and breadth of OSINT. The advent of the World Wide Web in 1990 has led to an exponential growth in information in digital form. The information age has resulted in the general public having the ability to publish information or multimedia quickly and cheaply to a worldwide audience. This explosion in readily accessible data has greatly increased the availability of OSINT from a wide variety of sources.

During the same period, there has been an accompanying explosion in computing power. The personal computer user now has the ability to store and instantaneously retrieve massive amounts of data inexpensively. As a result, a laptop computer equipped with two terabytes of hard drive storage can now store the entire contents of a large university library and retrieve that information based on keyword query in a fraction of a second. During World War II, a similar exhaustive search of such library holdings would have taken an army of researchers many months to complete.

Globalization has also played an important role in increasing the utility of OSINT. In many instances, the diffusion of wireless and mobile technology in what were traditionally considered underdeveloped countries has outpaced similar efforts in the United States. As evidenced by the heavy use of cell phones and Web 2.0 technologies such as Twitter during the Arab Spring uprisings, a repressive regime has limited ability to restrict information flows. Similarly, the near instantaneous information flow from the early uprisings greatly influenced later uprisings—fomenting pressures on regimes in the region and providing protestors with a viable means of emulating tactics, effective methods for coordination, and worldwide information dissemination.

Additionally, as the number of authoritarian regimes continues to decline around the globe, there are increasing pressures for governmental accountability, principally through enhanced transparency. Such transparency has greatly enhanced OSINT exploitation efforts by providing a wealth of new government-generated data that frequently outlines useful transactional data such as who is contributing funds to political campaigns or with what firms a particular government is contracting. Unsanctioned transparency sites such as WikiLeaks or opensecrets.org have provided a treasure trove of information from insiders who leak classified, proprietary or sensitive data on the web.

Lastly, OSINT has gained in importance in recent years due to a greater emphasis by the leadership of the IC and congressional oversight committees. Ambassador John D. Negroponte, the first U.S. DNI, declared OSINT "the source of first resort" and established an Assistant Deputy DNI for Open Source and created the Open Source Center (OSC)—all of which enhanced the stature of OSINT. Congressional interest in OSINT has resulted in hearings, commission recommendations, and ultimately increased funding and billets for open source officers (OSOs).

The subsequent shift away from the traditional IC policy of "need to know" or only sharing information with those who had an absolute need for the information, to a "responsibility to provide" has also increased the emphasis on OSINT. The 9/11 terrorist attack on the United States highlighted the need to share intelligence more widely. This departure from the overly protective IC culture has benefited OSINT as it tends to be of lower classification (but not always) and thus is more readily sharable with coalition partners, state and local homeland security officials, and even critical infrastructure owners.

Ultimately, the increased importance of OSINT has come as a result of the realization that it can provide information on a broad range of topics that was previously only available through the other INTs. OSINT's ability to provide global coverage at significantly less cost and lower risk has meant that the more limited, expensive, and dangerous collection capabilities can be reserved for the most intractable intelligence gaps. As technology, globalization, and communication tools such as social networking continue to redefine how we live our lives, the OSINT discipline will increasingly redefine the business of intelligence.

History of Open Source Intelligence

From the Civil War to World War I, the U.S. government made sporadic use of open sources for intelligence purposes. The more systematic U.S. exploitation of OSINT came at the onset of World War II with the establishment of the Foreign Broadcast Monitoring Service (FBMS) in February 1941. FBMS was established when Secretary of State Cordell Hull prevailed upon President Franklin Roosevelt to establish a government effort to support the nation's intelligence and counter-propaganda efforts. President Roosevelt agreed and directed the U.S. Treasury to allocate $150,000 from his emergency fund for recording, transcribing, translating, and analyzing foreign radio broadcasts. Originally focused on the Axis powers' shortwave propaganda broadcasts, FBMS was established as part of the Federal Communications Commission (FCC) National Defense Activities directorate.

FBMS was first headquartered in northeast Washington, DC, and a few months later opened its first bureau in a farmhouse in Portland, Oregon, from which it began to monitor Japanese broadcasts. Highlighting the value of OSINT analysis, the service's first analytic report was released one day before the attack on Pearl Harbor. The report stated, "Japanese radio intensifies still further its defiant, hostile tone; in contrast to its behavior during earlier periods of Pacific tension, Radio Tokyo makes no peace appeals. Comment on the United States is bitter and increased. . ."

It is important to note at this point that FBMS was solely focused on radio broadcasts and did not have responsibility for printed media. That responsibility was given to the Interdepartmental Committee for the Acquisition of Foreign Periodicals, which established an extensive worldwide network and acquired a valuable trove of publications. The committee's global network was very effective in acquiring vast numbers of books—for example, the Library of Congress received 5,000 Chinese books in 1945 that the committee purchased in Chongqing.

The Office of Strategic Services (OSS), created in June 1942, found OSINT and the work of FBMS invaluable. Legendary OSS Director William "Wild Bill" Donovan was an early convert to the value of FBMS when he served first as Coordinator of Information (1941–1942), prior to the establishment of the OSS. Donovan and his staff found FBMS products of such value that he paid for a wire service between FBMS and Coordinator of Information offices in Washington and New York. The wire was up and running by October 1941 and, a month later, the State Department also requested a wire to its headquarters, which initially ran for eight hours per day. A week after the attack on Pearl Harbor, the wire was expanded to twenty-four hours per day at six State Department locations. By late February 1942, the FBMS wire service was serving eighteen Department of War organizations and carrying an average of 25,000 words per day.

As OSS Director, Donovan wrote to thank FBMS for its "invaluable service," stating the following:

> These transcripts are of particular interest and value in that they indicate the different Japanese propaganda lines and often, though perhaps unintentionally, they contain intelligence which when combined with material from other sources contributes substantially to the political and economic intelligence now available on Japan.

On July 26, 1942, the FCC changed the organization's name to the Foreign Broadcast Intelligence Service (FBIS) (which would be changed again after the war to the Foreign Broadcast *Information* Service). By this point, the monitoring of foreign broadcasts had proved so valuable that the White House had a wire service installed to receive FBIS transcripts and analysis. The White House also established a direct telephone line so

President Roosevelt could listen to live broadcasts or even ask the FBIS staff questions—as British prime minister Winston Churchill did on one occasion while staying at the White House.

Like many wartime intelligence organizations, the FBIS was on track to be quickly disbanded when the war ended. Though FBIS as an element of the FCC shut its doors in December 1945, such a hue and cry came from the Departments of War and State, as well as the news media (which had been receiving some of the service's transcripts), that the War Department's Military Intelligence Division stepped in as temporary guardian on January 1, 1946. By the time FBIS was transferred to the War Department, its staff was at half its wartime peak figure of roughly 500.

FBIS remained part of the War Department for seven months, whereupon it was transferred to its permanent home as part of the Central Intelligence Group, which became the Central Intelligence Agency (CIA) with the passage of the National Security Act of 1947. As mentioned previously, the name of the organization was changed to the Foreign Broadcast Information Service (also FBIS). FBIS was given four goals by its new masters: to monitor pertinent foreign broadcasts, establish field stations and cooperative agreements with foreign governments, prepare translated daily transcripts of the foreign broadcasts, and distribute the information in accordance with approved distribution lists.

Open Source Intelligence in the Postwar Era

That FBIS survived the draconian cuts of the postwar era is testament enough to its value during the war to a wide range of consumers. Indeed, not even the more highly visible OSS was able to escape the budget ax as it shut its doors permanently on September 20, 1945. Ultimately, what saved the FBIS from extinction was its perceived value in the postwar years. Before World War II ended, FBIS analysts were already casting a concerned eye toward Moscow and warning of a possible threat from an emboldened Soviet Union. As the nation's leadership began to struggle with this future adversary, one of the few consistent sources of intelligence was FBIS, leading the *Washington Post* to opine that FBIS was "one of the most vital units in a sound postwar intelligence operation."

As part of the CIA, FBIS grew to become the preeminent collector of open sources of information in the U.S. government. It established a global web of foreign bureaus that both monitored and translated foreign broadcasts. When FBIS did not have the staff or access to monitor foreign broadcasts, it established bilateral agreements with the monitoring services of other countries—eventually establishing cooperative agreements with over a dozen countries.

For certain topics, OSINT was the preeminent intelligence source during the Cold War. A *Studies in Intelligence* article from 1957 alleged that 75 to 90 percent of what the CIA knew about the Soviet bloc's geography, economic difficulties, and scientific endeavors were based on the analysis of open source information emanating from within the Iron Curtain. OSINT frequently enhanced the community's situational awareness during crises. During the Cuban Missile Crisis of 1962, the FBIS monitoring of Radio Moscow broadcasts provided the first indications that Soviet premier Nikita Khrushchev had withdrawn Soviet missiles from the island.

Although OSINT exploitation yielded significant and valuable information, the importance of that information was not always immediately understood. The same *Studies in Intelligence* article claimed that, with the benefit of hindsight, CIA analysts realized that when the Soviet Union began its nuclear program, open sources had reported that the USSR was importing large quantities of mining equipment as well as specialized instruments from England and the United States.

To be sure, FBIS was not the only IC organization conducting OSINT exploitation during the Cold War. The IC had many small OSINT activities underway to meet the unique needs of their parent agencies. The Departments of State, Treasury, Agriculture (Foreign Agricultural Service) and Energy all engaged in small but effective open source units, as did each of the branches of the U.S. Armed Forces. Even the Library of Congress began leveraging open sources in 1948; the effort continues to this day as the Federal Research Division of the library, which still supports the U.S. government with open source analysis.

Although the IC OSINT operations during the Cold War were diverse, they frequently represented small, highly specialized endeavors that were isolated from broader IC analytic efforts. During this period, the IC failed to embrace the value of OSINT wholeheartedly. The primary reason for this reticence was the culture of the IC, which tended to place greater value on information that was collected clandestinely or at great peril. Second, few all-source analysts had the language skills, cultural literacy, and depth of experience with the media sources of their target countries. These analysts were generally unqualified to determine the validity of foreign news sources and sometimes would label open sources as unreliable or simply misinformation from adversaries.

This reticence to use open sources was further exacerbated by outside forces. As the world's telecommunications infrastructure continued to advance, intelligence professionals found themselves increasingly in competition with the news media. With the advent of the twenty-four-hour news cycle with the creation of the Cable News Network (CNN) in 1980 came near instantaneous reporting of world events. The CIA was simply unable to compete with the news media when it came to information dissemination; therefore, it highlighted its clandestine sources of reporting and shunned its open source reporting. This de-emphasis of OSINT had a significant effect on FBIS, particularly after the fall of the Soviet Union in 1991.

The U.S. military, however, began to develop a renewed interest in open source information as the Cold War came to a close. This resurgence was led by Marine Corps Commandant General Alfred Gray Jr., who in 1988 called for a greater focus on OSINT and advocated for additional resources to shift OSINT collection away from the Soviet bloc and refocus it instead on regions of instability and non-state actors. The U.S. Army followed suit in 1994 by tasking a reserve intelligence unit affiliated with Yale University to develop an OSINT course and handbook for the U.S. Army's Advanced Intelligence Officer Course. The DIA established an open source coordinator position in 1996, and by 1997, theatre-level open source elements began to spring up in the U.S. Pacific Command (USPACOM) and U.S. European Command (EUCOM).

Although this post–Cold War period was a relative boon for military OSINT, it also signaled a decline in the fortunes of FBIS. One contributor to this decline was the reticence of the FBIS leadership to embrace and exploit new information sources and technologies. FBIS belatedly expanded its mission in 1992 to include gray literature, commercial databases, and subscription services, which were increasingly providing a wealth of open source information. Well into the new millennium, FBIS largely ignored the information revolution taking place on the Internet and failed to exploit the medium systematically. As late as 2005, an independent U.S. government commission took FBIS to task for its lack of Internet exploitation, calling it "an unacceptable state of affairs."[7] This obsolete tradecraft and lack of initiative at FBIS led many in the CIA and across the U.S. government to question the service's value.

This ambivalence toward FBIS manifested itself in late 1996 when the CIA proposed a dramatic budget cut for FBIS that would result in the elimination of much of its foreign language translation capability and its overseas bureaus. To add insult to injury, the incoming director of Central Intelligence (DCI) George Tenet, during his confirmation hearings, opined that perhaps the CIA, given its clandestine nature, should not be in the business of OSINT. Ultimately, FBIS was saved from these drastic budget cuts not by its governmental consumers but rather by academics who, since 1974, had access to FBIS translations and transcripts through the Department of Commerce's World News Connection service and had successfully rallied to its defense with the intelligence committees in Congress.

The same year the CIA was proposing dramatic budget cuts for FBIS, the Commission on the Roles and Capabilities of the IC (or the Aspin-Brown Commission) engaged in an in-depth assessment of the IC. In its final report released in the fall of 1996, the commission castigated the IC for its failure to exploit OSINT effectively. The commission indicated that access to open sources in the IC was severely deficient and indicated that "a greater effort should also be made to harness the vast universe of information now available from open sources." The commission went on to state that open sources should be a top priority for the DCI both in terms of funding and attention.

With FBIS in a period of decline, another CIA open source activity began to bear fruit—the Community Open Source Program Office (COSPO). Established in 1994 by DCI James Woolsey, COSPO was tasked to develop, coordinate, and oversee the IC open source efforts. Under the leadership of Dr. Joseph Markowitz, COSPO focused on three key areas: establishing a collaborative and informative virtual private network called the Open Source Information System (OSIS), creating a one-way transfer system to allow analysts to move unclassified information seamlessly to their classified workstations, and to establish a virtual library called the World Basic Information Library (WBIL).

All three of these COSPO initiatives were successful and represented dramatic improvements for open source practitioners across the IC. COSPO expanded the amount of commercial open source information available to the IC and also provided a means by which the smaller and more isolated IC OSINT production units could broadly share the fruits of their labor. Ultimately, OSIS would have the greatest impact on the IC OSINT exploitation activities and would eventually attract well over 100,000 users across the whole of the U.S. government.

The success of COSPO did not go unnoticed by FBIS, whose leadership lobbied the DCI to make the heretofore autonomous COSPO subordinate to FBIS. Eventually succeeding in having the COSPO function transferred to its headquarters,[8] the FBIS leadership set about curtailing COSPO's community oriented activities and, inexplicably, created a competing open source information portal: fbis.gov (now known as opensource.gov). By the early years of the new millennium, FBIS had dismantled COSPO and threatened to close OSIS. The resulting outcry from OSIS users across the community led the DCI to remove OSIS from FBIS. It eventually became the Intelink-U network under the DNI chief information officer, where it remains (now renamed DNI-U) the preeminent OSINT dissemination platform for members across the IC and even federal, state, and local homeland security partners.

Open Source Intelligence in the Post–9/11 Era

As a result of the efforts to restructure the IC after the terrorist attack of September 11, 2001, greater coordination among the IC disparate OSINT activities was championed by multiple advocates. The 9/11 Commission Report, published in 2004, although not addressing the issue of open sources directly, did include one chart where they proposed a new Open Source Agency. The 9/11 Commission also did not address the need for open sources in its final report but the subsequent Intelligence Reform and Terrorism Prevention Act (IRTPA) of 2004[9] did place significant emphasis on OSINT. In Section 1052 of the IRTPA, Congress tasked the DNI with establishing a center for coordinating OSINT production, devising a means of integrating OSINT in the intelligence cycle, and ensuring that each IC element uses OSINT consistent with its mission and authorities.

In their final report to the president in 2005, the Weapons of Mass Destruction (WMD) Commission advocated the greater use of open sources of information that the IC has as well as the establishment of a "champion and home" for open source. The WMD Commission indicated that open sources provide four main benefits: the ability to quickly assimilate information on world events; a base for understanding classified reporting; the protection of sources and methods; and the ability to "store history." In terms of the role and new structure for the IC open source efforts, they stated the following:

> Open Source information has long been viewed by many outside the Intelligence Community as essential to understanding foreign political, economic, social, and even military developments. . . . We recommend that the DNI create an Open Source Directorate in the CIA to develop and utilize information processing tools to enhance the availability of open source information to analysts, collectors, and users of intelligence.[10]

In addition to the OSINT provisions of IRTPA, congressional advocates drove greater interest in the IC use of OSINT. Chief among those congressional proponents was Rep. Rob Simmons of Connecticut. Simmons had been the commander of a U.S. Army Reserve intelligence unit that wrote the U.S. Army's first OSINT handbook, as well as a clandestine service officer with the CIA and former staff director of the Senate Select Committee on Intelligence. He was well acquainted with the value of OSINT. Representative Simmons used his position to advocate a greater role for OSINT. In 2005, he injected OSINT related language into the 2006 National Defense Authorization Act that, for the first time, legally defined OSINT and directed DoD to establish a plan for increasing its use of OSINT. He subsequently held an open source business exposition and congressional hearings on the value of OSINT, all of which began to build momentum for the expansion of OSINT activities across the IC.

During the same year, the ODNI was established and the Assistant Deputy DNI for Open Source (ADDNI/OS) position was created, thus fulfilling the WMD Commission's call for an OSINT "champion." The ADDNI/OS was the IC senior OSINT officer, responsible for providing strategic direction, policy, resource allocation, and oversight to the IC OSINT efforts. The ADDNI/OS orchestrated the development of IC Directive 301 that established the National Open Source Enterprise—a program encompassing all sixteen IC agencies. ICD 301 delineated the authority of the ADDNI/OS and the role of the OSC, and enumerated the OSINT-related authorities and responsibilities of each IC element. The directive also established the National Open Source Committee as a senior executive/flag officer–level governance board.

The OSC was established in November 2005 to serve as a center of excellence for OSINT. The DNI renamed FBIS and provided additional funding and the mandate to become a service of common concern to support the IC OSINT activities. The OSC is not an element of the ODNI but rather remains a CIA entity (as was FBIS) with a broader responsibility to support the IC. To that end, the OSC embarked on establishing an Open Source Academy to provide open source training opportunities to the IC. In its first year of operation, the center significantly increased the number of OSINT products incorporated into the President's Daily Brief (PDB). According to the CIA *Studies in Intelligence* journal, the OSC grew to twice the number of staff members its predecessor FBIS had and has the ability to translate more than 30 million words a month.[11]

The ADDNI/OS succeeded in establishing an open source line item in the National Intelligence Program as well as providing resources and billets for OSO positions across the IC. The introduction of OSOs outside of the CIA for the first time enabled other IC agencies to develop a dedicated OSINT exploitation capability to meet their unique mission needs and with their specific authorities. The office of the ADDNI/OS was also instrumental in establishing a professional certification for OSOs, the development of the first IC-wide Open Source Collection Acquisition Requirements Management System (OSCAR-MS), and the establishment of an OSINT innovation center called Open Source Works (OSW).

As the enterprise matured, the Office of the ADDNI/OS began to transfer some of its responsibilities to the OSC. The WMD Commission had indicated that while there existed a "near-term" need for an OSINT champion and an institutional home, that in the long run, there would no longer be a need for either if the IC made adequate progress in valuing and incorporating OSINT. By early 2011, most of the ADDNI/OS responsibilities had been transferred to the OSC.

In mid-2012, the DNI designated the director of the CIA as the OSINT functional manager for the IC and codified the OSINT board of governors (comprising the IC agency heads) as the oversight element, and the National Open Source Committee as the IC OSINT coordination body. This OSINT functional management designation provides the CIA director the authority to "develop, coordinate, and oversee the issuance and implementation of IC standards on Open Source training and tradecraft, reporting, requirements, and evaluation measures."[12] The DNI, however, specifically reserved for himself the oversight role and the authority to develop higher-level IC policy relating to OSINT. The resulting CIA Director's OSINT Functional Management Implementation Plan reaffirmed the strategic goals of the ADDNI/OS 2006 National Open Source Enterprise Vision Statement, as well as the OSC role as a service of common concern where it is responsible for supporting the OSINT collection needs of the IC.

The establishment of an OSINT functional manager represents a maturation of the Open Source Enterprise (OSE) (the word *national* was dropped from the name in 2012) and the institutionalization of OSINT as a distinct INT. With this ongoing progress of the OSE, the shift from the need for an OSINT "champion" to that of initialization of the discipline is complete. The focus for the OSINT discipline in the near term is the WMD Commission's goal of true integration. They stated the following:

> It is our hope that open source will become an integral part of all intelligence activities and that, at some point in the future, there may no longer be a need for a separate directorate. We acknowledge that our recommendation could create one more collection specialty. But,

for now, open source is inadequately used and appreciated and is in need of the high-level, focused attention that only a separate directorate can provide.

For the time being, the CIA director as OSINT functional manager and the OSC as the service of common concern find themselves in the unenviable job of measuring their success by the extent to which they can work themselves out of a job.

Elements of Open Sources of Information

OSINT draws from a myriad of sources from the staid confines of academic and professional journals to the rough-and-tumble world of social media. In terms of media, OSINT draws from hard copy, broadcasts, and digital formats as well as the unconventional—such as graffiti.

Critical to foreign language open source exploitation is the need to have both language skills and cultural insight in order to exploit those sources fully. Conducting a solely English language search often returns only minimal information. Additionally, relying on English language summaries provided by foreign language websites and news sources is usually far less productive than translating from the original language texts. Foreign editors generally assume that English language readers are less interested in details and tend to summarize the news stories. For example, foreign language articles on drug trafficker arrests frequently include the arrestee's personal details—while that news source's English language version of the story would typically omit such details that are frequently judged too "in the weeds" for most American readers.

Some observers have incorrectly assumed that foreign language translation tools can overcome this foreign language hurdle. Although the accuracy of translation software may be improving, it will take decades to make any significant headway when it comes to cultural subtleties or regional differences. Consider that something as simple as ordering a carbonated beverage varies from region to region within the United States. Likewise, machine translation tools have yet to address idioms effectively. The Spanish idiom "*Eramos pocos y parió la abuela*" could be technically translated word for word as "There were few of us and then grandma gave birth," but a more accurate translation would indicate the writer was conveying that things went "from bad to worse," or "out of the frying pan and into the fire."

Understanding the target culture is frequently necessary to glean the most from a particular foreign open source. An in-depth exploration of culture is not possible, but here are some issues to consider. Concepts that are usually assumed to be universal can vary from culture to culture. For example, the concept of time tends to be past-oriented in Asian cultures; in Latin America, it tends to be present-oriented, and in the United States, we tend to be future-oriented when we consider time.

The issue of high-context versus low-context cultures is very important when exploiting foreign language open sources. In low-context cultures, those communicating tend to spell things out fully, while in high-context cultures, those who are communicating do so with the assumption that there is a great deal of commonality in knowledge, views, and experience. Examples of low-context cultures include Anglo-Saxons and Scandinavians while high-context cultures include Asians and Arabs.

Without strong foreign language skills and cultural understanding, the utility of exploiting foreign language open sources of information is severely limited. In short, there is no substitution for language skills and in-country experience. OSOs must also develop a deep understanding of the particular news sources they follow from the motivations of the publisher to the idiosyncrasies of the reporter.

Congress recognized this problem as well as the cost implications of keeping on the payroll numerous translators who might not be needed at all times, especially for more obscure or less commonly used languages. The solution was the creation of the National Virtual Translation Center (NVTC) in 2003. The NVTC is essentially a network of contract translators who are called in as needed to support various government customers.

Let us now look at the various media from which OSINT draws its information. We will begin with open sources drawn from the print medium, which include books, magazines, newspapers, and even traditional hard copy maps. Books have, for hundreds of years, been a mainstay of OSINT exploitation and academic research. Frequently, significant value is derived not only from the text itself but also from the footnotes and bibliography.

The 1975 political thriller *Three Days of the Condor* starred Robert Redford who played a CIA OSO who, by analyzing books, uncovers a CIA operation that costs his coworkers their lives. Hollywood's portrayal of the work of textual analysis is highly entertaining, though not particularly instructive. An excellent example of the analytical skills necessary for open source analysis can be found in the book *Counterfeit Spies* by Nigel West, which uncovers a number of bogus World War II secret agents by exposing significant errors, contradictions, and fallacies contained in their memoirs.

Magazines and newspapers also provide a wealth of open source information. Magazines and journals in particular have been very popular sources for OSOs as they tend to carry more lengthy and detailed coverage of a particular subject matter than that typically found in newspapers. During the Cold War, periodicals also typically yielded excellent photographs, which were far more useful than the grainy photos found in newspapers. Magazines like *Aviation Week* proved to be a treasure trove of technical details and photos for Soviet analysts as many classified details regarding U.S. military planes and space reconnaissance programs frequently found their way into the publication, leading many in DoD to derisively rechristen it *Aviation Leak*.

Newspapers provide the timeliest hardcopy assessment of current events. National and regional newspapers are useful; frequently the most detailed coverage of an event, organization, or individual comes from local newspapers. Even in nations where the press is controlled, decisions about what is published and what is not, or how it is presented, can be very revealing. For example, analysts working on the Soviet Union would study the arrangement of Soviet leaders atop the reviewing stand in Red Square as an indicator of relative rank and authority. An indicator of the real value of information contained in newspapers can be seen by the way in which many reporters pay for that information with their own lives. Coverage of terrorism, drug trafficking, and corruption in countries such as Brazil, Indonesia, Pakistan, Iraq, Russia, Mexico, and Somalia has led many journalists to begin self-censoring their reporting for fear of reprisals. Many journalists have taken to posting their sensitive content to blogs in a bid to continue their reporting with greater anonymity.

To the uninitiated, newspaper sections such as the obituaries and the classifieds are of little intelligence value, but to the experienced OSO it can provide a great deal of valuable information. During the first DNI Open Source Conference in 2007, the ADDNI/OS recounted the story of Berthold Jacob, a hapless reporter who gleaned from German newspaper obituaries and graduation and wedding notices sufficiently detailed information to uncover that Germany was secretly rearming in the mid-1930s—a violation of the World War I peace accords. Mr. Jacob, who was exiled in France, warned the world of the rise of the Nazi threat in a book published in 1936. The book included such a detailed order of battle for the new German military that Hitler was convinced he had a spy in his high command. Mr. Jacob was subsequently kidnapped and interrogated by the Gestapo, and much to their chagrin, he proved he had acquired the information from German newspapers.[13]

Classified notices have likewise often provided very useful OSINT sources. Competitive intelligence professionals employed by commercial firms have frequently perused the employment section of the newspaper to purloin important details from a competitor's job announcements. Frequently those announcements list vital details such as salary range, the customer, location of the work, and contract deliverables.[14] As with any open source, extensive experience with the particular source is essential to be able to uncover this valuable yet elusive intelligence.

Government publications and speeches by major political leaders are also an important OSINT trove. What is being said—or not—or the details being presented or omitted are all indicators of useful intelligence to the trained OSINT analyst, again in either open or closed societies. To use the Soviet Union again as an example, in the 1970s and 1980s Murray Feshbach, a demographer with the Census Bureau and then a professor at Georgetown University, noticed significant changes in the demographic statistics that the Soviet Union published. Feshbach assumed—correctly—that life expectancies were declining amidst a sociological and health crisis, both of which were signs of the inner rot of the late Soviet period.

The last component of hard copy open source materials is known as gray literature. The IC describes it as the following:

Gray literature, regardless of media, can include, but is not limited to, research reports, technical reports, economic reports, trip reports, working papers, discussion papers, unofficial government documents, proceedings, preprints, studies, dissertations and theses, trade literature, market surveys, and newsletters. This material cuts across scientific, political, socio-economic, and military disciplines.[i]

In short, it is generally characterized as hard copy documents of limited distribution that frequently lack bibliographic information—thus, ascertaining the author's identity, publisher, or publication date can be a challenge, if not impossible.

An example of gray literature is the previously mentioned report on Iraq filed with the Library of Congress by American archaeologists, which was used nearly 100 years later for soil composition and trafficability analysis by the DIA. A more current example was the acquisition of insurgent pamphlets, flyers, and underground newspapers by U.S. Army and U.S. Marine patrols in Afghanistan and Iraq that were successfully exploited by military intelligence and civil affairs personnel to provide greater situational awareness to U.S. units operating in those areas.

The broadcast medium of open source has three sub-elements: television, radio, and Internet-based broadcasts. With the advent of the Cable News Network came the twenty-four-hour news cycle, which dramatically altered both the timeliness of reporting as well as the breadth of coverage. The major news networks that have proliferated since the 1980s have developed an expansive network of affiliates that span the globe. In addition, the explosion of satellite and cable TV channels has increasingly segmented or targeted specific populations, which results in enhanced coverage of local and regional events as well as minority groups, offering OSOs far wider and more detailed coverage.

The radio sub-element of the broadcast medium has seen a dramatic expansion due in large part to the advent of digital radio signals in mid-1995 (in Europe) and satellite radio in 2001. Digital radio signals allow a traditional radio station broadcasting at a particular frequency to subdivide its signal into seven separate streams that can be used to broadcast different content on each. The two U.S. satellite radio providers each boast of over 100 channels to choose from, which, unlike traditional broadcast radio, can be received from anywhere in the United States.

For both TV and radio broadcasts, the Internet has dramatically altered both the breadth of coverage as well as the ease of acquisition. In the past, it was necessary to establish and staff listening posts to intercept foreign broadcasts. Today, many broadcasters also choose to stream their broadcasts over the Internet as a means of reaching a broader audience.

---

[i] Definition from the IC now-defunct Interagency Gray Literature Working Group.

Internet broadcasting has also lowered the cost of entry for organizations and individuals who wish to develop their own content. The ability to reach a worldwide audience via the Internet can now be attained with a few hundred dollars' worth of equipment and a high-speed Internet connection. The introduction of networks of amateurs who capture local police, fire, and emergency services' radio transmissions and their rebroadcast of those transmissions in near real time over the Internet is another area where the Internet has made OSINT exploitation easier. All of these Internet resources greatly expand the information available to OSOs from the comfort of their computer terminal.

The advent of the Internet and the World Wide Web have revolutionized the discipline of OSINT by making unprecedented amounts of information available and searchable. This major strength is also a major drawback as OSOs are constantly struggling with the vast amounts of data available. It is a proverbial needle in a haystack problem for OSOs, who must find the useful nuggets of information in a timely and efficient manner.

The OSO must also be able to correctly evaluate the source of reporting. The analyst must learn quickly the biases or political slants of various news outlets—none of which can claim to be entirely neutral. What they choose to report and how they choose to report matters a great deal—especially if the OSINT is being used as the basis for analysis for a reader who may be much less attuned to these nuances.

The open source analyst must discern and account for circular reporting—is the flurry of reporting the result of many witnesses separately reporting or extensive retweeting of one singular report? The bias of each source must be understood and analyzed, as well as the source's reliability or track record established.

Again, an exhaustive review of all Internet resources is not possible. A few key resources and issues will be discussed. One significant challenge with Internet exploitation is that of accessing the deep web. The deep web refers to content available on the web but that is not generally indexed by search engines. Websites with databases that generate content on the fly, such as newspaper sites, local tax assessment databases, and many social media sites are not indexed by search engines.

Many website owners may choose not to have their websites indexed by search engines by embedding code on their websites called the robot exclusion protocol. The vast size of the web can be a major impediment for search engines, which are able to discover and index only a small percentage of the web's entire holdings. Through a systematic exploitation of the web, it is possible to discover a wide array of deep web resources that are otherwise invisible to search engines.[15]

Web 2.0 technologies, such as social networking sites, blogs, and wikis, are very popular OSINT resources. Given that these types of sources are transient by their very nature, establishing the validity or provenance of particular postings can be extremely difficult. Through the use of content analysis, open source practitioners can, in some instances, determine the educational level, political affiliation, and underlying motivations of an individual who is posting content, provided there are a sufficient number of postings.

The instantaneous nature of technologies such as Twitter, Facebook, Flickr and YouTube, to name a few, have become ubiquitous information dissemination platforms that allow bystanders or participants in an event to broadcast information as it happens. As a result of the wide availability of sophisticated smartphones that serve as a means of collection, there has been an unprecedented explosion in handheld video and imagery that are of great value to OSOs. The inclusion of Global Positioning System (GPS) capabilities on many of these smartphones likewise provides specific information about the individual's whereabouts. As mentioned previously, these Web 2.0 technologies delivered critical OSINT during the Arab Spring uprisings in the Middle East and continue to provide situational awareness during major events from natural disasters to civil disturbances.

It is fair to say that the IC is just coming to grips with these new sources, as is everyone else. For example, the fact that perhaps 100,000 people in Tahrir Square in Cairo are using Twitter is interesting but it is of greater interest to discern who has the most Twitter followers and why. Who is this person? What faction or interest does he represent? Just as there can be deception in each of the other INTs, this is also true of social media. It is possible to buy thousands of seeming Twitter followers for a few hundred dollars. So, is the Twitter thought leader real, or are his followers illusory?

It is also important to note that the ease and speed with which these sites disseminate also increases the likelihood of short-term deception or false starts. Social media sites have no authentication mechanisms, merely measures of popularity and user feedback. For example, in the immediate aftermath of the Boston Marathon bombing, someone quickly identified a Pakistani-American as a likely suspect. This turned out to be wrong, but the false supposition took on a life of its own before it was authoritatively refuted. That said, given the plethora of social media sources available, long-term or large-scale deception would be extremely difficult. Source validation of social media is a critical challenge for open source professionals.

The last critical element in the digital realm of OSINT is that of commercial imagery and databases. Commercial imagery companies such as SPOT Image and DigitalGlobe provide standard imagery at approximately half-meter resolution (a photograph of high enough resolution where an object that is approximately eighteen inches long is distinguishable) and in some instances radar and infrared imagery products. High-quality commercial imagery can be purchased and downloaded from the Internet at the nominal cost of approximately $20 per square kilometer. Free services such as Google Earth also prove useful, but their images are generally dated and of a lower resolution. However, even at lower resolution, the ability to observe changes in a facility over time can provide the OSO and GEOINT analysts with valuable insights.

Commercial databases and content providers such as LexisNexis, Dialog, Jane's Information Group, the Economist Intelligence Unit, and Oxford Analytica have for many decades been the mainstay of OSOs, researchers, and librarians. The main benefit of using commercial sources is that the data have already been organized and vetted. Given the cost involved, the alternative of acquiring content for free from the web may seem attractive, but such efforts are not free; the process of finding, vetting, and organizing this data proves time consuming. In short, with OSINT you can either pay up front for quality content or pay on the tail end with significant investments in time and energy. In addition, many commercial databases have unique content not available via other means. Users are cautioned that although you may pay for commercial content or imagery, such payment generally does not allow you to further disseminate the content unless copyright permissions are negotiated in advance.

Last but not least are the OSINT elements that comprise the "other" category—that of graffiti and tattoos. It may not be immediately apparent that something as ephemeral as graffiti could be of intelligence value, but police and military officials have long exploited graffiti as a situational awareness tool. For example, during the Los Angeles Riots of 1992, the California National Guard was called upon by Gov. Pete Wilson to help quell the disturbances. National Guard commanders did not have a clear understanding of gang territories within the various sectors of the city in which they were operating. Los Angeles Police Department liaison officers assigned to those National Guard units were, however, able to quickly delineate gang territories for military commanders by simply reading the gang graffiti as the national guardsmen began patrolling their sectors.

A more recent trend in ephemeral open sources is the use of *narco-mantas,* or narco banners, by Latin American drug cartels. These banners are typically hung on bridges or in public places beside murder victims as a means of conveying a message as well as intimidating the authorities and populace. They are frequently paired with mutilated corpses for added effect. The banners are generally reactive in nature—used to respond to an arrest or an attack or to warn journalists who are reporting something the cartel finds unacceptable and even to communicate with the local or national government.

Police have exploited tattoos to identify gang members and gain valuable insights into gang member activity and hierarchy. Tattoos may likewise record historical information on gang member movements, as tattoo styles vary by region and with specific tattoo artists. Exploitation of tattoos by law enforcement has become so effective that many gang members are resorting to tattoos in hard-to-spot areas (such as inside the mouth), and some gangs are now discouraging the use of tattoos by new gang members.

How Open Source Intelligence Is Managed

The management of OSINT activities varies greatly from nation to nation and depending on the needs and structure of the organization conducting it. Within the U.S. IC, OSINT exploitation is managed through each step of the TCPED process. In this section, each TCPED element is covered with a review of any supporting systems and processes. (See the "TCPED Process" box.)

TCPED Process

- *Tasking*—Sending a request for information (RFI) to a collector
- *Collection*—Determining what to acquire and then acquiring it
- *Processing*—Getting the information into a useful format, such as transcribing and translating a foreign language radio broadcast into English text
- *Exploitation*—Validating and analyzing the acquired information and organizing the final product
- *Dissemination*—Sending the information to the requestor and sharing it with any other consumer who may need it

---

U.S. intelligence elements engaging in OSINT exploitation utilize OSCAR-MS. Created by the office of the ADDNI/OS in 2007, the system is the first IC-wide OSINT collection management system. OSCAR-MS provides a detailed inventory of OSINT organizations with a summary of capabilities and current production lines. The system augments the OSINT encyclopedic reference known as the National Open Source Enterprise Capabilities Manual, which serves as a desk reference on the IC OSINT capabilities.

Tasking

OSCAR-MS provides authorized users (typically an organization's collection management staff) with the ability to submit and track taskings—known as RFIs. RFIs come in two types: standing and ad hoc. Standing RFIs are long-term collection requests such as "provide any reporting on public comments made by government officials in Country X regarding Country Y's deployment of ships in the Persian Gulf." An ad hoc request is a more reactive and time-sensitive request dealing with a current event or operation such as "provide any photographs or video available from open sources regarding the flotilla of fishermen from Country X who are attempting to blockade naval vessels from Country Y deployed in the Persian Gulf."

By using OSCAR-MS, collection managers are able to ascertain which IC OSINT elements have the language and collection capability for a particular tasking and then submit that RFI to one or more collectors. Before an RFI can be submitted, the collection manager from the requesting organization must certify that he or she has searched the OSCAR-MS holdings and determined the RFI has not been previously submitted. This process minimizes redundant taskings from multiple IC organizations who are interested in the same information—a common problem in the past.

An OSINT element that receives an RFI can respond in one of three ways to the tasking. It can accept the requirement, at which point OSCAR-MS notifies the requestor that the RFI has been accepted. Alternatively, the OSINT collector who was tasked may reject the RFI if it is duplicative in nature or falls outside his or her mission space. For example, the Federal Bureau of Investigation (FBI) OSINT cell would likely reject a request for collection on violations of territorial sovereignty in Africa, as monitoring international territorial disputes is well outside the bureau's mission space. A third option is for the collector to inform the requestor that while he or she has the capability to fulfill the request, he or she does not currently have the ability to do so because of time, personnel, or budget constraints. If the request is an urgent and high-priority need, the requestor may wish to provide additional funds to the collection activity to fund the RFI collection or can advocate for the RFI, at which point a lower-priority collection task would be dropped.

Collection

Once a task has been accepted for collection, the OSINT element will begin the process of acquiring the raw open source information needed to fulfill the requirement. The best approach when conducting OSINT acquisition is to begin with the end in mind. Given the vast amounts of information available through open sources, a collection effort that begins indiscriminately collecting information will prove a big hindrance when it comes time to process and analyze the data.

RFIs should be broken down into EEIs if not provided already by the requestor. In short, the collector should determine the following:

- What specifically is the question I am trying to answer?
- What are the most critical elements of this question?
- How much time do I have to acquire the information so I provide ample time for processing and analysis of the acquired information?
- What are the best sources for this type of information?
- How should I collect and store this information?

The last question is a very important one as it carries numerous implications for collection. First, there is the issue of OPSEC, where, depending on the sensitivity of the RFI and the sophistication of the target, significant precautions may be required so as not to betray sources and methods during the acquisition phase. A careless open source exploitation effort may end up divulging valuable information to the target, which can jeopardize the mission or put the collector's life in danger.

For open source acquisition activities that are Internet-based, the collector must consider that much Internet content is ephemeral in nature. It is not enough to simply print out or bookmark a resource, as such content may often disappear in a matter of days. Printed material is of little utility if the product must be disseminated widely. A means of archiving digital data is required for all but the smallest of OSINT tasks.

A means of keeping track of which websites have been exploited is also an important means of limiting duplication of effort and maximizing the effectiveness of current and future collection. By maintaining a database or spreadsheet with metrics on each site visited, collectors can begin to record critical information on the value, credibility, and utility of the site in question, which will be of great value during the exploitation phase.

Processing

Frequently, the open source information acquired during collection requires additional processing before it can be exploited. Foreign radio and TV broadcasts may need to be translated and transcribed. Foreign language content, likewise, would need translation. Commercial imagery and hand-held photography may need to be rotated, cropped, or annotated. During processing, it is important that a copy of the original open source materials be preserved in case questions arise that may require returning to the original for verification or further analysis.

With the use of databases, spreadsheets, and link analysis tools, frequently the data acquired through open sources require significant amounts of processing in order to get the data into a format that the software can use. Social networking or link analysis software may require the data be imported in a particular format such as comma delimited data fields such as the following: First Name, Last Name, Date, Type of Interaction, Name of Person or Entity Interacted With or "John, Smith, 20130704, Purchase, XYZ Corp." Obviously, creating an input file with delimited fields from newspaper articles would require an extensive amount of processing.

Exploitation

It consists of two parts: information vetting and analysis (which includes writing and editing the final product). Vetting of the information acquired from open sources is the critical first step. As mentioned previously, all open sources of information have an inherent bias. The nature of the bias is as varied as the source's underlying motivation for going through the trouble of collecting, organizing, and publishing that information. As secondhand users of the information, OSOs must be able to validate and verify the information as well as account for any inherent biases during the vetting process.

To vet open sources of information, criteria must be established. The following open source evaluation criteria were developed by the Department of Homeland Security (DHS) Office of Intelligence and Analysis Open Source Team. DHS vets information based on three factors: the validity of the information itself, the credibility of the source, and the frequency with which the source reports. Stated another way, the information is assessed based on how plausible the information is, how trustworthy the source is, and how good a track record the source has.

Department of Homeland Security Open Source Intelligence Evaluation Criteria

Information Evaluation	
Confirmed	Confirmed by other reputable independent sources; logical in itself; consistent with other information on the subject
Probably true	Not confirmed; logical in itself; consistent with other information on the subject
Possibly true	Not confirmed; reasonably logical in itself; agrees with some other information on the subject
Doubtfully true	Not confirmed; possible but not logical; no other information on the subject
Improbable	Not confirmed; not logical in itself; contradicted by other information on the subject
Cannot be judged	No basis exists for evaluating the validity of information
Source Evaluation (Credibility)	
Reliable	No doubt of authenticity, trustworthiness, or competency; has a history of complete reliability
Usually reliable	Minor doubt about authenticity, trustworthiness, or competency; has a history of valid information most of the time
Fairly reliable	Doubt about authenticity, trustworthiness, or competency; has provided valid information in the past
Not usually reliable	Significant doubt about authenticity, trustworthiness, or competency; has provided valid information in the past
Unreliable	Lacking in authenticity, trustworthiness, or competency; history of invalid information
Cannot be judged	No basis exists for evaluating the reliability of the source
Source Evaluation (Frequency)	
Constant provider	Source's primary purpose is to provide information on the target or subject
Frequent provider	Source often provides information on the target or similar subjects
Limited provider	Source occasionally provides information on the target, subject, or similar subjects
New or unknown provider	Source's first known instance providing information on the target or subject

Once the vetting process is complete, the analytical phase begins. OSOs and other analysts use a wide variety of analytical methodologies. Just about every analytical methodology used in all-source analysis is used in OSINT analysis. A description of analytical methodologies used by the IC can be found in Mark Lowenthal's *Intelligence: From Secrets to Policy* and Robert Clark's *Intelligence Analysis: A Target-Centric Approach.*

The proper analysis of open source information frequently requires greater depth of cultural and language skills than many all-source analysts possess. OSOs require this depth of knowledge because they are routinely called upon to collect the raw data (which is frequently in a foreign language and loaded with cultural nuances) as well as to analyze the data. All-source analysts, on the other hand, generally receive their information in the form of finished reporting, which has been collected and vetted by single-source analysts. OSOs, given the cultural and linguistic skills necessary for their job, tend to specialize in a particular country or region and thus develop a level of expertise that is not common with all-source analysts who tend to shift countries or regions during a career.

With the advent of Web 2.0 technologies such as social networking applications, one analytical methodology that has gained in importance with OSOs is social network analysis (SNA). SNA seeks to depict, measure, and understand the structure evident in a group of individuals connected by one or more interactions or relationships. By studying the interactions prevalent in social networks, OSOs are able to analyze their targets better by ascertaining how the network is structured and operates; why the interactions occur; and in some cases, even predict future interactions.

SNA is a powerful tool for OSOs. It is particularly well suited for OSINT analysis because SNA lends itself well to the dynamic process that is OSINT exploitation. One of the central tenets of SNA is that social networks are dynamic and constantly evolving—much like the stream of information gleaned from open sources. SNA researchers have also demonstrated that the structural influences of the social network can affect the actions and perceptions of the individual(s) within. As the use of social networking applications continues to rise, so will the importance of this analytical methodology for OSINT analysis.

Dissemination

Once the OSINT product is complete, it must be disseminated to the requestor or the designated audience. With the advent of the DNI "responsibility to provide" dictum in response to the 9/11 terror attacks, the IC has focused its efforts on information sharing with any consumers having a legitimate need for the information. To that end, OSINT products, many of which are at the unclassified level or with the more restrictive For Official Use Only caveat, have become a common means of disseminating intelligence to non-intelligence or nonfederal consumers.

By far, the most popular method of dissemination for IC OSINT products is via the IC unclassified intranet fabric known as DNI-U (previously called Intelink-U and originally designated as the Open Source Information tion System, or OSIS). DNI-U not only provides a protected intranet at the Unclassified/For Official Use Only level but also contains a wide variety of collaborative technologies that are heavily used by customers across the IC, the federal government, as well as state and local consumers.

The OSC utilizes the opensource.gov restricted portal on the Internet as a means of disseminating its reporting, but due to a cumbersome interface, it has a much smaller user base. In addition to these two dedicated OSINT dissemination platforms, OSINT dissemination is often accomplished via other information portals such as FBI Law Enforcement Online, the Department of Justice's Regional Information Sharing System, and the Department of Homeland Security's Homeland Security Information Network. OSINT products are also routinely disseminated on the classified networks as well.

Who Produces Open Source Intelligence?

Open source exploitation is ubiquitous as a means of gathering intelligence for governments, corporations, the news media, and many non-state actors. Unlike the other INTs that have high entry costs or significant risks, OSINT is the most accessible INT given its low risk and cost. Additionally, the speed at which OSINT can be acquired and the degree to which it can be shared with others are major advantages other INTs cannot equal.

Within the U.S. government, numerous organizations conduct OSINT exploitation, both within the IC as well as across the non-intelligence elements of the government. The OSE (formerly the NOSE) consists of all the OSINT elements found within the seventeen members of the IC. Established by the Assistant Deputy DNI for Open Source in 2006, the OSE is a governance and budgetary framework governed by IC Directive 301 with oversight provided by IC representatives to the National Open Source Committee and the OSINT Board of Governors.

Within the OSE, the largest player is the OSC at CIA, which serves as a service of common concern, providing open source collection, transcripts, and translations to meet the needs of the CIA. The content acquired by the OSC on behalf of the CIA is then made available to the OSE, the broader federal government. The OSC also provides training and professional development resources for OSOs across the IC.

Within the CIA, responsibility for OSINT analytical products falls to the CIA Directorate of Intelligence. In order to meet this responsibility, the Directorate of Intelligence established the OSW element. The OSW, with its expert OSINT analysts, most of whom have native fluency and extensive in-country experience, provides strategic-level analytical products that provide unique insight and perspectives. The OSW is unique within IC OSINT elements as it was designed from the ground up to be a center of innovation for open source tradecraft, analytical methodologies, and related technology—all operating at the unclassified level. By working outside the highly constraining classified environment, OSW can quickly leverage outside expertise and the latest in methods and technologies in a manner that is simply impossible to carry out otherwise, given the security constraints of the classified world. In late 2013, OSW was transferred from the Directorate of Intelligence to the OSC.

The next largest player within the OSE is DoD, which has extensive open source activities at the national, theater, and tactical levels. At the national level, DoD OSINT efforts are managed by DIA with oversight provided by the Defense Open Source Committee. Within DIA itself, open source exploitation is not centralized but rather is distributed across the agency based on the needs of each office.

Another national-level DoD intelligence agency engaged in OSINT exploitation is the National Geospatial-Intelligence Agency (NGA), which focuses on commercial imagery and maps. NSA conducts OSINT exploitation in support of its SIGINT mission. NSA's needs for processing massive amounts of data and for machine translation support have greatly benefited the OSE as the agency's insights and technologies are leveraged by other agencies.

A number of national intelligence centers have OSINT centers of excellence dedicated to support their unique mission sets. Chief among them is the National Center for Medical Intelligence (NCMI) located at Ft. Detrick, Maryland, which is a sub-element of DIA and has a long history of providing the highest quality OSINT products relating to epidemiology and environmental health in foreign operating environments, as well as the medical capabilities available in each nation around the globe.

Another component of DIA, the Missile and Space Intelligence Center (MSIC), located at Redstone Arsenal in Huntsville, Alabama, has likewise distinguished itself by exploiting technical literature and producing top-notch OSINT products related to missiles and directed energy weapons as well as related command, control, communications, computers, intelligence, surveillance, and reconnaissance (C4ISR) systems. Of particular interest are MSIC partnerships with local universities where undergraduate and graduate students engage in unclassified OSINT research in support of the MSIC mission.

At the theater level, the unified combatant commands (COCOMs) have varying degrees of OSINT capability. The largest and longest standing OSINT effort is located at the EUCOM with its nexus at the Joint Analysis Center in Molesworth, England. Additional major OSINT producers among the joint commands include the USPACOM, U.S. Special Operations Command (USSOCOM), USCENTCOM, and U.S. Transportation Command (USTRANSCOM). These OSINT elements are generally regionally focused but in some cases have a more narrow focus, such as supporting special operations at USSOCOM and combat operations at USCENTCOM.

With its focus on worldwide transportation and logistics, USTRANSCOM OSINT activities are global in nature.

Each of the armed services engage in their own OSINT exploitation efforts both in a formal dedicated capability and extensively at the tactical level, done informally by intelligence officers and enlisted personnel on an ad hoc basis. The U.S. Army is the most advanced both in terms of OSINT related doctrine and production. Doctrinally, the U.S. Army is the only service to have formally articulated how OSINT exploitation is conducted within the broader scope of military intelligence efforts. The U.S. Army published *Field Manual (Interim) 2–22.9 Open Source Intelligence* in late 2006, which was updated and superseded in 2012 by the *Army Techniques Publication 2–22.9* with the same title.

The U.S. Army also boasts of a number of OSINT producers that are recognized centers of excellence in the OSE at the national level. Overseas, the main U.S. Army OSINT producer was the Asian Studies Detachment at Camp Zama, Japan. Utilizing primarily retired Japanese military attachés whose salaries were funded by the Japanese Government, the detachment provided a unique OSINT perspective on Asia. Regrettably, due to budget cutbacks, the detachment has shut its doors. In the European theater, the U.S. Army's 66th Military Intelligence Brigade located in Wiesbaden, Germany, has been a provider of OSINT products since the late 1990s and currently supports the OSINT requirements of the U.S. Army Europe and U.S. Army Africa.

The most renowned U.S. Army OSINT element is the Foreign Military Studies Office at Ft. Leavenworth, Kansas, which, according to their website, specializes in OSINT exploitation on "foreign perspectives of defense and security issues that are important for understanding the environments in which the U.S. military operates." Their publications on the Soviet experiences in Afghanistan were widely read by the U.S. military prior to the launch of Operation Enduring Freedom in response to the 9/11 terror attack. The Foreign Military Studies Office pioneered the use of virtual OSINT teams by populating an encyclopedic reference wiki called the World Basic Information Library (originally created by COSPO) with reservists from across the country working from their home computers.

The Marine Corps is an avid consumer of OSINT, given the nature of its mission. For many years, the Marine Corps Intelligence Activity (MCIA) in Quantico, Virginia, has produced high-quality OSINT-derived country handbooks that are very popular within the IC and the broader U.S. military. In addition, MCIA produces small laminated "smart cards," which serve as a quick reference guide for deployed marines; they contain language and cultural, political, and environmental information for the area to which they are deployed.

The catastrophic Haitian earthquake of 2010 resulted in the deployment of the 22nd Marine Expeditionary Unit to provide humanitarian support. As operations began to move into full swing, the Washington, DC, area was hit by the "snowmageddon" snowstorm, which dumped upwards of thirty inches of snow on the Capital Region. As movement within the DC region was severely restricted, the one source of intelligence for Marines in Haiti not affected was MCIA OSINT efforts. MCIA personnel exploiting OSINT from their homes in the DC area were able to provide tailored and highly time-sensitive intelligence support to the 22nd unit on the ground in Haiti. These OSINT products have the added benefit of being able to be shared widely with nongovernmental organizations and the military support from other nations, which caught the attention of the Marine Corps' most senior leaders. Thus began the ongoing effort to inculcate OSINT exploitation, termed Expeditionary OSINT, into Marine Corps Doctrine.

The U.S. Air Force has a center of excellence for OSINT within the National Air and Space Intelligence Center (NASIC) at Wright-Patterson Air Force Base in Dayton, Ohio, which focuses on OSINT exploitation on foreign aerospace forces and weapons. The U.S. Navy Office of Naval Intelligence (ONI) produces OSINT products focused on the maritime operational environment with a particularly strong focus on technical topics. As with the U.S. Army and the U.S. Marines intelligence personnel, the U.S. Air Force, U.S. Navy, and U.S. Coast Guard military intelligence personnel conduct extensive amounts of informal OSINT exploitation at the tactical level. Modern military operations are growing increasingly reliant on OSINT even if the service doctrines have, in many cases, yet to reflect that reality.

Other large IC OSINT producers include the DHS OSINT team located within the DHS Office of Intelligence and Analysis, which is the preeminent OSINT element within the domestic elements of the IC (DHS, FBI, Coast Guard, and DEA). The Department of State's Bureau of Intelligence and Research (INR) procures foreign publications, maps, and geographic data on behalf of the OSE and conducts a significant amount of public polling overseas. The Department of Energy, principally through its various national laboratories, engages in extensive OSINT exploitation on a wide variety of technical topics in support of the IC and the broader U.S. government.

Beyond the IC, the three largest OSINT production elements include the Federal Research Division of the Library of Congress, the Defense Technical Information Service and non-IC media monitoring efforts used by public affairs, civil affairs, and psychological operations elements of the DoD. The Federal Research Division, leveraging the unique and extensive holdings at the Library of Congress, provides OSINT products to the U.S. government on a fee-for-service basis. DTIC, though not an intelligence element, manages a large digital repository with significant open source–derived reports on scientific and technical capabilities, which are widely used by the IC.

International Open Source Intelligence

Given its ubiquitous nature, OSINT is practiced in almost every nation. In terms of a formalized structure, the now-defunct COSPO established the International Open Source Working Group (IOSWG) in the mid-1990s as a collaborative framework for OSINT exchange among member nations. Dissemination of IOSWG content was accomplished via a segregated section of the OSIS (now DNI-U) called OSIS International.

The IOSWG had twelve member states: Australia, Canada, Denmark, France, Germany, Great Britain, Israel, Italy, the Netherlands, Norway, Sweden, and the United States. Members would provide (to varying degrees) OSINT products to the rest of the IOSWG via OSIS International with representatives coming together for an annual conference and partner-hosted training opportunities. The IOSWG framework was eventually dismantled by the OSC in favor of bilateral exchange agreements. This bilateral approach made exchanges easier to manage for the OSC but came at the significant cost of loss of access to internationally produced OSINT by the rest of the U.S. OSE.

In terms of a formal OSINT structure and capability, after the United States, the next largest purveyor of OSINT is Great Britain. OSINT activities within the kingdom are guided by the U.K. Joint Intelligence Committee and operationally fall under the Ministry of Defence's Deputy Chief of Defence Intelligence, who is responsible for producing intelligence analysis and production. Britain's media monitoring capability is found within the British Broadcasting Corporation (BBC) Monitoring Service, which has been monitoring foreign broadcasts since 1939 and predated U.S. monitoring as previously discussed in the history section.

Australia established its own Open Source Centre as responsibility for the production of OSINT shifted from the Department of Foreign Affairs and Trade to the Office of National Assessment. The Centre focuses its open source exploitation efforts on international developments that can affect Australia's national interests. It principally serves the Australian national intelligence community, but interestingly, it also makes its products readily available to state and territorial departments and agencies via its Open Source Centre portal.

Israel, given the threat posed by Islamic extremist-inspired terrorism, has a highly developed open source exploitation capability geared toward understanding and tracking Internet-based radicalization, terrorist group activities, and general threats to the Israeli national interest. Hatzav, the Israeli OSINT element, is part of the famed Unit 8200, or the Israeli National SIGINT Unit of the Israeli Defense Forces (IDF). Hatzav is said to collect up to 50 percent of the basic intelligence required by the IDF.

In China, the Chinese State Security organization (Guojia Anquan Bu) began by providing open source information to the Communist Party of China in the 1940s.[16] The Russian Foreign Intelligence Service (SVR) is also known to have a long-standing formal OSINT element derived from its predecessor, the KGB. During the Cold War, the KGB placed heavy reliance on OSINT exploitation against the United States and Western Europe. Ultimately, most nations engage in OSINT exploitation, but not every nation chooses to establish a formal OSINT element.

International organizations such as the European Union Commission's Joint Research Centre were known to operate OSINT sections. NATO has produced a number of handbooks and manuals on OSINT in the past.[17] In addition, many law enforcement organizations around the world have established OSINT cells. OSINT units were established within Interpol and Europol, but such efforts languished due to lack of command interest. The U.K. Scotland Yard and the Royal Canadian Mounted Police are known to have dedicated OSINT units. Within the United States, all federal law enforcement agencies conduct OSINT exploitation, and on the local level the New York City and Chicago Police Departments and the Los Angeles County Sheriff's Department also have OSINT squads.

Private Sector Open Source Intelligence

OSINT, as a critical element of competitive intelligence, is practiced globally in the private sector. Every major multinational corporation engages in competitive intelligence and, as such, engages in OSINT exploitation. The major advantage of OSINT exploitation is that, unlike traditional corporate espionage, there are no ethical or legal limitations (since the information is derived from open sources) and thus little risk of arrest or public embarrassment.

Additionally, there are a number of firms that provide commercial open source content via subscription service or access to proprietary databases. The most popular commercial database firms include Dialog, Factiva, Jane's Information Group, and LexisNexis. Popular subscription-based OSINT purveyors include the Economist Intelligence Unit, iJET, IntelCenter, and Oxford Analytica. Geospatial OSINT products can be purchased from commercial imagery firms such as DigitalGlobe and the French firm SPOT Image.

There are also a number of private-sector OSINT firms that produce custom products on contract based on a specific customer tasking. Dedicated OSINT companies include CENTRA Global Access, Eurasia Group, Information International Associates, InfoSphere, and Plessas Experts Network to name a few. Many government contracting firms also engage in OSINT as part of their national security consultancy.

Types of Targets Open Source Intelligence Works Best Against

Determining which targets OSINT works best against is factored on a case-by-case basis. Generally, OSINT works well against most targets, whether they are individuals, organizations, technologies, locations, or governments. In our increasingly interconnected world, it is practically impossible to remain obscure, and this greatly improves the chances there will be open sources of information on the topic.

The more advanced a country's telecommunications infrastructure is, the more fertile the OSINT ground becomes. In the digital age, we are increasingly leaving more and more electronic footprints with our commerce, communications, and entertainment activities. The rapid expansion of inexpensive cell phones and cell service around the world has allowed many nations to leapfrog costly infrastructure upgrades. This, in turn, allows the populace the ability to instantly interconnect and use Web 2.0 applications such as blogs, Twitter, and Facebook, as demonstrated by the 2010 Haiti earthquake and the Arab Spring uprisings.

In light of recent events, the old notion that OSINT exploitation is not successful against closed or repressive societies has had to be abandoned. Even in the most isolated country in the world, North Korea, a great deal of information regarding the new regime of Kim Jong-un has come from open sources. In a clear departure from previous secret missile launches, the North Korean government invited the international media to cover the failed launch, which provided significant OSINT exploitation opportunities. The confirmation of the North Korean First Lady Ri Sol-ju, with her name and photograph, did not come from some highly placed clandestine source but rather through news footage from the regime itself and through the public pronouncements of Kim Jong-il's former personal sushi chef who met her while visiting Kim Jong-un.

In other repressive regimes with strict Internet controls, the ability to block Internet access to certain sites or manipulate information has proven largely impractical. The populace's ability to circumvent the censorship by Chinese and Arab governments is so commonplace as to be socially acceptable. Recent efforts by the Communist Party of China to cover up its corruption or inadequate responses to disasters by censuring or manipulating open sources of information have proven counterproductive, with the party ultimately having to admit publicly its failings. In short, although it is obvious OSINT exploitation works best in open societies with transparent governments, it can and does prove very useful against countries or organizations on the other end of the spectrum.

As a general rule, OSINT is excellent at providing background information and target atmospherics. As alluded to in Dr. Joseph Nye's often-cited metaphor, OSINT can frame the intelligence question with background information, which enables our more limited clandestine collection capabilities to fill in the gaps while minimizing the risks associated with intelligence collection. Skillful OSINT analysis can also be predictive in nature from determining when the environment is volatile and likely to erupt into violence to accurately assessing when an adversary is merely bluffing or saber rattling.

OSINT is also critically important during a crisis or ongoing incident where the need for situational awareness is paramount. Moving at the speed of the digital age, OSINT is the most time sensitive of the INTs, with OSOs frequently able to respond hours, if not days, before other collectors. The ubiquitous nature of cell phone cameras and video, coupled with dissemination tools such as Photobucket and YouTube, have resulted in the ultimate situational awareness tool—instant and persistent surveillance.

Finally, artful OSINT analysis can provide early warning indicators that may tip and cue other INTs. An example can be found in Google's ability to determine the peak of the flu season in a country or region based on Google searches by individuals in that country or region searching for flu symptoms. This capability has become so well known and popular that Google has created a dedicated resource online called Google Flu Trends available at www.google.org/flutrends.[18] Google has also developed a resource to track dengue.[19]

Ultimately, there is no rule regarding which targets OSINT works best against. The challenge with open source information is not determining whether the needed information exists or not (because chances are it does) but rather figuring out where it might reside. The ADDNI/OS stated the following at the 2007 DNI Open Source Conference:

> We must come to terms with the fact that the font of human knowledge resides largely outside of the Intelligence Community and [is] available principally through open sources. Increasingly, the information we seek is out there; we just need to be smart enough to uncover it.[20]

Future Trends in Open Source Intelligence

OSINT as a discipline is likely to undergo dramatic changes in the coming years. In the same way the new information economy is affecting publishing, the news media, and businesses by driving the need for new decentralized business models, OSINT will likely devolve from a centralized and highly structured activity to many activities that are as diffuse and specialized as the open sources they target. Smaller and more specialized and responsive OSINT activities will be driven by, and collocated with, the operational elements they support.

The ODNI, recognizing that the OSC cannot fulfill the OSINT needs of everyone in the IC, has shifted to a construct where OSC resources and personnel are gradually reduced and its mission refocused on serving a functional manager role. The DNI outlined this new focus in a 2012 letter to the CIA director (who is the executive agent for the OSC), indicating that the OSC should focus on "develop[ing], coordinat[ing], and oversee[ing] the issuance and implementation of IC standards (and not higher-level IC policy) on Open Source training and tradecraft, reporting, requirements, and evaluation measures." With the IC utilization of OSINT increasingly becoming an integral part of all intelligence activities, the WMD Commission's prediction that eventually there will be no need for a centralized OSINT directorate appears to have been prescient.

Another likely trend in OSINT is the fusion or greater instantaneous integration of disparate data sources. Consider the common act of uploading a photo to a social media site such as Facebook. The user takes a picture of his or her friends at the local park with a mobile phone and uploads the photo to the site. The phone's built-in GPS capability also provides geo-location information, and the user labels or tags each individual in the picture. These tags not only identify the individuals by name but also provide a link back to that individual's Facebook profile. This simple act provides unprecedented amounts of open source information all fused instantly in one source. The implications for OSINT exploitation and its utility are profound.

Cell phones have become indispensable and constant companions for most people in the world today. As the phone technology and the underlying cellular communications infrastructure continue to advance, our current expectations of privacy and anonymity will be undermined. Add to this the growing popularity of webcams and the OSINT discipline will have to incorporate new methodologies and technologies for exploiting this persistent and ubiquitous source of photographs and video.

Another area of change for OSINT will be the coming primacy of social networking tools and technologies. We are quickly moving toward the day when social networking sites become the primary means of communicating; receiving news; shopping; and engaging in discourse with our network of friends, business associates, and members of our affinity groups. The social networking medium's ability to enable those functions and add rich layers of contextual data will become the critical focus for OSINT exploitation in the future.

The inclusion of SNA methodologies as a basic core competency for OSOs will soon become imperative. As OSOs begin to exploit SNA methodologies and tools, this will drive the development of new collection methods and analytical models for use throughout the IC. Ultimately, the complexity of OSINT-enabled SNA, coupled with the imperative of visual depictions of social networks, will drive the development of immersive environments for SNA. The ability to utilize virtual reality technologies to aid OSOs in walking through and interacting with three-dimensional depictions of social networks is the wave of the future.

Though OSINT has always played an important role in intelligence, most observers would agree that its importance and the quality of OSINT products will continue to increase as our information age continues. Ultimately, due to the ever-growing quantity and quality of actionable intelligence available through open sources, intelligence elements around the world will restructure their tactics, techniques, and procedures to reflect the growing reality of OSINT as the source of first resort.

References

1. National Defense Authorization Act for Fiscal Year 2006, Pub. L. No. 109-163, sec. 931 (2006).
2. Ibid.
3. Intelligence Community Directive 301: National Open Source Enterprise, Office of the Director of National Intelligence, July 11, 2006, http://fas.org/irp/dni/icd/icd-301.pdf.

4. Oversight and Investigations Subcommittee of the Committee on Armed Services of the U.S. House of Representatives, *Intelligence Successes and Failures in Operations Desert Shield/Storm*, 103rd Cong., 1st sess., August 16, 1993, Committee Print No. 5, 12.

5. Major Mats Bjore, "Six Years of Open Source Information: Lessons Learned," Open Source Quarterly, 1996.

6. Dr. Joseph Nye, (keynote address, Security Affairs Support Association, Fort George G. Meade, MD, April 24, 1993).

7. The Commission on the Intelligence Capabilities of the United States Regarding Weapons of Mass Destruction, *Report to the President of the United States*, March 31, 2005, 378.

8. J. Niles Riddel, Deputy Director, FBIS, "National Security and National Competitiveness: Open Source Solutions" (paper presented at the 1st International Symposium, Washington, DC, December 2, 1992), https://www.fas.org/irp/fbis/riddel.html.

9. The Intelligence Reform and Terrorism Prevention Act of 2004, Pub. L. No. 108-458 (December 17, 2004).

10. The Commission on the Intelligence Capabilities of the United States Regarding Weapons of Mass Destruction, *Report to the President of the United States,* March 31, 2005, 377, 379.

11. "The Scope of FBIS and BBC Open-Source Media Coverage, 1979–2008." *CIA Studies in Intelligence* 54, no. 1 (March 2010): 17–37.

12. Director of National Intelligence, *Endorsement of OSINT Functional Management Implementation Plan*, July 23, 2012 (E/S 00427).

13. Eliot A. Jardines, Assistant Deputy Director of National Intelligence for Open Source, Remarks and Q&A 2007 ODNI Open Source Conference, July 16, 2007. http://www.dni.gov/files/documents/Newsroom/Speeches%20and%20Interviews/20070716_speech_3.pdf.

14. Burt Helm, "How to Use Competitive Intelligence to Gain an Advantage," *Inc. Magazine*, April 2011.

15. Lee Ratzan, "Mining the Deep Web: Search Strategies That Work," *Computerworld,* December 11, 2006.

16. Federation of American Scientists, *Chinese Ministry of State Security*, http://www.fas.org/irp/world/china/mss/history.htm.

17. Florian Schaurer and Jan Storger, "The Evolution of Open Source Intelligence (OSINT)," *The Intelligencer*, Winter/Spring 2013.

18. Google, "Flu Trends," http://www.google.org/flutrends/about/how.html.

19. Google, "Dengue Trends," http://www.google.org/denguetrends/intl/en_us/about/how.html.

20. Ibid.

3

Human Intelligence

Michael Althoff

What It Is

HUMINT is the acronym for human intelligence and is usually associated with espionage or the clandestine acquisition of secrets by a human source as well as the intelligence produced from this collection discipline. The fundamental elements are the clandestine method of collection, the secret nature of the material collected, and most importantly the human collector. Although the other intelligence collection disciplines (INTs) discussed in this book (except Open Source Intelligence [OSINT]) are engaged in the clandestine collection of secrets as well, only HUMINT utilizes people as its source.

HUMINT has a unique place in the intelligence collection strategy of any nation, which further distinguishes it from the other INTs; it is visible in meeting one of the principal challenges to any country—assessing the threat posed by an adversary. Each of the other INTs makes valuable contributions to understanding the threat from another country, but it is often HUMINT that provides confirmation of the true nature of the threat—that is, is it real or fake? HUMINT derived from human sources who are able to sit in leadership or inner circle meetings and report on plans and intentions and policy decisions provides a unique perspective into what a country really wants to do. So, too, does the HUMINT from documents obtained by a human source that delineate foreign, domestic, economic, military, or weapons research and development (R & D) plans and intentions as well as their implementation. One of the most cited examples of this kind of HUMINT from the Cold War era involved Oleg Penkovsky. Penkovsky was a highly placed but disillusioned Colonel in Soviet military intelligence. He provided evidence that debunked the idea that the Soviets possessed superior missile technology to that of the United States. Perhaps, more importantly, he acquired intelligence on the intentions of the Soviet leadership during the Cuban missile crisis, which helped shape the U.S. response and avoided a nuclear war.

It is also important to understand what HUMINT is not. HUMINT collection is too often romanticized as an adventurous and daring calling involving constant danger; incredibly handsome men; alluring femme fatales; and evil, crafty villains. The practitioners of the art of collecting HUMINT know full well that it is less James Bond or even Austin Powers than it is George Smiley, the British Secret Intelligence Service (SIS), or Military Intelligence, Section 6 (MI6), character from John Le Carré's novels. Most HUMINT is collected overtly and not through clandestine means. Much of the daily exchange that happens in diplomacy, for example, is HUMINT, but is overt. The same can be said of the activities of military attachés who are posted abroad. The key common denominator is the involvement of humans as the source, whether secret or open.

The identification and manipulation of human beings willing to betray their country—commit treason—is largely hard, unrecognized work involving long hours, tedium, and persistence that is only occasionally punctuated by adrenaline-pumping fear and danger. The risks are real as tragically demonstrated by the deaths in 2009 of seven Central Intelligence Agency (CIA) officers when a source blew himself up at their compound in Khost, Afghanistan. Such events, however, are the exception rather than the rule.

HUMINT is the preferred means of intelligence collection by non-state actors as well, to include terrorist organizations, narcotraffickers and criminal groups in addition to legitimate commercial entities. Perhaps this is because, in business parlance, the cost–benefit ratio is potentially so positive. The collection of HUMINT does not require the monetary investment in infrastructure, personnel, and technology that characterizes the other INTs. The payoff can be huge compared to the investment in dollars and cents. This is also why HUMINT is highly valued by traditional national intelligence and law enforcement agencies as an essential component of a country's overall intelligence collection capability. There is a downside to all of this, however, because the cost of failure in the HUMINT realm can be devastating, resulting in loss of life or great national embarrassment when an intelligence collection operation goes awry.

The covert efforts of the CIA, MI6, KGB (*Komitet Gosudarstvennoi Bezopasnosti*—Committee for State Security; now SVR, or *Sluzhba Vneshnei Razvedki*—External Intelligence Service), Chinese Ministry of State Security (MSS), and Mossad to acquire HUMINT and protect their nations' security are well known from the news media and movies. The Federal Bureau of Investigation (FBI); the British Security Service, or Military Intelligence, Section 5 (MI5); the Russian FSB (*Federal'naya Sluzhba Bezopastnosti*, or Federal Security Service); Shin Bet, and other domestic law enforcement organs also recruit clandestine human sources or use undercover officers to penetrate criminal enterprises, drug cartels, and terrorist organizations to obtain HUMINT. What they collect can then be used to disrupt the criminal or terrorist schemes of these groups. Not to be outdone, these same transnational groups try to reverse the process and compromise or recruit law enforcement members to gain the HUMINT they need to protect their interests and remain viable.

HUMINT can also encompass industrial espionage, or the efforts by one company to steal the secrets of a competitor, whether in the same country or somewhere else in our global economy. The reasons why a company may conduct a covert operation to gain commercial HUMINT vary, but the goal is usually the same—learn what another company is doing to protect your own firm now and in the future.

Sharing HUMINT among foreign intelligence services or law enforcement agencies is another essential component of any HUMINT collection program. This is particularly important when one country does not have formal relations with another country (e.g., the United States with Iran and North Korea), but a liaison partner has such relations. HUMINT sharing about an adversary is also valuable when that country or group has a particularly proficient counterintelligence (CI) capability, such as Russia, China, or some terrorist organizations. The HUMINT collection efforts of intelligence service partners against these types of hard targets are a force multiplier to the acquisition of valuable intelligence. Liaison-supplied HUMINT may fill in critical gaps, but it must be evaluated continually, since not all foreign partners use the same standards in vetting their human sources or in authenticating the HUMINT they produce. Caution should also be exercised with HUMINT obtained from foreign partners, since they may have their own agendas in supplying some or all of the HUMINT they acquire about a particular country, non-state actor, or topic.

A classic example of the value of sharing intelligence between liaison partners is what has become known as the Farewell dossier. In 1980, the French Directorate of the Surveillance of the Territory, or *Direction de la Surveillance du Territoire* (DST), recruited KGB Lieutenant colonel Vladimir I. Vetrov, who was code-named "Farewell." Vetrov gave the French some 4,000 documents that detailed an extensive KGB effort to clandestinely acquire technical know-how from the West. French President Francois Mitterrand offered to share this HUMINT treasure trove with U.S. President Ronald Reagan. Instead of simply using this material to improve U.S. defenses against the KGB efforts, the Department of Defense (DoD), FBI, and CIA in early 1982 began developing an asymmetric counterattack. The KGB "wish list" of Western technology was used to feed back to Moscow, through CIA-controlled channels, the items on the list augmented with "improvements." These improvements were designed to pass acceptance testing by Soviet scientists and engineers but would eventually fail randomly in actual service. Flawed computer chips, turbines, and factory plans found their way into Soviet military and civilian factories and equipment. Misleading information on U.S. stealth technology and space defense flowed into Soviet intelligence reporting. The result was a disaster for the credibility of the KGB. Unfortunately, Vetrov met an untimely end (an occupational hazard for spies). In 1983, Vetrov was apparently part of a love triangle in which he killed a fellow KGB officer and attempted to kill the woman involved. During the ensuing investigation, his espionage was discovered and he was executed. In some cases, murder—especially if it is a crime of passion—can be forgiven; treason cannot be forgiven.

HUMINT may also be acquired from defectors who have left their homeland secretly and are willing to share intelligence with their new-found protectors. One of the most dramatic defections during the Cold War involved Victor Belenko, a lieutenant in the Soviet Air Force who escaped from Russia in 1976 by flying his MiG-25/Foxbat fighter aircraft to Japan. The materiel exploitation of this aircraft (Belenko also conveniently brought along the fighter's technical manual) and the hours of debriefing he underwent provided the United States with much valuable information about the state of Soviet aircraft weapon systems technology, as well as Soviet Air Force tactics and doctrine. The MiG-25 was eventually returned to the USSR, minus a few parts. Belenko went to the United States, where he was granted citizenship and given a generous trust fund.

High-profile defectors, such as Saddam Hussein's son-in-law Hussein Kamel, who defected to Jordan in 1995, are more problematic. How do you handle a defector like Kamel, a known human rights abuser? How do you go about vetting and using the HUMINT from such sources? Controversy still exists, for example, about the use of the intelligence he provided on Iraqi weapons of mass destruction (WMD) programs. Ultimately Kamel and his brother, who was also married to a daughter of the Iraqi dictator, chose to return to Iraq and were summarily executed by their father-in-law.

Émigrés, on the other hand, have moved from their native land of their own accord, and though they may provide secrets to their new country of residence, in most instances they do so overtly rather than in secret. During the Cold War, émigrés from the East were quite willing to tell Western intelligence organizations what they knew about life and conditions behind the Iron Curtain.

Such an overt rather than clandestine collection method that still results in the acquisition of secret information or intelligence suggests that the definition of HUMINT needs to be broadened to include this alternative means of obtaining secrets. Another example would be the secrets acquired by the overt interrogation of prisoners and detainees as well as debriefings of individuals who volunteer or willingly give up intelligence. This would, for example, include a category of subjects known as legal travelers. Legal travelers openly visiting a country that is off limits to citizens from other countries can also overtly collect intelligence simply through observation. The insights these visitors could provide just by being in a denied area nation would be invaluable because of the basic "ground truth" HUMINT they discover, which no satellite or eavesdropping antenna can capture.

The definition of HUMINT can therefore be expanded to include both covert and overt collection, but useful intelligence remains the object of the collection and humans the means of acquiring it. Mere "information" is not the goal of HUMINT collection. Certainly information may be a by-product of any of the INTs, but it is secrets that remain the primary focus of each of their collection efforts. Spy satellites, for example, are able to provide imagery of troop movements or nuclear weapons testing and development that an adversary wants to remain hidden but which would be invaluable intelligence to the country collecting the imagery. The overhead reconnaissance performed by both these and commercial satellites can also provide imagery that is not secret, such as the visible effects of climate change or the migration of populations. What is gleaned from this imagery might ultimately raise national security concerns, but it is information, not intelligence.

There is considerable value nonetheless in the collection of information by intelligence services. They generally prefer collecting information readily available to the public because of the reduced risks and the cost effectiveness involved. The more information that can be obtained openly about a country or subject of interest, the less the other modes of collection—especially human sources—will be tasked. (See the "How Human Intelligence Is Managed" section for a discussion of tasking for HUMINT.) In open, democratic societies, there is a wealth of information available through the media, universities, research labs, and commercial entities. Exchange students, visiting academic, scientific or commercial delegations, as well as intelligence officers use their freedom of access to openly collect information of interest to their countries. Although humans are the means of collection, these sources seek information available to everyone and not the HUMINT or closely guarded secrets that humans can acquire.

What It Collects

Now that we understand what HUMINT is—the clandestine or overt collection of intelligence by human sources and the product thereby derived from such collection—and what distinguishes it from the other intelligence disciplines, we can look at what it collects. One of the most important collection requirements for any intelligence service is to learn the plans and intentions of an adversary—whether the targets are countries, commercial entities, terrorist groups, or criminal enterprises. National-level intelligence services, with the mandate to protect their country's security, focus upon an enemy or potential enemy's plans and intentions in its foreign, domestic, and military policies to ascertain the threat posed by that opponent. A leader's perceptions and those of his or her closest advisors, the foreign policy and negotiating strategies to be pursued, the international relationships to be established or strengthened, the domestic economic and foreign trade policies to be enacted, and the defense posture to be set, including new weapon acquisitions as well as weapons-related R & D, are just some of the critical elements that would go into the formulation of the threat assessment of an adversary.

Assisting in their formulation of the potential threat posed by the newly independent Estonia was likely one of the reasons that the Russian foreign intelligence service (SVR) recruited Hermann Simm in 1995. The Russian government was interested in the threat to Russians residing in an independent Estonia and in ensuring the security of Russia's borders from the threat posed by Estonia's new friends in the West. Simm's position in the Defense Ministry in charge of Estonia's national security system gave the SVR the potential to learn about both. Responsible for all of Estonia's classified military documents, the issuance of security clearances and its cyber defense systems, Simm's value as a spy significantly increased when Estonia joined the North Atlantic Treaty Organization (NATO) in 2003. He then gained access to NATO military secrets, which were high on the SVR target list, especially as relations with NATO deteriorated. Simm was ultimately compromised by the sloppy tradecraft of his handler and arrested on September 21, 2008, but not before delivering to the Russians over those years thousands of documents and becoming the most damaging spy in NATO history. Hermann Simm pleaded guilty to espionage on February 25, 2009. He was sentenced to 12.5 years in prison and fined around $1.7 million to replace the security systems in Estonia that he had compromised.

Threats to a country are no longer posed just by other nation-states. Threats to the homeland now exist from terrorist groups, criminal enterprises, and narcotraffickers in addition to the threats of cyber attacks from state-sponsored groups or independent hackers. These very different adversaries present significant challenges for intelligence services and law enforcement agencies trying to collect HUMINT on adversary plans and intentions in order to mitigate the threat each poses. Recruiting spies to commit espionage against their country is difficult enough. The task is made more difficult with terrorists, criminals, or hackers because of the ideological or financial bonds that may join them together, along with the fear of death to them and reprisals against their families if they are discovered. The alternative of trying to infiltrate someone into these groups may be even more problematic given that the person must look and speak like those in the group and have the type of background and bona fides that demonstrate commitment to whatever the cause or criminal enterprise might be.

In addition to collecting HUMINT about the secret plans and intentions of adversaries, intelligence services and law enforcement agencies also seek HUMINT about those adversaries' capabilities—especially their weapons systems. Whether these are conventional, nuclear, biological, or chemical weapons, HUMINT has and will likely continue to play a key role in ascertaining the threats posed by an enemy's current and projected arsenal. HUMINT in combination with the intelligence produced by the other INTs can give a country's leadership and defense establishment what it needs to develop the weapons and countermeasures to thwart an adversary's weapons systems and protect national security.

The Russians recognized the opportunity to protect their national security when Jeffrey Delisle, a Canadian Navy sublieutenant, walked into the Russian embassy in Ottawa in July 2007 and volunteered to give secret information to the Russian military intelligence service (*Glavnoe Razvedyvatelnoye Upravleniye*, or Main Intelligence Administration [GRU]). Delisle worked at a highly classified naval intelligence facility in Halifax, Nova Scotia. His access to military secrets in databases shared among the "Five Eyes" intelligence group of Canada, the United States, the United Kingdom, Australia, and New Zealand could give the GRU considerable insight into the technological capabilities and threats posed by its Western adversaries. For the next four years, Delisle copied secret computer files onto a USB stick and pasted the files into e-mails, which he then sent to the Russians. After returning from a trip to Rio de Janeiro where he met his Russian handler in September 2011, Delisle came to the attention of Canadian authorities for carrying conspicuous amounts of cash and behaving suspiciously when queried about his activities while in Brazil. After monitoring him for several months and intercepting some of the messages he sent to his GRU handler, Delisle was arrested by the Royal Canadian Mounted Police in January 2012. On February 8, 2013, Jeffrey Delisle pleaded guilty to selling classified information to Russia and was sentenced to twenty years in prison minus time already served and fined the almost $112,000 he had been paid by the Russians. The full extent of Delisle's espionage remains classified, but the Russians probably got their money's worth, considering Delisle's access. The damage to the Canadians was not just the loss of intelligence and the potential threat to human sources but the prospect that there would be less intelligence sharing from their partners until the partners were convinced that the Canadians could adequately protect the secrets being shared.

Threats to a nation's security also come from an enemy's civilian and military intelligence services. The collection of CI HUMINT about the plans, intentions, capabilities, requirements, and most importantly successes of opposing intelligence organizations is critical to the preservation of any country's security. This is why one of the highest priorities for every intelligence service is the penetration of its adversaries' intelligence establishments. In view of the high value of CI HUMINT, it is not surprising that its acquisition poses one of the most difficult challenges for HUMINT operations, given the extraordinary CI countermeasures that intelligence services implement to protect their crown jewels. These might include such things as periodic polygraphs, limited or completely banned contact with foreigners, or internal monitoring of intelligence officers' activities. Nonetheless, as seen throughout the Cold War on both sides, the acquisition of a human penetration of an intelligence service, whether through recruitment or volunteering, provides some of the most valuable HUMINT that can be collected.

HUMINT is not limited to adversaries or potential adversaries, however. As events over the past few years have shown, nations customarily conduct all sorts of intelligence collection against states that may be deemed "friends." The German uproar over alleged U.S. Signals Intelligence (SIGINT) against Chancellor Angela Merkel—and the Turkish uproar over German SIGINT against them—are pertinent examples. This type of collection can extend to HUMINT. The motive for this type of HUMINT is often the question of intentions, which is always a key intelligence requirement. Even among friendly nations there may always be lingering doubts about reliability or plans, which can have consequences for both parties. The Japanese, for example, kept Nazi Germany completely in the dark about plans to attack the United States and bring it into the war in 1941.

However, conducting HUMINT, or any other intelligence collection, against friendly states runs even higher risks than other collection given the consequences if these are revealed. For example, Israel ran a HUMINT operation against the United States via Jonathan Pollard, a U.S. Navy intelligence analyst, in the 1980s, who volunteered his services to Israel (and South Africa). Although the Israelis were aware of the consequences if they were caught, the material Pollard offered seemed too good to turn down. Pollard was caught in 1985, causing a major rift in U.S.-Israeli relations at the time and ever after, as Israel repeatedly requested that he be released, which the United States has refused. (Pollard was sentenced to life in prison but under the sentencing rules in effect at the time, he is eligible for parole at the end of 2015.)

Nations do create limits on their intelligence collection, including HUMINT. The Five Eyes nations do not collect on one another. Germany, after the alleged NSA revelations, reportedly requested to be admitted to this "club" and was refused.

Why It Matters

HUMINT is an integral part of any country's intelligence collection program because it, like Communications Intelligence (COMINT), often is the only means available to determine *exactly* what an adversary—whether a country, terrorist group, drug cartel, criminal enterprise, or opposing intelligence service—intends to do. It may provide the initial warning of a new threat to a nation's security on which the other INTs are then able to focus and confirm. On the other hand, HUMINT is sometimes viewed as the collector of last resort because of the difficulty and length of time involved in acquiring intelligence via human sources. It is therefore often the case that one of the other INTs will acquire intelligence, such as troop movements or nuclear testing, that HUMINT is then tasked to corroborate and possibly amplify. This symbiotic relationship among the various collection disciplines is visible too when human operations enable SIGINT or MASINT collection efforts and when SIGINT or Imagery Intelligence (IMINT) facilitates HUMINT operations.

The importance of HUMINT in protecting a nation against threats also applies to its role in supporting a nation's military planning, strategy development, and weapons acquisition and operations both large and small. HUMINT provides valuable strategic-level intelligence to military policymakers and can also provide critical tactical-level intelligence to operational commanders on the battlefield as well as enhance the tactical intelligence acquired through SIGINT and IMINT for war fighters and strike teams alike. As will be discussed later, HUMINT from unvetted sources—especially in a threatening environment such as a war zone or military operation—must be handled very carefully. Corroboration from other human sources, but preferably from the other INTs, should be required if possible to establish the validity of the intelligence. While HUMINT matters, its value is significantly enhanced in combination with the other collection disciplines.

History

Throughout most of recorded history, the gathering of intelligence has been accomplished by human agents rather than the technical means that became dominant during the twentieth century. For governments of empires, kingdoms, and nation-states, HUMINT from early days has had two main objectives: internal security and knowledge of military opponents. Merchants in the ancient world also needed intelligence about markets, prices, competitors, and risks and relied extensively on agents to obtain such information.[1] In many ways, these topics remain today the objectives of HUMINT collectors—governmental and commercial.

The early history of intelligence is therefore largely the history of HUMINT. The Old Testament describes a classic HUMINT operation, where Moses sent out spies to bring back information on the land of Canaan. The mission Moses gave them was "… to see what the land is, and whether the people who dwell in it are strong or weak, whether they are few or many, and whether the land they dwell in is good or bad …" In the fifth century BCE, Chinese general Sun Tzu developed the first known formal exposition of HUMINT in his classic work on strategy, *The Art of War.* At about the same time, the Egyptian pharaohs employed spies to identify disloyal subjects and to locate tribes that the pharaohs could conquer and enslave. After about 1000 BCE, Egypt's HUMINT efforts focused more on political and military threats from their regional rivals—first the Greeks and then the Romans.

The Greeks and the Romans, in their turn, relied on HUMINT for political and military intelligence. Greek city-states routinely collected HUMINT about other city-states' military strength. The Roman Empire, for intelligence support to its military and governing operations across three continents, relied on a massive network of agents. It also conducted domestic espionage to identify internal threats, such as learning in advance about the plot to assassinate Julius Caesar in 44 BCE. But Caesar—like many subsequent national leaders—ignored his intelligence service's warning and suffered the consequences.[2]

In the Middle Ages, nation-states such as France and England developed HUMINT capabilities using their diplomatic services. The most extensive HUMINT network in Europe, though, was that operated by the Roman Catholic Church. This was also a time when HUMINT-enabled COMINT flourished, a tradition that continues today. HUMINT assets purloined letters, intercepted communications, and eavesdropped on government and commercial conversations.

Venice in the late Middle Ages began establishing permanent embassies abroad with one of their primary purposes being the collection of commercial and economic intelligence on Venice's trading partners and competitors. Venice's leaders wanted to ensure that the city's commercial monopolies were protected and that its trade was unhindered. To do this, the city's rulers operated a secret intelligence service that was the envy of the rest of Europe.[3] Embassies have been used as platforms for collecting HUMINT ever since.

Building on the Venetian model, the courts of Europe soon began to organize their own secret services. One of the most successful of these was developed and operated by Sir Francis Walsingham, spymaster to Queen Elizabeth I. At least one historian attributes the birth of modern espionage to Walsingham and the organization of spies, code breakers, and analysts he built.[4] His spies kept the English Court informed of Spain's efforts to overthrow the Virgin Queen, and his covert actions in this regard delayed the sailing of the Spanish Armada.[5] His thoughts on the Spanish problem were written in 1587 and titled "Plot for Intelligence out of Spain." It now resides in the British National Archives and may be the oldest collection plan in existence.[6]

In the first part of the nineteenth century, during the Napoleonic Wars, both France and Britain maintained organizations for the purpose of gathering HUMINT. One historian has described Napoleon's efforts this way:

> Napoleon drew his information from many agencies, by many means, and paid well for it. Much of it came from his diplomatic service, every French ambassador and consul (like those of other European nations) having his own spy net and staff of bright eyed junior diplomats, who made friends with loose-tongued officials and occasionally did romance their plump wives.[7]

Europe's autocrats tended to turn inward after the fall of Napoleon and concentrate on internal security, giving rise to modern secret police organizations. The generally recognized originator of this concept was Joseph Fouché, Minister of Police in revolutionary and postrevolutionary France and under Napoleon. Fouché had the clandestine operator's skill at intrigue and manipulation. He also was proficient at changing loyalties; in their turn, he betrayed French leaders Robespierre, Napoleon, and Louis XVIII. Fouché's establishment of a centralized police organization, his use of disinformation, double agents, informants, bribery, and intimidation all in support of the political leadership have earned him acknowledgment by some as the architect of the modern police state.

By the middle of the nineteenth century, the increasing competition among Europe's nation-states fueled a demand for intelligence. Newly formed nations such as Germany developed effective HUMINT operations in neighboring countries. Bismarck's intelligence chief Wilhelm Steiber established Germany's Information Bureau and deployed a network of agents and informants. The network was crucial to Prussian expansion and to Berlin's victory in the Franco-Prussian War of 1870 to 1871. One story has it that when the chief French peace negotiator arrived in Versailles, Steiber had him installed in a house that had previously served as the headquarters of the Prussian Secret Service in France. Steiber himself, disguised as a butler, met the French plenipotentiary at the door and personally attended to his every need. All the while, Steiber was collecting information on the Frenchman's instructions from Paris to give to Bismarck. British intelligence historian Hughes-Wilson assesses the following:

> Steiber's achievements ... changed the nature of intelligence forever. From being the private plaything of Kings, ministers and generals, intelligence now became part of the bureaucratic fabric of the nation state, both in peace and war. Intelligence was no longer some private world, but was recognized as part of the political military mainstream in every developed capital.[8]

The U.S. experience with HUMINT contrasts with that of European nations because of the different nature of the threats it faced in North America. European empires, kingdoms, and nation-states confronted enduring internal and external threats. Their HUMINT services therefore tended to endure. The political and military threats to the United States were more sporadic until World War II. Consequently, U.S. HUMINT organizations were created in response to threats and tended to disappear when the threats did.

George Washington created the first of such organizations during the American Revolution. Washington's experience in the French and Indian War had impressed on him the value of good HUMINT sources. Recognizing the inherent weakness of his military position, he relied on intelligence to improve his odds against the British. He created a relatively professional and successful secret intelligence bureau after the failure of a mission by Nathan Hale, whose amateur efforts and abysmal tradecraft led to his capture and hanging.[9] Washington often acted as his own spymaster and wrote his own requirements for his agents to collect against. Washington's spies used many of the same techniques still employed today, including trusted intermediaries who facilitated communication between agents (known as cutouts), dead drops, cover, and safe houses. For the duration of the war, Washington's network of agents kept him informed of British military movements and intentions. Washington also understood the value of CI—especially when one of his commanders, Benedict Arnold, proved to be a traitor. Washington was deaf to British pleas that he not hang Arnold's British contact, Major John Andre, who had been caught with incriminating intelligence when in civilian dress.

The intermittent presence of U.S. HUMINT organizations continued throughout the nineteenth century. No formal standing intelligence organization existed in the United States except in times of conflict. During the Mexican War, some 200 full-time spies from all levels of Mexican society provided reporting to General Winfield Scott, helping him to wage a successful campaign against superior numbers.[10] At the heart of this operation was the Mexican Spy Company, a group of Mexican criminals run by a bandit named Manuel Dominguez. Motivated apparently by money and U.S. Army protection from imprisonment, these highwaymen ranged from Veracruz to Mexico City and kept Scott accurately informed of the Mexican Army's movements.[11] The Mexican War would be the first time the U.S. military used large numbers of foreign nationals as agents to conduct HUMINT collection operations.

When the Civil War started, neither side had an organized HUMINT framework. Over the course of the conflict, this would change. Union armies in both the Eastern and Western theaters eventually developed fairly sophisticated HUMINT organizations. Although Confederate forces used spies and scouts, they appear not to have been nearly as successful or as sophisticated as their Union counterparts. Initially, the Union army contracted its HUMINT activities to Alan Pinkerton. Pinkerton was more effective at CI than at HUMINT collection, and his military intelligence career ended with that of his sponsor, General McClellan. Eventually, the Union armies in the East developed their own capability in the Bureau of Military Information (BMI) under the command of a former New York lawyer named Colonel Sharpe. The BMI provided the Army of the Potomac, through its network of spies, interrogations, debriefings, and cadre of analysts, a detailed and highly accurate picture of the Confederate army of Northern Virginia's movements and order of battle.[12] The BMI also furnished strategic-level intelligence to the Lincoln administration. Operatives like Elizabeth Van Lew, who lived in Richmond, submitted detailed reports about the political and economic conditions inside the Confederate capital.[13]

In the West, General Ulysses Grant used Major General Grenville Dodge as his intelligence chief. Dodge created one of the largest intelligence networks of the war, including over 100 agents. Many of their identities remain unknown, because Dodge used code names and numbers for most of them. His espionage network is known to have operated in Vicksburg, Meridian, Selma, Mobile, Chattanooga, and Atlanta. He successfully recruited the services of Unionists in Northern Alabama who supplied valuable intelligence. From late 1862 until the summer of 1863, it is estimated that these agents completed over 200 intelligence-related missions.[14] In the Vicksburg Campaign, Dodge's intelligence was absolutely vital to Grant, both in determining

Confederate General Pemberton's force strength and plans and in keeping abreast of the activities of Johnston's and Bragg's armies, which were desperately seeking ways to relieve Pemberton.

Dodge faced many of the same budgetary and bureaucratic obstacles that his successors in HUMINT have subsequently confronted. To avoid paper trails in the U.S. Army's paymaster department, he funded many of his agents through the proceeds of captured Confederate cotton and other contraband sold at auction. Angered by Dodge's tactics, his superiors in the U.S. Army and the War Department demanded documentation of his activities to include pay vouchers and the names of his sources and operatives. Dodge refused, fearing for the safety of his people. Grant, who clearly valued Dodge's work and its results, supported him. Dodge kept the vouchers in his personal files the rest of his life.[15]

After the Civil War, U.S. intelligence organizations again shrank to insignificance. But not long after the war's end, U.S. attention began to turn outward. Expanding U.S. international commerce and other interests drove a need for political, military, and economic intelligence about overseas regions. For military intelligence, that need was served by attachés.

Early in the nineteenth century, European nations had begun posting military and naval officers to their diplomatic establishments abroad. By the middle of the century, most legations included at least one military or naval attaché. These officers performed a number of protocol functions, but it was common knowledge that their primary mission was to obtain intelligence concerning the military forces of the countries in which they served.[16]

During the 1880s, the United States began to follow the European lead. In 1882, the U.S. Navy established the Office of Naval Intelligence and tasked it with the mission of observing and reporting on the maritime activity of foreign navies.[17] At the end of that decade, the U.S. Navy and U.S. Army began assigning attachés to U.S. diplomatic missions abroad to collect military-related intelligence.[18] Despite such developments, these intelligence organizations remained small and did not actively conduct much in the way of covert HUMINT collection operations. What was known about foreign militaries and the threat they might pose to the United States was largely dependent upon open sources supplemented by military attaché and diplomatic reporting.[19]

The First World War resulted in a surge of intelligence services, including those of the United States. It also gave rise to the use of neutral countries, such as Switzerland, as platforms for running HUMINT operations inside the belligerent nations.[20]

During the interwar period, U.S. intelligence activities, including HUMINT, again shrank in size. Germany, Japan, and the Soviet Union, on the other hand, expanded their HUMINT capabilities substantially during the 1930s. The USSR was particularly effective in recruiting HUMINT assets who performed well for decades.

It took the outbreak of World War II, however, to shake American intelligence out of its lethargy. As the war progressed, U.S. HUMINT capability grew in size, sophistication, and importance beyond anything previously experienced. Those who served in the Organization of Special Services (OSS) would form the nucleus of the U.S. HUMINT capability well into the Cold War. The OSS did not achieve many intelligence break-throughs per se, but it proved to be an invaluable training ground for the founders of the CIA.

When the OSS was disbanded in November 1945, its components were given over to those agencies willing to take them. Espionage, for example, went largely to the War Department, which was not much of a stretch as the OSS had been part of the Joint Chiefs of Staff structure during the war. However, the passage of the National Security Act of 1947 and the stand-up of the CIA changed the nature of U.S. HUMINT. Although the act did not specify that the CIA would become the center for HUMINT, CIA did so, in part responding to the absence of other agencies willing to take responsibility. The center of gravity became the CIA civilian controlled Directorate of Plans (DDP)—later the Directorate of Operations (DDO) and now the National Clandestine Service (NCS). The individual military services nonetheless have continued to rely on both overt and clandestine HUMINT capabilities since 1947, with the U.S. Army being the largest contributor. Today, the military's clandestine HUMINT effort resides primarily within the Defense Intelligence Agency's Defense Clandestine Service.

The onset of the Cold War saw a significant increase in the size, sophistication, and capability of U.S. HUMINT across all of the domains noted previously: plans and intentions, weapons developments, internal strengths and weaknesses, and CI and counterespionage. Given the fact that the DDP/DDO was responsible for covert action as well as HUMINT, these two activities often merge in some people's thinking, but their goals are quite different. HUMINT is about collecting intelligence. Covert action is about creating preferred political outcomes in such a manner as to be undetected. There is an intelligence collection aspect attendant to covert action in terms of assessing the conditions and the chances for success, but the two should be thought of as distinct activities.

The changing requirements of the military have often driven the development of specialized HUMINT organizations. During the Cold War, for example, the U.S. Military Liaison Mission, which was originally established to help monitor the Potsdam Conference agreement among the occupying powers of Germany, evolved into a HUMINT operation that collected intelligence against the Soviet military forces occupying Germany. It gathered valuable intelligence on the status of Soviet forces and their equipment. In the current era of global terrorism, the unique mission of the military's Special Forces has both made new demands on HUMINT and at the same time supplemented overall HUMINT capability.

How Human Intelligence Is Managed

Requirements and Tasking[21]

The quality of HUMINT reporting is in part a function of the quality of the requirements the HUMINT collector receives. There are a number of elements that identify a good HUMINT requirement. These include specificity, identification of potential sources, priority, and time urgency of the intelligence needed. It is usually helpful if the collector knows who wants the information being collected; why they need it; why it is important; and if it is not for an already recruited asset, some clues about where or who to go to get the HUMINT. When formulating a HUMINT requirement, it is important to differentiate between a request for information and a real gap in intelligence. The potential risks involved in HUMINT collection make it imperative that scarce collection resources not be used to get information that might already reside in an existing database somewhere. Thus, the first step in developing a HUMINT requirement is to scrub the existing databases to ensure the information need identified constitutes a real gap in intelligence and, further, that it is something HUMINT is best able to satisfy as opposed to collection by technical or open source means. Once this has been done, the building of a requirement can proceed.

The specificity of the requirement is crucial for HUMINT as opposed to other collection sources. For example, let us say that we have an interest in the possible WMD program of another state. SIGINT and Geospatial Intelligence (GEOINT) collectors can do large-scale collection against large swaths of territory that may turn up significant intelligence to help us determine the state of the program. In contrast, human collectors require more vectoring to specific cities, sites, institutions, and people where the required information is likely to be found.

The U.S. Intelligence Community (IC) has a structured yet flexible formalized requirements system. This requirements system serves a variety of functions. It identifies gaps in intelligence suitable for HUMINT collection that have been articulated by policymakers and operational military commanders and that have been further refined by knowledgeable analysts and collection management officers. It prioritizes these requirements and sometimes assigns them a time urgency—that is, a need to be collected within a certain time frame. It provides accountability by assigning specific collectors who have the requisite capability to acquire the needed intelligence. The system also provides feedback in the form of evaluations and assessments. Such assessments can help determine where new capabilities need to be developed, what the value and extent of current capabilities are, how available resources can be most efficiently allocated, and how additional resources can be justified in the budget process.

The National HUMINT Requirements Tasking Center, or NHRTC, manages the requirements system largely through the National HUMINT Collection Directive (NHCD) process. In this process, the NHRTC invites the interested parties on a particular topic to submit their requirements. The primary players are usually members of the IC but can also be drawn from other interested parts of the government. The NHRTC aggregates these requirements, breaks them down into logical subsets of the broader topic, and assigns them a priority. These priorities are drawn from the National Intelligence Priority Framework (NIPF). The NHRTC then invites the community of HUMINT collectors to review the requirements in a given NHCD and to make a commitment to collect against those requirements for which they have or can develop a capability to successfully collect against.

This requirements system is not static. It is constantly being added to and refined. The goal of the NHRTC is to review and revise completely as well as assess the collection against a given NHCD. Nominations for new NHCD topics can be submitted for NHRTC consideration by any member of the IC. New requirements may be added to an existing NHCD at any time through the submission of intelligence collection requirements, or ICRs as they are known. Further, depending on urgency of a need, special opportunity to collect against a need or the seniority of a particular requestor, HUMINT collectors can be tasked directly outside of the NHRTC process. For example, questions arising from those receiving the President's Daily Brief (PDB) or from the National Security Council (NSC) become high-priority requirements that are conveyed directly to HUMINT collecting agencies for transmission to collectors in the field. These are often in response to fast-moving events such as the Arab Spring or the reported use of chemical weapons in Syria. Such requirements will then be captured by the NHRTC after the fact.

This requirements process has some notable strengths and is a significant improvement over what existed just a decade ago. It does the following:

- provides greater collector accountability,
- standardizes reporting formats and products,
- provides feedback to users,
- reduces the number of requirements on the books,
- lessens the likelihood of duplication among scarce collector resources,
- is more inclusive of the wide range of governmental agencies and departments that have something to offer in the HUMINT arena, and
- still retains flexibility to meet urgent or unanticipated needs.

Collection

Once HUMINT requirements are validated and transmitted to the field, the collectors go into action. If the requirement calls for clandestine collection, then members of a country's clandestine services take the lead. Friendly liaison services may also be contacted when appropriate to assist in obtaining the intelligence needed to respond to the requirement.

HUMINT requirements may be sent to government and military installations throughout the world—that is, wherever the requirements could possibly be answered by agents and contacts alike or where others with the potential information could be approached and queried. They can also be sent only to specific field components for a particular recruited asset or agent, who has or is likely to have access to the intelligence that will answer the requirement(s).

To clarify a bit of nomenclature, the individuals sent out to do the recruiting are called case officers; the people they recruit are spies. Spies (which intelligence agencies call "agents") are recruited through what is known as the acquisition cycle, which consists of a well-trained case officer spotting, assessing, developing, and recruiting that asset. Based upon the standing HUMINT collection requirements for each station—such as the British Secret Intelligence Service section of an embassy, also called the *rezidentura* by the Russians—case officers will look to spot potential agents with access to the kind of secrets that will respond to those requirements. The case officer will then look for some way to meet the target so that the case officer can begin the process of assessing whether the individual has the type of access that would warrant continued contact. If it is determined that the potential agent has the kind of access to secrets that would be of interest and is amenable to continue meeting with the case officer, then the case officer will try to develop a relationship with the person. During this developmental phase, which can take weeks, months, or even years, the case officer continues enhancing rapport with the individual while assessing his or her potential as an agent. As part of this assessment, the case officer will try to determine if the individual is a dangle—that is, someone purposely placed in front of the case officer by another intelligence service to learn as much as possible about the tradecraft and requirements of the case officer's organization. For example, intelligence services highly prize learning about the type of covert communications their adversaries use for their agents, the location of safe houses, and dead drops where agents leave intelligence collected and receive payments or new pieces of technology ("spy gear") to facilitate collection. Requirements are also another valuable target for dangles because they give insight into what an opposing intelligence organization and government does not know. This would include topics ranging from where a political leader stands on a particular foreign policy issue, such as sanctions against a country that is proliferating WMDs, to the capabilities of a new weapons system. Armed with such information, an intelligence service could feed back (as in the Farewell case) false or misleading information to deceive an adversary. The case officer will also look for vulnerabilities in the potential agent, which might motivate him or her to commit espionage. These could be such things as opposition to one's government or its policies, revenge for perceived slights by an employer, or simply money, whether it be out of personal greed or to meet the medical or educational needs of a family member. The Russian and Chinese intelligence services have been known to use blackmail or sexual entrapment to recruit sources; most other intelligence services eschew such methods.

They would prefer an agent who is willing and motivated to spy rather than one who feels coerced.

Assuming that the agent believes the target has access to the required intelligence and may have reasons to accept being recruited, permission must be given by the case officer's parent service, which will also review the case. When the determination is made by the case officer and his or her intelligence service to recruit or pitch a developmental target, it is usually with some level of confidence that the person will accept the pitch and if not that at least the pitch will *not* be reported to the person's government, intelligence service, terrorist cell, or drug cartel. No case officer wants his or her intelligence service affiliation exposed or to create an international incident or possibly be killed for making a recruitment pitch. Cold pitches—that is, pitching someone who has just been met—sometimes works but often is done more to annoy the intelligence service or government of the person pitched. Anyone who is cold pitched and who reports it to the appropriate authorities will be identified as someone who is viewed as vulnerable by an opposing service and likely removed from the position he or she holds or returned home. This can be a particularly effective tactic against an aggressive case officer from an adversary's intelligence service. Pitches are also sometimes made by a case officer under the pretense that he or she is actually working for another country's service. These "false flag" pitches are used for example in the Arab world where a target may be more likely to spy for another Arab country rather than for Israel.

When the pitch is accepted, the two remaining elements of the agent acquisition cycle—handling and termination—come into play. Handling an agent is done initially by the recruiting case officer, who in some instances may continue in this role throughout the duration of the agent's espionage work. Usually, however, the agent and the handler will change locations over time, necessitating other case officers taking on the handling responsibilities for the asset. In the pitch, the case officer will have already discussed the financial or other benefits to be provided to the agent for his or her efforts. Subsequently, the case officer will establish the HUMINT to be collected and the type of communications that will be used for the agent's clandestine work, such as personal meetings; brush passes; or impersonal contact through dead drops, steganography, satellite, or other forms of covert communications. The recruiting case officer will also give the agent some tradecraft instruction in such things as signaling for meetings, how to arrive at a personal meeting without surveillance, the location of and method for loading a dead drop site, and how to use any covert communication devices. For the duration of the handling phase—that is, for as long as the agent continues to work as a spy—the case officer will discuss with the agent at face-to-face meetings the current state of the agent's personal life, any changes in access to secrets, new collection requirements, and possibly follow-up questions to previous requirements or to materials or documents the agent already provided. Administrative details, such as arrangements for future meetings and financial matters, are discussed at these meetings as well.

All clandestine collection relationships come to an end at some point whether by mutual agreement or not. An agent with a lengthy and productive career who retires from his or her job and thus loses access to intelligence of interest might be exfiltrated from his or her country of residence or terminated amicably by the handling case officer if the person chooses to remain there. In the latter case, this might include financial or other recognition such as a medal (which the agent would be shown but could not keep) acknowledging the agent's contribution over the years. Recontact information would also be provided should the asset ever need to contact the intelligence organization again. Recruited agents who simply lose their access or their motivation and are no longer able to accomplish what they agreed to do in accepting the original pitch and cannot be redirected to collect other secrets, may also be terminated with the case officer's appreciation for their efforts. In this situation, the asset could receive some financial remuneration, as well as the option to recontact the handling officer if his or her situation changes. But the recruited agent who simply does not perform to expectations or who is caught in deceptions or in peddling information to other intelligence services will be terminated expeditiously and without the possibility of any future contact.

Case officers are not found just in civilian intelligence services throughout the world but also in military organizations such as the Russian GRU and Chinese People's Liberation Army (PLA). Trained in much the same way as their civilian intelligence counterparts, these military intelligence personnel focus primarily on recruiting agents with access to military secrets such as an adversary's battlefield plans, intentions, strategy, and in particular the capabilities of current weapons systems and development of new ones. Just as their civilian colleagues, military case officers also have as one of their highest collection priorities the penetration of opposing military intelligence organizations.

While satellites now provide much of the intelligence on another country's roadways, bridges, railways, airfields and ports, the military attaché still retains responsibility for reporting on such fundamental information. The attaché's observations on the ground can confirm or even expand this crucial building block of intelligence for military planners, who need it especially when military forces must be deployed against an enemy. Attaché observations of joint military exercises also provide an opportunity to observe strategies, their implementation, the effectiveness of the military units involved and of their leadership—all basic elements to understanding the tactical and strategic military capabilities of another country. This intelligence, along with the insights of the attaché, are unobtainable by technical collection means and therefore make attachés an essential component in any nation's military intelligence collection effort.

The attaché is also valuable as another pair of eyes and ears inside a foreign country to report not just about military matters, but also about political and economic issues and problems facing the host country. This type of ground truth reporting adds additional perspective for military and civilian analysts, military commanders and policymakers. It is essential therefore that military attachés have sufficient training in the language of the country to which they are assigned along with a broad and deep understanding of its culture, and political and economic systems. This knowledge, combined with the attaché's military expertise in weapons systems, offensive and defensive strategy and tactics, and the host country's military establishment, will allow an attaché to fulfill his or her HUMINT mission and contribute to the security of the nation he or she represents.

HUMINT collection, whether civilian or military, covert or overt, requires a considerable amount of support both in the field and from the collector's headquarters. This can range from responding to messages, transmitting requirements, disseminating reporting, providing technical equipment (spy gear) to aid in collection, or assisting an operative in establishing or maintaining their "cover." HUMINT operatives living in foreign countries usually require some kind of cover or false identity unless of course they are "declared" as representing an intelligence service to their host country counterparts. Cover has been defined as "The role played by an intelligence officer to conceal his true purpose for living or traveling abroad."[22] For intelligence services throughout the world there are generally two types of cover—official and non-official. The former might be another government position held by a case officer overseas, while the latter is a deep cover position abroad that could be within a government office, commercial entity or some other kind of organization. The Russians for example favored journalist and trading company cover for many years, while Chinese intelligence officers have been found in overseas Chinese companies and posing as students in foreign universities. Operatives under non-official cover are called NOCs by U.S. and British intelligence and "illegals" by the Russians. The ring of Russian illegals broken up in the United States in June 2010 had a variety of covers including real estate broker, journalist and working in finance and academia. NOCs must have excellent believable documentation to back up their cover stories or legends, since they must live their cover each and every day. Maintaining official or non-official cover has become increasingly difficult, however, with the development of biometric identification systems and the easy availability of biographic data on the internet.

Intelligence services sometimes find it necessary to expand cover beyond individuals in order to conduct espionage or support covert operations. They will therefore establish cover companies or proprietaries. The CIA's Air America is perhaps the most famous proprietary in the history of U.S. intelligence. It was a real operating airline, but used to support clandestine operations throughout Southeast Asia until it was disbanded in 1976. More recently some intelligence services have formed companies in other countries for the purpose of acquiring embargoed technology, equipment and knowledge, particularly regarding nuclear expertise, missile delivery systems, and weapons of mass destruction. The other type of proprietary is "notional," which as its name suggests exists in name only. Its purpose is to provide an undercover case officer with a real mailing address, phone number, and other business paraphernalia such as business cards and letterhead stationery, to backstop the officer's employment cover and thereby thwart an opposing intelligence service's investigation efforts to penetrate his or her cover legend. Notional proprietaries can also be used as mail drops where recruited agents can send correspondence to what appears to a suspicious counterintelligence organization as a legitimate business.

While cover is an important component of HUMINT collection tradecraft—"the methods by which an intelligence agency conducts its business"[23]—it is not the only one. In order to meet a potential or recruited asset securely a number of tradecraft practices can be employed. An obvious and important one involves the case officer using various means of transportation—car, bus, taxi, subway, walking—to defeat an opposing service's surveillance, thus allowing the meeting to take place undetected. To further ensure that the meeting is covert, countersurveillance by members of the case officer's service may be employed to detect whether there is any opposition surveillance of either the case officer, asset or both. The case officer may also use disguises as part of his or her tradecraft to identify and lose surveillance. Having a safe house or apartment that is rented by another person and utilized only for the purpose of conducting clandestine meetings is another tradecraft element that can enhance an agent's security. Sometimes case officers other than the original recruiter or handler must meet an asset. The tradecraft employed would require some form of recognition signal to be used for the safety of both individuals. This might be something as simple as a rolled up magazine or newspaper under a specific arm followed by a verbal parole or identifying question and answer so that each knows the other is the person to be met. Movies and TV have provided numerous examples over the years of such identifying exchanges.

When personal meetings cannot occur, impersonal communication must be utilized. There are several tradecraft practices that can be used to enhance communications security and thereby the security of the agent. Secret writing with lemon juice or other liquids has been employed for centuries when information had to be conveyed covertly. One-time pads, invented in the early 20th century, use two identical pads with randomly selected letters and numbers. When transmitting a message, the sender uses the page for that day to encrypt the information. The receiver uses the same page to then decrypt the message. During World War II and the Cold War, microdots were used by agents to send the information they had collected to the intelligence organizations for whom they worked. The advantage of the microdots was that they could hold large amounts of information in a tiny space that could then be pasted into letters, postcards, newspapers or books and go undetected by prying counterintelligence organs. Further advances in technology and the development and global expansion of the

Internet have seen the use of steganography become a preferred method of communication and tradecraft practice by intelligence services. Data is encrypted and inserted into images that may be visible in emails or on readily accessible websites. Unless a counterintelligence service knows where to look and has the capability to decrypt the message once found, the communication remains secure.

Less technically advanced, but a nonetheless fairly reliable tradecraft practice for protecting secret communications and spy gear is the concealment device. This could be any item in an agent's possession—piece of furniture, pen, knickknack, toothpaste tube—which is altered to hide anything from counterintelligence professionals that might incriminate the asset as a spy. Concealment devices are also used extensively for passing collected intelligence at dead drops. Western services, for example, have used artificial dead rats and hollowed-out stones as concealment devices to further reduce detection by opposing services.

A continuing challenge for HUMINT is that it is collected by many organizations for many purposes. While this challenge is not nearly so pronounced for the technical collection disciplines, HUMINT collection often requires that you must deal with different bureaucratic structures, an overlap in authorities, and intelligence-sharing issues. The principles of source protection and "need to know" can further complicate matters. Legal restrictions or the nature of collection may necessitate separating foreign from domestic collection, as in the United States, United Kingdom, Russia, and Israel. But countries such as China combine the two in order to better track people as they move into and out of the country. Because the military is the biggest single customer, most countries have separate organizations to handle military HUMINT and further subdivide it into national and tactical levels. Homeland security and local law enforcement have ongoing issues about where the boundary between them exists—for example, the FBI versus the New York Police Department about jurisdiction on issues related to terrorism.

Processing

After HUMINT is collected in response to a requirement, it needs to be put into a format for dissemination that will protect the source or agent and get the intelligence to those who need it in a timely fashion. Unlike the technical collection disciplines, HUMINT requires little in the way of processing "raw" data. The sensor is not a sentient being that records observations and thoughts. The product a user gets from technical collection is simply a report, in a standardized format, that responds to all or part of a requirement. HUMINT reports, on the other hand, may be reviewed at several levels before dissemination. In some cases, especially with terrorist reporting or intelligence about fast-breaking events, HUMINT may be disseminated directly from the field to consumers by the civilian or military intelligence field component.

Since the protection of sources and methods remains of paramount importance, reviews are also used to determine the classification of the HUMINT—whether it is to be disseminated electronically or in a more restricted way (including via hard copy only)—and how widely the HUMINT is to be distributed to consumers. Reports officers or collection management officers may sometimes combine several reports on a similar topic into a more meaningful and comprehensive single report, but they must never during the review process "spin" the HUMINT to fit preconceived policy perspectives or to avoid raising hot button issues with senior government officials. Having reports officers who are professionals, subject matter experts, and of the highest integrity and who are sufficiently removed from collection operations so as to maintain their objectivity helps ensure that the HUMINT disseminated accurately conveys what the source provided. In addition, the prospect of further reviews up the chain of command reduces the potential for inflating or spinning the intelligence, no matter whom the customer might be. The accuracy and reliability of the intelligence product is paramount if an intelligence service wants to be relevant and valued by its government masters.

Perhaps the most important aspect of what might be called HUMINT processing is characterizing the reliability of a source. Because it involves human beings, HUMINT has a much larger element of subjectivity in it than is found in the technical collection disciplines. Reports that are the result of direct collector observation of an event, policy decision, facility, or weapon system are usually very reliable. But because much of HUMINT comes from sources other than a trained collector—that is, recruited agents; developmental sources; professional, personal, and official contacts; acquaintances, etc.—the veracity of their information must be carefully vetted. This is a process shared by both collectors and analysts.

How does a collector insure the information received is not deliberate misinformation or being fabricated by a source to gain attention or favorable treatment of some kind? These are the kinds of questions source vetting or asset validation is designed to answer. This can be done in some cases through testing sources by asking them to obtain answers to questions for which the answers are already known or by giving them operational tests to perform so as to assess their reliability. Corroborating information can also be sought from other sources to include that which can be obtained from technical collectors. In addition, a thorough evaluation of the stream of a source's reporting is very useful in determining whether the source is being responsive to the requirements posed, and is providing secret information that fits with his or her access to that information, and whether the intelligence is accurate. Validity of reporting over time is often considered the best test of a source's veracity. Finally, whenever possible, sources can be subjected to a polygraph test. For many sources, however, especially those on the battlefield or who are reporting on terrorist or criminal activities, determining reliability sometimes comes down to the judgment and instinct of the collector.

This is especially true in the case of one-time sources and volunteers or "walk-ins" who provide what appears to be highly significant information. Vetting is not a one-time event; even for the most credible sources it must be a continuous and rigorous activity.

The importance of vetting a source for accuracy becomes most clear in those instances in which a source provides highly significant information that is used to inform policy or military action and turns out to be false. The extensive untrue and misleading reporting from East German sources during the Cold War is but one extreme example of what can occur when validating HUMINT reporting assets is not done or not done thoroughly.

East Germany was considered a hard target because of its inaccessibility to Westerners so that when East Germans were recruited (perhaps when posted to East German embassies abroad) or volunteered to spy, they were considered valuable assets for the insights they could provide to what was happening in their country. Since the East German sources could not be met personally very often because of the travel restrictions into and out of the country and given the highly proficient counterespionage capabilities of the East German intelligence service (Stasi), covert communications were required to task these assets and receive their intelligence reports. It was also the case that little if any operational testing was possible, let alone polygraphs, because of the limited time available for face-to-face meetings on those rare occasions when such meetings did occur. The intelligence provided by these agents, though not significantly insightful, was considered valuable by the analysts and policymakers who read it, primarily because it was all that was available. There was nothing outside of the intelligence reports from these East German sources to confirm or contradict what they were reporting. Although some within the IC questioned relying too extensively on this limited body of intelligence, the situation continued until the Berlin wall fell. At that time, it was learned that almost all of the East German reporting assets had either been dangles or had been turned by the Stasi and become double agents. Intelligence produced by any East German assets, especially in the last ten years before the wall fell, was therefore considered compromised, even though not all of it had been completely false. Some of the reporting was sufficiently accurate to help establish the credibility of the source and, by extension, the reliability of other Stasi-controlled East German assets reporting on similar topics. The lesson learned from this experience is that just because the targets are denied areas, the number of assets limited and therefore the ability to corroborate reporting extremely difficult, this does not reduce the collectors' responsibility to validate these sources and their reporting. In fact, the experience with the East German reporting should make collectors and analysts even more wary.

A more recent and dramatic example involved an Iraqi expatriate source living in Germany known as "Curveball." Originally a source who came to the attention of the German intelligence services, Curveball provided information purporting to describe how the Iraqis had built mobile vans for the production of biochemical weapons. This information fit nicely into the preconceptions of some within both the U.S. intelligence and policy communities. Despite debriefing by expert analysts and the skepticism of some, Curveball's information was used by then Secretary of State Colin Powell at the United Nations to support military action against the regime of Saddam Hussein. Unfortunately, Curveball had fabricated this information; it was totally false.

The characterization of a HUMINT source by reports officers can be a source of tension between the reports officers and the analysts. Although phrases such as "a reliable source," "a source with known access," and "a source whose reliability is still uncertain" are all intended to help the analysts weigh the value of the source and his or her intelligence, they also serve to mask the source, as noted previously, for reasons of protecting the source's identity. Therefore, analysts may believe that they still do not have a good feel for the source's ultimate reliability. This turned out to be one of the problems with Curveball. Analysts could either accept or reject the intelligence but had little substantive means of doing so. It is also important to understand that at some point the HUMINT apparatus of an intelligence service may have a vested interest in a source, given all of the time and effort that has gone into recruiting him or her. The HUMINT managers and collectors may be more willing to accept the value of their source than are the analysts receiving the intelligence. It is imperative, therefore, that the reports officers and analysts have established solid lines of communication to avoid any misunderstanding by analysts of a source's reliability, which may vary based on access and knowledge base.

Foreign Collectors of Human Intelligence

As noted previously, all intelligence services use human sources to collect intelligence. Some HUMINT collectors such as the United States, Russia, and China have a global presence and an extensive range of collection requirements. Others such as the United Kingdom and France, though highly proficient, have a limited presence throughout the world and fewer HUMINT collection priorities on matters affecting their national security interests. A brief examination of how these services operate provides a useful glimpse into the way other countries make use of HUMINT collectors.

Russia

The SVR is tasked with collecting HUMINT overseas on subjects of interest to the Russian leadership. In addition to the traditional political, economic, and scientific collection topics, the SVR now also focuses on terrorism given the threat to Russia posed by both domestic and foreign terrorist groups. The SVR is the successor to the First Chief Directorate of the KGB and has continued the efforts of the KGB to recruit and run spies such as Aldrich Ames and Robert Hanssen or to run networks of illegals like those uncovered in the United States with the arrest of Anna Chapman in June 2010. The SVR is responsible for the residencies (*rezidentura*) at Russian embassies throughout the world and for liaison relationships with other intelligence services—especially regarding terrorist groups. Just as their U.S. and Chinese counterparts, SVR officers will also be tasked to collect as much open source information as possible to reduce the need for acquiring human assets.

The FSB came out of the KGB Second Chief Directorate (CI) and is responsible for internal CI and security, including defeating the HUMINT collection efforts of other intelligence services against Russia. Perhaps because Russian President Vladimir Putin was once in charge of the FSB or because of its important role in acquiring HUMINT for Russia's domestic counterterrorism effort, the FSB seems to have become the preeminent intelligence service in Russia today.

The GRU is Russia's military intelligence service. It did not change its name or its mission after the fall of the Soviet Union. The GRU is responsible for the collection of military and Science and Technology (S&T) HUMINT but also has SIGINT and IMINT capabilities to encompass the broader spectrum of military intelligence required by the Russian civilian and military leadership. The GRU posts its personnel under the cover of the military offices at Russian embassies across the globe.

China

The Chinese MSS oversees the Chinese HUMINT collection effort, which is centered in its Second Bureau. Here, the requirements for foreign HUMINT collection are established and forwarded overseas to its intelligence officers and agents. The Second Bureau also has the responsibility for recruiting spies so it is involved in each aspect of the agent acquisition cycle. Just as in many other intelligence services, MSS officers use diplomatic, commercial, or journalist cover to conceal their activities from local services. The MSS, however, also makes use of the large number of Chinese living, working, studying, and traveling overseas to address some of its HUMINT collection requirements, especially regarding technology and economic intelligence. These individuals are recruited by the MSS First Bureau (Domestic).

The acquisition of military HUMINT is the responsibility of the Second Department of the PLA General Staff Headquarters. The Second Department uses both defense attachés and recruited agents to collect intelligence—especially on military-related technology and the R & D associated with it, as well as to obtain open source material on these areas of interest. Analysis of military HUMINT is also done within the Second Department where finished intelligence is produced for dissemination to the Chinese civilian and military leadership.

Great Britain

MI6 is comparable to the CIA and its overseas focus to collect HUMINT about threats to national security.

MI5 is the counterpart to the FBI and is responsible for the domestic security of the United Kingdom. It focuses upon threats to the British homeland, whether from Irish rebels, terrorist cells, WMD proliferators, organized crime, drug traffickers, or foreign intelligence services. MI5, like the FBI, will attempt to recruit sources or insert penetrations into these groups in order to collect the HUMINT necessary to disrupt their plans. Media reports of MI5 arrests and disruption of terrorist cells in the United Kingdom are often the result of such HUMINT operations with help sometimes from the HUMINT obtained overseas by its colleagues in MI6 or from friendly foreign intelligence services.

France

The DGSE (*Directoire Generale de la Securite Exterieure*—General Directorate for External Security) is the French version of the overseas intelligence service. Although the DGSE is under the French Ministry of Defense, its HUMINT collection mission is not limited to military issues but encompasses the full range of requirements needed by the French civilian and military leadership. DGSE officers are posted throughout the world at French diplomatic missions in order to collect HUMINT and recruit assets as well as to maintain relationships with foreign intelligence services—especially throughout Europe and in many of the former French colonies. The French also use French civilians or "honorable correspondents" from a variety of occupations to obtain HUMINT during the course of their business, academic, or other professional activities and travel. In addition to collecting HUMINT, the DGSE is also responsible for disseminating the intelligence to French consumers and for producing finished analysis for the French intelligence community.

The DGSE has been particularly adept against the threats from terrorists to France and its worldwide interests. They are joined in this effort by the DGSI (*Direction Generale de la Securite Interieure*—Directorate General of Internal Security) which replaced the DCRI (*Direction Centrale du Renseignement Interieur*—Central Directorate of Homeland Intelligence) on May 12, 2014. The DCRI had been created on July 1, 2008, by combining the DST and the RG (*Direction Centrale des Renseignements Generaux*—Central Directorate of General Intelligence). The DGSI is under the Ministry of Interior, and not surprisingly, its HUMINT collection effort is focused upon the domestic threats from terrorist cells, criminal groups, cyber attacks, economic espionage, and foreign intelligence services. Given France's considerable experience in thwarting terrorist activities domestically and in its former colonies, the DGSI has extensive relations with the domestic intelligence services and law enforcement organs of its European neighbors on countering terrorism in the twenty-first century.

Best Targets

As discussed in the first section on what HUMINT collects, there are a multitude of topics for which human sources provide the best but not necessarily the only intelligence required by policymakers and military leaders. The following list of intelligence topics, while not exhaustive, demonstrates the breadth of issues that HUMINT can address.

Plans and Intentions

This is what sets HUMINT apart from the other intelligence disciplines, for it is through human sources that these specifically human ideas can be ascertained. The tasking may be about the plans and intentions of the following:

- a nation's leadership for its foreign, domestic, economic or military policies,
- a country's defense establishment regarding strategy or weapons R & D,
- terrorists and cyber attackers on where and how to strike and by whom,
- narcotraffickers on expanding production or changing delivery modes and locations, and
- intelligence services on increasing offensive and defensive counterespionage operations against an adversary.

Terrorism

HUMINT can provide the names of personnel within terrorist organizations, their movement, responsibilities, the financial sources of the group, and how they recruit and communicate. HUMINT can also enable SIGINT and IMINT for additional collection.

Weapons Development and Proliferation

Through HUMINT, new weapons—whether chemical, biological, radiological, nuclear, or conventional—can be identified even before any testing is conducted that might be detected by the other collection disciplines. Such intelligence can be invaluable in developing effective countermeasures to an enemy's new weapons system. Human sources may also provide advance warning of where these new weapons might be shipped so that the other INTs can track them and potentially have them interdicted.

Counterintelligence

Human penetrations of opposing intelligence services can provide insights into their tradecraft, collection requirements, targeting priorities, morale, communications methods, vulnerabilities, and any recruitment successes in one's own or in an allied service. HUMINT can also enable SIGINT collection on the communications of other intelligence organizations.

Tactical and Strategic Intelligence for the Warfighter

One of the highest priorities for both civilian and military HUMINT collectors during wartime is providing real-time intelligence—both tactical and strategic—to military leaders so that they can make informed battlefield decisions, gain their objectives and most importantly protect the soldiers on the ground. The HUMINT acquired could come from direct observation, elicitation from friendly civilians, debriefing of recruited assets and interrogation of enemy personnel.

Foreign Military Combat Capabilities

Observations of other military organizations' capabilities by human assets is one way to acquire this intelligence. Another is for a recruited source to obtain documents related to an adversary's military exercises and the evaluations contained therein. This could help negate the denial and deception efforts of an opponent against satellite collection platforms.

Cyber Threats

Human penetrations of state-sponsored or independent hackers may reveal their organization, leadership, capabilities, and most importantly targets. Such HUMINT could enable more concentrated SIGINT collection and the implementation of countermeasures to defeat their attacks.

Political Instability

Intelligence from recruited sources and volunteers alike is often one of the earliest indicators of rising instability in a country. HUMINT warning to domestic policymakers or interested foreign governments about a potential coup or one in progress may be critical in deciding how best to deal with the situation.

Threats to Economic Stability

HUMINT plays a significant role in warning about threats whether to the homeland, government, communications infrastructure, or economy. In today's global economy, HUMINT about possible disruption from attacks on an economy may be crucial in preventing or limiting the damage to an individual country or to the world's financial system.

Emerging and Disruptive Technologies

The warning capability of HUMINT again may be important in identifying new technologies being researched and developed by both governments and non-state actors well before any indicators are picked up by the other collection disciplines.

Transnational Organized Crime

HUMINT derived from penetrations of criminal organizations may provide essential insights as to the leadership, internal structure, communications, and relations with other groups and routes for transporting their illicit cargoes. The HUMINT acquired can often assist SIGINT and GEOINT collectors in tracking these criminals and aiding law enforcement in stopping their shipments of drugs, weapons, or other humans.

Future Trends

Human Intelligence in the Digital World

The Internet Age and the explosion of social media have created both new opportunities and challenges for HUMINT collection. From agent recruitment to requirement generation and the timely delivery of intelligence to consumers, intelligence services are adapting to the digital world in which they must now operate. This is not to say that traditional HUMINT sources and methods, requirements concerning plans, intentions and threat warning, or modes of processing and disseminating HUMINT have been abandoned. Intelligence services continue to retain their traditional methodologies regarding HUMINT, but they are adapting as they must to remain relevant and protect their individual country's national security.

For example, the early phases of the agent acquisition cycle—spotting, assessing, and developing—can now be accomplished to some degree over the Internet. Individuals with particular skills or with current or potential access to secrets can be identified through resumes on employment websites, responses to advertisements for job vacancies, or via chat rooms devoted to topics of interest to an intelligence service. Volunteers who want to provide intelligence no longer have to take the dangerous step of walking into a foreign embassy or covertly expressing their interest in a note or personal aside to a case officer. They can simply send an e-mail to an intelligence service's website to begin the process. Intelligence services, too, will monitor social media in an effort to identify sources with access who have vulnerabilities that might be exploited.

Beyond the cyber recruitment process, tasking and responding to short-fuse requirements can also be facilitated through the Internet. Using the Internet for secure, encrypted, covert two-way communications can reduce the danger of exposure to a source (and a case officer) from a personal meeting or from using a dead drop. HUMINT, especially in fast-breaking situations, must be collected, processed, and disseminated expeditiously yet in the most secure manner possible in order for it to meet the demands of political and military leaders. This can be a serious challenge in this era of twenty-four-hour news networks and global telecommunications.

The digital world adds a new dimension to the challenge of developing effective cover for case officers. Appearing to be somebody you are not has become a bigger challenge than ever. The days when a business card and somebody to answer a fake business phone at a notional proprietary were enough to at least provide an effective light cover are long gone. Especially for young people with a large digital footprint, it is hard to hide your true identity from a persistent and information technology (IT) savvy foreign CI service. The irony is that having a small digital footprint can also raise suspicions. The advent of inexpensive and sophisticated biometrics further complicates the use of false identities in HUMINT collection operations.

Intelligence services, while recognizing the advantages of the Internet and social media, also understand that these have inherent CI risks. For example, fictitious volunteers on the Internet can be used to occupy an opposing service and thus prevent them from finding or working with legitimate volunteers. Tying up the resources of an opposing service is a CI goal of any worthwhile intelligence organization. Social media can also be used by an intelligence service to mislead opposition elements that are threatening the domestic political stability of a country or to ferret out opponents by posing as sympathizers to their cause. More than ever, HUMINT derived from sources in this burgeoning and fast-paced cyber world must be placed in its appropriate context and used judiciously by analysts and decision makers.

Increased Interaction of Human Intelligence with the Other Intelligence Collection Disciplines

As was noted previously, HUMINT often enables the other collection disciplines to perform their functions. Thus, sensors placed along a route identified through HUMINT where nuclear material is likely transported will help the MASINT collectors. Similarly, HUMINT about the general location of a biological or chemical weapons lab will assist GEOINT in targeting the area by satellite and increase imagery analyst focus as well. SIGINT will continue to use HUMINT acquired on the communications of a nation, terrorist group, or criminal enterprise to refine its collection. This trend will likely continue if not expand in the future as countries use enhanced denial and deception techniques to conceal their political and military plans, intentions, weapons R & D, and anything else they wish to hide from technical collection platforms.

So, too, HUMINT collection will be challenged and need to utilize the capabilities of technical collection even more in the future. More countries are introducing biometrics to monitor travellers, and more intelligence services are expanding video surveillance. So the opportunities for personal meetings between case officers and their potential or recruited agents may become fewer as well as more difficult and time consuming in their planning and execution. Communications monitoring of an intelligence service's

CI components or imagery of a meeting site are two ways in which SIGINT and GEOINT can assist HUMINT collection. They can also be invaluable as HUMINT collection increasingly focuses on non-state actors such as terrorist or criminal elements and weapons proliferators.

Rebuilding Trust

Intelligence services in the West and particularly in the United States have lost the trust of citizens, allied services, and recruited agents alike following revelations such as those by Edward Snowden and by WikiLeaks. In fact, this trend has been going on for several decades as both print and electronic media have published sensational accounts about the HUMINT collected (or missed) by various intelligence organizations. These stories have often spurred popular debate about the legality of the methods used in acquiring the HUMINT and even the accuracy of the intelligence itself, leading to a loss of public trust in the agencies responsible for carrying out the HUMINT collection mission.

The leaking of classified HUMINT to the media also results in the loss of trust from a friendly service that sees the intelligence it shared publicized on the front page of a newspaper, announced over the airwaves, or nowadays published online. Despite assurances that the intelligence would be protected and remain secret, the service providing the HUMINT can only view its revelation as a breach of trust and force it to question whether any intelligence will ever be shared again with the service from which the leak came. At a time when issues of global terrorism, weapons proliferation, and international organized crime require intelligence services throughout the world to share more rather than less intelligence, such a loss of trust in HUMINT sharing could have significant consequences.

The human source who learns that the intelligence he or she provided has been revealed in the media will come to distrust the service as well for its demonstrated inability to keep a secret. The publicized HUMINT may have more damaging consequences for its source than those resulting from its content, since the leaked HUMINT could compromise the source's identity. The fewer the number of individuals with access to the HUMINT, the easier it is for counterespionage organs to discover the source. Thus, the more leaks an intelligence organization experiences, the less likely new agents will agree to recruitment by that service, because of the increased danger of having their identity revealed. Intelligence services now and in the future not only have to protect their assets from discovery through leaks but also must be extremely vigilant to protect their source(s) whenever they use actionable HUMINT acquired by the penetration of a small terrorist cell, hacker group, or criminal gang to disrupt these adversaries' activities.

The trend of revealing HUMINT will have to be addressed if trust is to be rebuilt—at least with friendly liaison services and especially with potential or recruited agents. This may require stiffer penalties for those leaking classified HUMINT. It also may necessitate reviewing the process for grant-ing individuals access to HUMINT and reducing the number of those with a real need to know it. Such measures would run counter to the information revolution that emphasizes more people having more access to more infor-mation on a daily basis. It might also mean reversing the trend of giving greater access to a larger number of military personnel in order to enhance support of the war fighter. Finally, while reducing leaks can help rebuild trust among liaison partners and agents, the only way trust might be rebuilt with a nation's citizenry is through an honest discussion of the value of secrecy in protecting a nation's security. Once the need for that secrecy is understood and accepted as only applying to the protection of the sources and methods of intelligence collection, then perhaps some trust can be reestablished.

Change in Collectors and Operating Locations

The trend intelligence services have experienced in the late twentieth and early twenty-first century away from HUMINT collection that could be addressed through traditional operations and personnel can be expected to continue and intensify. This has required a reappraisal of where the HUMINT will be collected and by whom. The intelligence needed to answer the requirements about threats from terrorists, weapons proliferators, inter-national criminal enterprises, or cyber hackers is unlikely to be obtained by those under most current types of cover. Rather, new and more innovative kinds of cover unrelated to official government positions will need to be increasingly employed. This will likely mean added danger to case officers as fewer of them will be operating with the safety net.

At the same time, the case officers who will have to meet and establish relationships with those who have access to the secrets of these groups will also have to be different. They will have to look like, speak like, and have sufficient cultural or technical backgrounds that allow them entree to these very hard targets. More attention, therefore, will have to be directed at recruiting case officers with those ethnic and religious backgrounds or technical skills that will facilitate working against the nontraditional targets that intelligence services focus on now and in the foreseeable future. The United States has a distinct advantage in this regard because of its multiracial or multi-ethnic population. To fully exploit this advantage, however, will require a significant change in current security practices and policies. The resulting diversity will both enrich intelligence organizations and enhance their chances of successfully meeting their HUMINT collection challenges.

Organizational and Resource Challenges

As budgets face greater scrutiny and the possibility, in some cases, of a steep decline in dollars available for intelligence collection, a number of vital questions will have to be addressed. How does the United States determine how much HUMINT it needs and can afford in the near future? How should the HUMINT community be best organized to meet its post–Iraq and Afghanistan missions? How best to strike a balance resource wise and organizationally between the strategic needs of the President and senior civilian policymakers and the more operationally and tactically detailed needs of military commanders? How does the IC deal with the generation of case officers trained in the fast-paced, adrenaline-pumping world of tactical intelligence collection, who must now adjust to the more traditional role of recruiting agents and obtaining HUMINT in a more benign environment? There are no easy answers to these questions, but the answers once derived and implemented will largely shape the size, capability, and direction of American HUMINT in the next decade.

Throughout history, HUMINT has helped shape the fate of empires and nations. It has been glorified and vilified in countless books, motion pictures, and television programs. The emergence of technical collection disciplines has not diminished the importance of HUMINT in regard to ferreting out the important secrets and vulnerabilities of others. Rather, scientific and technical advances over time have enhanced the age-old methods of HUMINT tradecraft, not replaced them. A professionalized, sophisticated, and agile HUMINT capability therefore remains an essential part of any powerful nation's security apparatus.

References

1. Frank Santi Russell, *Information Gathering in Classical Greece* (Ann Arbor: University of Michigan Press, 1999).
2. Adrienne Wilmoth Lerner, "Espionage and Intelligence, Early Historical Foundations," http://www.faqs.org/espionage/Ep-Fo/Espionage-and-Intelligence-Early-Historical-Foundations.html#ixzz344Tsil4z.
3. John Hughes-Wilson, *The Puppet Masters* (London: Weidenfield & Nicolson, 2004), 60.
4. Stephen Budiansky, *Her Majesty's Spymaster* (New York: Viking, 2005).
5. Hughes-Wilson, *The Puppet Masters*, 81.
6. Ibid., 77.
7. John R. Elting, *Sword Around a Throne* (New York: The Free Press, 1988), 115.
8. Hughes-Wilson, *The Puppet Masters*, 248.
9. Thomas B. Allen, *Tories* (New York: HarperCollins, 2010), 174–175.
10. Brooke Caruso, *The Mexican Spy Company: United States Covert Operations in Mexico, 145–1848* (Jefferson, NC: Mc Farland & Company, Inc., 1991), 158.
11. Caruso, *The Mexican Spy Company*, 154.
12. Edwin C. Fishel, *The Secret War for the Union* (Boston: Houghton Mifflin, 1996).
13. Elizabeth R. Varon, *Southern Lady, Yankee Spy* (Oxford, UK: Oxford University Press, 2003), 174.

14. William B. Feis, *Grant's Secret Service* (Lincoln: University of Nebraska, 2002), 128.
15. Ibid., 127–128.
16. Col. John F. Prout, "The First U.S. Naval Attaché to Korea," *Studies in Intelligence* 49, no. *1* (2005).
17. John P. Finnegan, *Military Intelligence* (Washington, DC: Center of Military History United States Army,1998), 11.
18. Prout, "The First U.S. Naval Attaché to Korea."
19. Ibid.
20. Allen Dulles, *The Craft of Intelligence* (New York: Harper & Row, 1963), 26.
21. The material in this section was largely derived from an interview conducted on October 15, 2013, with Mr. Ronald Romich, the former principal deputy of Community HUMINT Management Office and vice chair of the National HUMINT Committee.
22. Joseph C. Goulden, *The Dictionary of Espionage: Spyspeak into English* (Mineola, NY: Dover Publications, Inc., 2012), 43.
23. Ibid., 233.

4

Signals Intelligence

William N. Nolte

Signals Intelligence, or SIGINT, is that form of intelligence derived from the collection and processing of various forms of electronically transmitted data and information; those forms being the communication of human language material (communications intelligence, or COMINT); and data derived from electronic emission devices, primarily radar (electronic intelligence, or ELINT). In some services, the interception of telemetry and other instrumentation signals (foreign instrumentation signals intelligence, or FISINT) is also included within SIGINT. For these purposes, when necessary we will include FISINT as a component of SIGINT.[i]

As for the matter of evolution, the relationship of cryptology—the making and breaking of codes and ciphers—to SIGINT is an important one. Most importantly, the relationship is not one of precursor to successor but an ongoing process, as will be noted from time to time. Even today, news media often refer to the National Security Agency (NSA) and its United Kingdom counterpart, the Government Communications Headquarters (GCHQ), and similar organizations as their nations' "code making and code breaking" agencies. This remains true; it is not, however, completely true, and the percentage of employees at these agencies who actually work on building or solving codes and ciphers is relatively small—far smaller for certain than the percentage engaged in this core function at predecessor organizations in the 1930s or 1940s. That change—very much linked to technologies in communication and information generation and storage—will be part of this account. At the start, however, it must be emphasized that this is not the story of cryptology, its concepts, or its methodologies but rather the inclusion of all of those into an expanded process that over time has placed increased emphasis in how signals are communicated and what can be learned from the communications process

---

[i]One point of confusion is the difference between FISINT and Measurement and Signature Intelligence, or MASINT. The distinction is relatively straightforward: In FISINT, the information being collected is derived from an instrument *intentionally* placed on a platform, a launch vehicle, for example, to transmit various information (altitude, speed, trajectory) back to the persons or organization controlling the exercise or activity in question. In MASINT, the data or information is not the output of such a sensor but rather information (heat, radiation, vibration) emanating *naturally* from a process, a machine, or some other phenomenon.

itself, in addition to what can be learned from being able to exploit the contents of the messages or data being communicated.[ii]

One important issue deriving from the dual mission of cryptology—the making and breaking of codes—also needs to be addressed as part of our evolutionary review. At its basis, cryptology has both an offensive and a defensive mission. For most of history, the defensive mission—that is, the creation of methods that would protect a country's own communications—was generally perceived to be the more important mission. To prove the point, if a nation had to choose between protecting its own secret information and communications or exploiting the weaknesses of the codes of other nations—but could not do both—which would it choose? Almost certainly, in most times and places, it would choose the former. To the generations of cryptologists recruited and trained in the period after the First World War, under pioneers such as William F. Friedman in the United States, that would almost certainly have been the case. The training of that period emphasized both missions, and among the key objectives of the code breaking function was acquiring an appreciation of the code-making skill of adversaries (or potential adversaries) and learning if those adversaries had succeeded in penetrating one's own cryptographic systems. If one could also derive useful information on whether the adversary was planning to take such actions as declaring war, staging a sneak attack, or otherwise behaving badly, that was of course important to the diplomats, political leaders, and military officials who needed to counter such actions, but such reactions were not the primary professional focus of the cryptologists themselves.

One consequence of the extraordinary achievements in Second World War Allied COMINT, as it would have been known at the time, was a shift in balance between the offensive and defensive missions. The defensive mission may have continued to be reflected in the designation of the U.S. cryptologic service as the NSA, rather than the National Signals Intelligence Agency, but over time, the emphasis in budgeting and attention focused on the SIGINT role. The defensive role, under the terms *communications security* (COMSEC) or *information assurance* (IA) remained important. It was, after all, reassuring to know during the Cold War that nuclear launch codes could not be tampered with. But a noticeable shift in emphasis had taken place from the 1950s through the end of the Cold War. As we discuss the continuing impact of the ongoing information revolution on the SIGINT and COMSEC missions, we will need to address a subsequent (and significant) readjustment in emphasis—one that promises to continue as SIGINT organizations deal with the cyber environment—in both its offensive and defensive dimensions. Does SIGINT, as it has been known for the past thirty to forty

---

[ii]Cryptologists make a distinction—a real and important one in their terms—between codes and ciphers. Readers interested in that distinction and with sufficient interest in the subject to explore it should begin with David Kahn's *The Codebreakers* (New York: Macmillan, 1967). That distinction will be observed loosely if at all here.

years, become subsumed by a broader cyber model? This question has conceptual implications; it also has significant organizational implications, as noted, in the current U.S. experience in which the U.S. Cyber Command and the NSA share the same leader but remain different organizations. Even that arrangement leaves uncertain, again in the U.S. case, the overall coordination of cyber efforts, and the roles of such organizations as the Department of Homeland Security (DHS). This introduction will not resolve issues of this sort or even predict their outcome. At best, it will provide an overview of a complex twenty-first-century national security issue.

Signals Intelligence: The Cryptologic Base

More than forty years after its first publication, David Kahn's *The Codebreakers* remains the seminal work in public understanding of the long-secret world of codes and ciphers. For centuries, if the subject was mentioned at all, the discussion involved secrecy, "black chambers,"[iii] and even the occult. Occasional, indirect references appear from time to time in histories and in language. Even in the latter, however, such references are often so obscure as to conceal their origin in the world of secret communication. To "see the writing on the wall" is a frequently used image, but few, at least before publication of *The Codebreakers,* could have traced its origins to the Book of Daniel and the prophet Daniel's ability to analyze for King Belshazzar the mysterious message "Mene, mene, tekel, upharsin," leading Kahn to call Daniel the world's "first known cryptanalyst."[1]

In its most basic form, the protection of a message from unintended viewing by a party other than the author and the intended recipient by means of codes or ciphers does not take us into SIGINT. The letters or other characters used in both the message in its "clear"—that is unencrypted—form and its encrypted analog are symbols to be sure. But the aspect of signaling is not present. Over time, however, in such simple forms as semaphore systems— land-based as well as naval—the communications process required transmission over at least some time and some distance. Even the flying of a pennant identifying a ship's nationality represented a form of signaling (as flying a "false flag" to gain advantage represents a simple form of signals deception).

Two sequential technologies of the mid- and late-nineteenth century— telegraphy and the radio, the latter known in its earliest period as "wireless telegraphy"—dramatically altered the nature and volume of "signaling" in national security affairs (as well as in commerce and other fields), with resulting changes in the intelligence value of both the protection of signals and the content they convey and in efforts to defeat such protective efforts.

[iii]The term *black chamber* has a long history of use in referring to an organization dedicated to communications intercepts and code breaking. The original black chamber appears to have been the *cabinet noir* established by King Henry IV of France in 1590 with a mission of opening, reading, and resealing letters of intelligence interest.

From Morse Code to the First World War

In 1844, Samuel F. B. Morse demonstrated the first commercially successful electronic telegraph, with his famous message "What hath God wrought." In the words of David Kahn, Morse and the telegraph "made cryptology what it is today." As in later evolutions of both cryptology and SIGINT, the achievement was one involving both physical science (in the ability to move a message-carrying current over distance) and procedural or conceptual developments of equal consequence. In telegraphy's case, one consequence was Morse code, a product of its inventor's understanding that some letters in English are used more frequently than others and the development of a system that efficiently used this understanding in assigning coded equivalents to letters and numbers. Frequency counts remain a tool of cryptology into the twenty-first century.

In its commercial usage, Morse code was employed in support of twin objectives of economy of words and confidentiality. The economic objectives applied in commercial and military alike;[iv] the confidentiality objective would become dramatically more important within a short period after Morse's famous message. In reality, of course, Morse's code was what cryptologists would refer to as an "open code," its series of dots and dashes readily available to anyone in the public (as generations of Boy and Girl Scouts would learn).

Almost immediately, nations and their military instruments employing the telegraph realized the need to further encrypt their communications to add protection suitable to their needs. In the American case, this became critical in the Civil War, in which both the Union and Confederate forces employed a range of methodologies to protect their own communications while attempting to disrupt or exploit the communications of the other side. Even in this early period, some measure of the shift from cryptology—as understood to mean the making and breaking of codes and ciphers—to the broader SIGINT and signals security operations of the twentieth century, starts to become apparent.

As a simple example, in any war of the late-nineteenth century, an army encountering the telegraph line used by an adversary faced an immediate choice. They could sever the line, disrupting the enemy's communications, or tap the line, hoping to intercept the enemy's message traffic and exploit the information gained from this source. As later generations would learn and relearn, the decision in these cases is not always easy. Could the discovery of the line and its exploitation be kept secret? Could the code or cipher the enemy was using be broken? Was it even worth thinking that the enemy wanted the line tapped for the purposes of passing deceptive information? Some of these questions

---

[iv] A frequently cited instance of the humor that could result from the efficiency sought in "telegraphic English" involved the actor Cary Grant. When a journalist inquired of Grant's age by telegram, the text read, "How old Cary Grant?" Grant's reply: "Old Cary Grant fine. How you?"

remained a generation or so away for their full implications to be clear, but the telegraph marked an important event in the development of SIGINT.

In 1897, Guglielmo Marconi opened his first wireless telegraphy on the Isle of Wight, having previously received a British patent for "Improving the Transmission of Electrical Impulses and Signals." Telegraphy was suddenly removed from the inconvenience of stringing cables from point to point. Communications could now be "broadcast" to many recipients at once, opening enormous opportunities in commerce, entertainment, and other fields. The loss of the cables did have, nevertheless, the disadvantage, from a security perspective, of that broadcast feature. Not for the last time, the downside to a given technology was directly related to its advantages.

In the national security arena, wireless telegraphy or radio, as it would ultimately be known, offered enormous opportunities to naval services, which had benefited with the rest of society from telegraphic links between bases and other facilities but which had been shut out of any operational use at sea. Radio lifted that barrier, and soon both navies and merchant marines carried radio equipment and operators, employing the familiar, reliable Morse code. (Bandwidth and power for voice communications over any distance were still years away.) By 1903, an International Radio Telegraphic Conference took place in Berlin, marking the speed with which this new technology established its role.[v]

In the traditional military domains—ground warfare and naval warfare—naval services had, as noted, benefited less from the invention of wired telegraphy and telephony. It should come as no less a surprise to realize that the advent of wireless communications produced a resultant and immediate reaction on the part of naval (including merchant marine) services to exploit the prospect of the new media. Telegraphy was quickly and broadly adopted as a standard shipboard communication device for a range of missions including the development of standard codes for, among other purposes, distress signals.

Military applications moved apace, with the development in most navies both for procedures and doctrines for the use of wireless communications and for procedures that acknowledged the dangers of their inherent "broadcast" nature. As had been the case with cryptology over the centuries, the emerging field of SIGINT almost immediately demonstrated the interaction between development to protect one's own communications and the use of that development to exploit the communications of adversaries potentially less effective in the protection process. Like cryptology, SIGINT would develop, almost from its inception, an ongoing tension between offensive and defensive components.

Albeit in primitive form comparable to the technology itself, SIGINT activities, offensive and defensive, were already under development within the

---

[v] The 1903 conference did many things, but it was not this event but its 1906 successor that established SOS as the international radio distress signal, the most famous procedural signal in the history of radio.

first decade after the appearance of Marconi's wireless. Britain's Royal Navy intercepted (and read) communications from Tsarist Russian naval elements deploying to the Pacific in the Russo-Japanese War (1904–1905), a reflection on the time lag, at least within the Tsarist service, between the employment of wireless communications and the development of wireless security regimes. Such activities were as rudimentary as those taking place to discover the military uses of the era's other technological marvel, the airplane. Both would develop at dramatically enhanced speeds after August 1914.

The First World War

The use of wireless communications (not to the exclusion of wired communications, by any means) and its development in the First World War very much paralleled that of airpower during the same period. What was in August 1914 a new, promising but undefined technology at the start of the war would over the next four years become an integral component of military and naval operations.

Many aspects of the communications component of the war involved SIGINT core cryptologic disciplines. All of the nations at war in 1914, joined by the United States in 1917, expanded both their offensive and defensive cryptologic activities. As noted before, SIGINT may address, strictly speaking, only the *offensive* aspect of such activities, but for our purposes, it makes little sense not to include security and counterintelligence (CI) developments in this review. They are, in the end, complementary and integrated entities, not inherently separate ones.

Offensively, for example, Britain made it an early priority to sever Germany's undersea cables, forcing the Germans either onto the cable systems of other nations, including Britain, or moving to wireless communications. In either case, the security of German communications would, from that point, depend on the skill of the Germans devising Germany's codes and ciphers, aligned against the skill of the Allied personnel working to defeat those cryptographic systems. Within days of the cutting of the cables, the Admiralty had assigned Sir Alfred Ewing to create what would become "Room 40," a name that survived long after the Royal Navy's cryptologic branch had moved from those original quarters.[vi]

Similar developments took place at this time within the services of Britain's allies, as with the Central Powers, and, more slowly, in the still neutral United States.[vii] In each case, the developments included those taking

---

[vi] In the Admiralty building in Whitehall.

[vii] Some belligerents experienced serious failures in adapting to the new environment. Tsarist Russia had a long history of using cryptology as a tool of state security. Russia's inability to apply this experience to the new wireless environment in the early months of the war produced disastrous consequences, as at Tannenberg (August 1914), when many military instructions were communicated over the air "in the clear," and were intercepted by German forces who used the information to produce one of the war's early and strategic victories.

place within the traditional fields of code making and code breaking but also in the expansion of cryptology into the development and exploitation of the means by which communications—encrypted or not—were passed from one terminus to another. The evolution toward SIGINT as a concept was well underway early in the First World War. Britain's most spectacular cryptology success during the war is described in the box "The Zimmermann Telegram."

The Zimmermann Telegram

In January 1917, with the United States still tenuously neutral in the First World War, the German foreign ministry, with Germany's resources draining in a war already stalemated for over two years, proposed a military alliance with Mexico, offering the latter the return of territories lost to the United States in the nineteenth century.

Britain intercepted the communication, and the analysts in Room 40 reduced it to plain text rather quickly. That was, relatively speaking, the easy part of the problem. The real question was how to exploit this achievement without revealing its source. In the end, they were able to build the cover story that they obtained a copy of the message by "hand on collection"—that is, by stealing it, in Mexico. With this cover story in place, but not without some concern, the British confronted the United States with the telegram, fearing all the while that the Germans would see through the cover.

An important event in itself, coming as the United States entered the final debate over its entry into the First World War, the Zimmermann Telegram illustrates that beyond the making and breaking of codes and ciphers, the protection of sources and methods remains central to both signals intelligence (SIGINT) and information assurance (IA).

In many instances, this included the simple interception of signals "broadcast" by an adversary, then turning the intercepted material over to trained cryptanalysts to "break" and exploit the information. In other cases, this meant the gleaning of information from aspects of the communication itself, or of characteristics of the communicated material beyond the content of the underlying message. In the first place, direction finding, the ability to track an intercepted signal and using two or more receivers to "fix" the signal's point of origin, was soon in place by all sides in the war. The technology may have improved somewhat between the First and Second World Wars, but audiences of any number of movies on the latter have noticed scenes in which specially equipped vehicles rush through the streets of some city while headset-bearing operators operate a small wheel that moves an antenna on the roof of the vehicle. This is direction finding in its most basic but effective form. What would become in the Second World War "the Battle of the Beams" was already underway a generation before.

Perhaps even more important in the development of SIGINT from its cryptologic base was the revelation that even in the event of failure to break the cipher protecting a message, useful information could be obtained (and exploited) from the "externals" of the message traffic. Externals in this sense mean any information other than the plaintext content of the encrypted message. What, if anything, can be learned from the origin of the message and its recipient, either by name or by location? Does each communicating entity appear to have the authority to initiate communications with the other? Does one entity appear to initiate communications to a set of others?

In many cases, the information derived from such questions can only be inferred. Does, for example, a pattern showing one entity initiating communications with a set of other entities, each of which replies but which rarely initiate communications with each other or with the primary initiator, reflect structure? Could this be a hierarchy with the originating entity reflecting a headquarters, with the others as subordinate units? This may be simply an inference, but combined with other information, it may be a useful inference and one that once confirmed can provide a continuing flow of information involving movement, expansion (or compression) of the entity involved, and even operations.

By the same token, what about the volume of information flowing between communicants, even if, as assumed, the cryptographic system holding the plaintext remains unbroken? Does careful recording and study of the patterns of communication correlate with patterns of activity? In the periods before an offensive, for example, does the adversary increase the flow of information until, let's say, twenty-four hours before the offensive, then dramatically reduce that volume in the last day?

The brilliant cryptanalytic achievements of U.S. and British cryptanalysts in the Second World War have received (and deserve) enormous credit. But, for our purposes, the development of early traffic analytic techniques in the First World War is an achievement of perhaps equal importance. As cryptographic systems of the twentieth century became more sophisticated and more resistant to exploitation, traffic analysis offered the emerging SIGINT entities a redundant capability largely unavailable to their predecessor black chambers. An inability to "read the writing on the wall" no longer denied cryptologic organizations the capability to supply information of interest and value to consumers—military and civil—with the need to know an adversary or potential adversary's capabilities and intention. That achievement continues to bear fruit into the twenty-first century, as traffic analysis evolves into "network analysis."

The Continued Evolution of Signals Intelligence: The Interwar Years

The end of the First World War produced significant cuts in national security establishments, including their cryptologic elements. Perhaps more than in most postwar periods, the 1920s experienced the hope if not the possibility that the carnage from 1914 to 1918 would force the world to make it truly a "war to end all wars." This was of course not to be, as the rise of both Soviet and Nazi totalitarianism (and Japanese militarism) ultimately presented the United States and its former French and British allies with challenges they could not ignore.

In the 1920s, however, revulsion at the extraordinary waste of the Great War produced concerted efforts to eliminate conflict, through the League of Nations and a series of arms limitations agreements, the latter focused on naval expenditures. In the United States, cuts in the national security establishment left a small naval cryptologic unit in place, along with a small effort jointly funded by the War Department and State Department. That unit achieved one of the great cryptologic achievements of the era, breaking the systems in use by the Japanese in their arms control negotiations and thereby providing enormous advantage to the United States in setting limits on Japanese naval strength. This achievement, led by Herbert Yardley, one of the most prominent of American cryptologists (the other being William F. Friedman), represented a high water mark in interwar cryptology.[viii]

Another important development in cryptology during the 1920s was its first application to domestic uses, specifically in law enforcement. (See box "The Rum Runners.")

The Rum Runners

Following the terrorist attacks of September 2001, the United States (and other countries) have paid additional attention to homeland security. In reality, of course, domestic security had never been completely ignored. As a result, some elements of signals intelligence (SIGINT) (and cryptology) have entered domestic security considerations. The invention of the telephone was followed, one suspects rapidly, by awareness that telephones could be tapped. In the United States, this practice, on behalf of law enforcement agencies, was immediately controversial and subject to challenge on civil liberties grounds. By the 1920s, again in the U.S. example, the controversy had largely been resolved by court decisions requiring court orders for phone taps *related to domestic law enforcement*. The situation as it pertained to taps placed on foreign intelligence or other national security grounds remained unresolved through the end of the century.

During the period when alcohol production was outlawed in the United States, suppliers of illicit liquor often used codes (as did other smugglers) to communicate their plans and operations. The U.S. Treasury Department (of which the Coast Guard was then a component) maintained a code breaking element to deal with these cases. The leading figure in this effort was Elizebeth Friedman, the wife of William Friedman. Because of her testimony in several trials against rum runners and others, Mrs. Friedman was for many years the most public figure in American cryptology.

[viii] Yardley may be considered one of the last of the traditional code makers or code breakers. Friedman's career pointed to a different era in which his texts and his protégés were to play such a significant role.

In 1929, the incoming secretary of state, the veteran statesman Henry Stimson, ordered Yardley's black chamber closed, on the grounds that gentlemen do not read other people's mail. Within a short period of time, the U.S. Army had replaced Yardley's bureau with a new Signal Intelligence Service (SIS), headed by William Friedman. In the same period, Britain also was adjusting its cryptologic capability, creating in 1919 the Government Code and Cypher School, incorporating the previous army and navy elements that had operated through the First World War. Postwar optimism notwithstanding, cryptologic organizations continued to operate within the security establishments of all the great powers. From its earliest inception, as the Cheka, the Soviet Union developed capabilities based on a significant tsarist tradition. Well before the emergence of Hitler, Weimar Germany had created the Abwehr, including a radio interception and cipher component.

Beyond government, the interwar period was a period of significant development of cryptographic equipment from a number of brilliant commercial inventors. The American Edward Hebern, the Swedes Boris Hagelin[ix] and Arvid Gerhard Damm, and the German Arthur Scherbius introduced equipment intended for a commercial market but with obvious military and diplomatic applications, as will be seen. All, including Scherbius's Enigma, operated on variations of rotor or wired rotor technology.

It was Yardley who brought cryptology its greatest notoriety in the interwar period. Angered at the closing of his cipher bureau, he published in 1931 *The American Black Chamber,* revealing the U.S. success in reading Japanese ciphers in the 1920s. The book created a great sensation, effectively ending the prospect that Yardley would ever be employed again by the U.S. government and leading Japan to a fundamental review of its cryptologic security.

Beyond the traditional code making and code breaking parameters of cryptology, most military services continued development of such related techniques as radio communications and radio security guidelines, direction finding, and traffic analysis. In almost all of the powers, scientists were researching the use of radio signals not to communicate but to determine the range and bearing of targeted objects. Radar would become a major component in the development of SIGINT not just as an extension of traditional cryptology but also of what would become known as ELINT. The Second World War would mark the key period in that development.

The Evolution of Signals Intelligence: The Second World War

For nearly thirty years, the role of intelligence in the Second World War occupied a decidedly secondary place in the historiography of the period. This all began to change in 1972, with the publication of J. C. Masterman's

---

[ix] Hagelin was Swedish but of Russian origin.

The Double Cross System, detailing British success in rounding up German agents in the United Kingdom at the beginning of the war.[2] Two years later, F. W. Winterbotham's *The Ultra Secret* revealed the role of cryptology in defeating Nazi Germany.[3] Finally, in 1978, the extraordinary R. V. Jones published *Most Secret War,* focusing on the role of British scientific intelligence developments in the war effort, especially in winning the "battle of the beams," in many ways the world's first ELINT war.[4] It is the stories highlighted in the Jones and Winterbotham books that will occupy us here.

The story of World War II intelligence, especially SIGINT, which we can now describe as the combined effect of COMINT and ELINT, begins before the outbreak of war in 1939. On the COMINT side, U.S. Army cryptologists and their navy counterparts (in a unit designated OP-20-G) were working against the systems installed by Japan in the aftermath of the *American Black Chamber* disclosures. Across the Atlantic, French and British experts were working to break and exploit German systems, including the machine system that would turn out to be the famous Enigma. Polish cryptanalysts, working with limited resources (and as it turned out, limited time) were also working against Enigma.

Beyond cryptology, developments in traffic analysis and other components of what the British called Y service continued, as did intense effort to turn the experimental success of radar into an effective early warning system. The intensity of the time is confirmed by two extraordinary incidents. First, in July 1939, the Polish Cipher Bureau hosted British and French representatives at a conference in Poland at which the Poles gave their guests the results they had achieved on the German Enigma system. Within a few months, the Polish cryptologists would be fleeing across Europe to escape capture by the Germans. Later British success against Enigma would, at least, have been significantly delayed had it not been for this extraordinary act of generosity on the part of a doomed ally.[5]

In 1941, while the United States remained officially neutral, a delegation of four U.S. cryptologists visited the United Kingdom to conduct a dramatic exchange of information. The U.S. team, led by Frank Rowlett, one of the junior cryptologists hired by Friedman in 1930, had achieved great success against the Japanese machine encipherment system designated by the Americans as Purple. (Unlike Enigma, Purple operated not through a set of wired rotors but through a process of "stepping," using conventional telephone switching devices.) Over several days, the Americans exchanged their Purple discoveries for information on what the British had learned about Enigma and other German systems. "Magic," the project term for the exploitation of Purple, and "Ultra," the handling system for Enigma, instantly became two of the most intimate secrets held by the Anglo-Americans, nearly a year before U.S. entry into the war and two years before a formal arrangement on U.S. and U.K. cryptologic cooperation came into being.[6]

Pearl Harbor and Midway: Cryptanalytic Success versus Signals Intelligence Success

In December 1941, as the diplomatic crisis between the United States and Japan deepened, Japan provided its negotiators in Washington with a final diplomatic note, carefully timed to break off negotiations before the attack on Pearl Harbor began. Through the night of December 6 and 7, code clerks in the Japanese embassy in Washington struggled to process the fourteen-part message before the ambassador's scheduled meeting with the secretary of state for 1:00 p.m. (Washington time) on December 7.

A few miles away, U.S. cryptologists[x] were also working on the message encrypted in the diplomatic system the Americans called "Purple." Shortly after 9:00 p.m. on December 6, they delivered all but the final portion to the White House, leading President Roosevelt to conclude that "this means war." The fourteenth and final portion was available to Chief of Staff George C. Marshall late in the morning of December 7, still several hours before the attack. Marshall could have called Hawaii on a secure ("scrambler") phone, but the decision was made to use an encrypted telegram, deemed more secure. Through a variety of delays and mishaps, the message was not delivered to commanders at Pearl Harbor until 11:45 a.m. local time, two hours after the attack was over.

In a sense, Pearl Harbor represented an impressive cryptanalytic success but a signals intelligence (SIGINT) failure, the difference being that if the goal of cryptanalysis on its own is to achieve plaintext, the role of SIGINT must be thought of more broadly—that is, in obtaining information that can change outcomes in military or diplomatic situations.

The role of cryptology in the U.S. naval victory at Midway in June 1942 has been frequently recounted. It was worth noting here briefly because it shows the movement toward SIGINT as an integrated effort of collection, analysis, and subsequent signals deception, all employed in support of a great operational success.

In early 1942, uncertain about Japan's next step, possibly an invasion of the Aleutians or an attack on Midway Island, the U.S. Navy learned, through the Magic intercepts, that the code name for a future target was AF. In an attempt to clarify Japanese plans, authorities in Hawaii asked the base at Midway to broadcast—in unencrypted form—that the island's water supply was in jeopardy. Within days, the Japanese noted information that AF was facing a water shortage. The deception had worked, and the United States took steps to intercept the Japanese invasion force on the favorable terms of knowing the enemy's intent without revealing that knowledge.

Cryptographic success notwithstanding, as the late author Ronald Lewin noted, "The battle is the payoff." SIGINT did not *win* the battle of Midway, but it put the navy's pilots and crews in position to turn the tide in the Pacific through acts of exceptional heroism and self-sacrifice. In that sense, it represents a step forward in the development of the SIGINT process, based on but extended beyond its cryptanalytic roots.

---

[x]The fourteen-part message was processed by both army and navy cryptanalysts. As part of the Magic handling arrangement, the two services processed intercepted traffic on alternating days, sharing some other resources, including language talent, as well. SIS and OP-20-G had moved to develop capabilities in the front end of the intelligence process, with a small set of field intercept stations in the continental United States, Hawaii, and the Philippines (later Australia). But on the "back end"— that is, on processing and dissemination, work remained to be done to create a fully mature SIGINT system.

The continuing U.S. success with the Purple code turned out to be a decisive factor in the Battle of Midway (see the box "Pearl Harbor and Midway").

In the end, the U.S. and U.K. relationship through the course of the war focused on Germany (and to a lesser extent Italy). The loss of Britain's East Asian empire in late 1941 and early 1942 minimized British effort against Japan, except for the China-Burma-India theater. Soon after the U.S. entry into the war, American cryptologists began to arrive at Government Code and Cypher School facilities, both in London and at Bletchley Park, Buckinghamshire. Through a combination of some of the best scientific and mathematical expertise available to both countries, including the British mathematician Alan Turing, several noteworthy technical devices were developed. The most important of these probably were the "bombes," enormous electromechanical "computers" that extended dramatically the computational power available to the cryptologists attacking Enigma.

Since the appearance of *The Ultra Secret,* the story of World War II cryptology has been extensively told. Much of the emphasis in this literature has been on the story of Ultra itself—that is, the cryptologic effort of the European theater. It remains an extraordinary story, filled with achievements in mathematics and engineering, of course, but also with the narrative of the mechanisms developed to protect this most secret source of strategic information. It is in the development of those mechanisms, along with the parallel achievements taking place in the use of radar and other electronic devices, that completes (for its time) the evolution toward what can truly be called SIGINT.

Generations of intelligence recruits, now joined by students in intelligence studies programs in many universities, have become familiar over the decades with the intelligence process or, as it is sometimes called if not practiced, the intelligence cycle. From the definition of intelligence requirements by the users of intelligence, through collection by a range of mechanisms, through processing (to include analysis of a signal, decryption, and translation), through analysis of the revealed information, and finally to dissemination back to the consumer crafting the initial process, the presence of this cycle, with many variants, is at the heart of defining the modern set of intelligence sources, prominently, human intelligence (HUMINT), and various forms of technical intelligence, including SIGINT.

The presence of components of this process in the Second World War is fairly apparent. COMINT was an important instrument even before the term itself was common. Information and operations involving radar and other instruments, the core of what would later be known as ELINT, also made its presence felt—sometimes dramatically. But the integration of the two had not yet taken place. Nevertheless, it was clear that code making and code breaking, the traditional cryptologic core, had been joined by additional disciplines developed in response to new or refined technologies.

For all the participants in the Second World War, traffic analysis—the focus of the British Y Service and analog organizations in other countries—proved as valuable in the Second World War as in the First World War. The use of wireless communications had become central to mid-twentieth-century warfare, placing a premium both on maintaining the security of friendly communications and, from the other side, exploiting those of adversaries. Effective analysis of the "externals" of a communication, apart from solving the underlying plaintext of any message being conveyed, proved to be an extraordinary weapon in establishing the location, movement, or order of battle of an adversary's forces.

The brilliant Allied cryptanalytic successes against German and Japanese systems have tended to obscure the equally important success of the "code makers" within the World War II cryptologic organizations. Roosevelt and Churchill would marvel at the results pouring out from Magic and Ultra, while giving relatively little thought to the effort that went into protecting their own communications.[xi] That imbalance may in itself be a tribute to the men and women who focused on the defensive part of the Allied effort, but even in a chapter focused on SIGINT as an offensive tool, it is worth noting that balance and even integration across offensive and defensive capabilities remain an important consideration, as will be seen in our discussion of cryptology and SIGINT in the early twenty-first century.

Research had also become a larger and broader component of the cryptologic and SIGINT effort. Research on codes and the mathematics of encipherment remained critical, but research into advancing the art of collection technology and on the capabilities of tools such as radar made that research an increasingly important component of the overall process, a lasting development in a field that, after all, worked in a communications environment itself undergoing significant change. After an almost imperceptible interval, the cryptologic developments of the Second World War would be put to use again, confronting different adversaries.

Signals Intelligence in the Cold War

As the brief post–World War II era moved toward the Cold War, the intelligence and cryptologic communities faced the new challenges presented by the Soviet Union, its allies, and its clients. During the early years of the Cold War, HUMINT and IMINT access to the interiors of the Soviet Union and Communist China (after 1949) was extremely limited. Policymakers,

---

[xi] The late Frank Rowlett, one of the first Friedman hires at the U.S. Army's SIGINT Service, could, even decades later, bristle at the attention given Enigma—a fully exploited machine in his view—and the relative indifference to counterpart systems he had helped develop, which had never been broken but which, alas, received far less fame.

therefore, placed major emphasis on SIGINT to answer questions about what was going on inside these exceptionally capable information control regimes. (See the box "Venona" for an example.) These efforts were complicated by the loss of access to Soviet encryption systems through espionage by a Soviet agent, Sergeant William Weisband.

Venona

Even during the Second World War, the U.S. army, with support from the British and the Australians, had been working on a Soviet agent communication system based on one-time pad cryptology. The security feature of the one-time pad is as simple as one can be: don't reuse the pad. Soviet violation of this procedure gave army cryptologists the opportunity to break into the system, slowly and tediously. This became the basis for the Venona disclosures of the 1990s.[7] Although debates continue on some aspects of the information revealed in Venona, especially the association by cover names with many of the major espionage cases—Alger Hiss, Ethel and Julius Rosenberg—of the late 1940s and early 1950s, Venona altered the historiography of the early Cold War period, providing evidence of an extensive Soviet espionage effort that achieved success in penetrating official Washington and major activities such as the Manhattan Project.

Adding to the complexity of the early Cold War environment, the United States and its Allies had, predictably, demobilized quickly after the surrender of the Germans and Japanese in 1945. President Harry Truman committed the United States to a government operating along the lines of "economy and efficiency," including an almost immediate end to Lend-Lease arrangements. That decision intensified the financial crisis in Britain, which emerged from the war victorious but virtually bankrupt. Moreover, the publics in both countries, let alone in recently liberated but significantly destroyed and dispirited Europe, were hoping for if not expecting an extended period of peace.

By 1947, however, troubled by Soviet behavior in Eastern and Central Europe, Truman began to rebuild the American national security apparatus. The National Security Act created a National Security Council (NSC), a Secretary of Defense (the Department of Defense [DoD] was created in 1949), and the Central Intelligence Agency (CIA), along with a separate air force. Within a short period, the Secretary of Defense ordered the U.S. Army's cryptologic component (renamed the Army Security Agency), the U.S. Navy's COMINT element (soon to be the Naval Security Group) and the air force's new security service to be linked under the Armed Forces Security Agency. This new entity, with little authority over the individual service components, would survive as a limited condominium until late in the Korean War.[xii]

Uncertainty about the role of COMINT in the national security environment was apparent in other ways as well. From the creation of the CIA, U.S. intelligence had been coordinated by the U.S. Intelligence Board (USIB), led by the director of Central Intelligence. Parallel to USIB existed a U.S. Communications Intelligence Board, a reflection of uncertainty on the mission and use of SIGINT assets.

By 1949, with the rising Soviet threat in Europe and the fall of nationalist China to the communists, the peaceful world envisioned in 1945 had given way to something more dangerous—especially given the spread of nuclear weapons. The CIA began efforts to penetrate the Soviet landmass with human agents, while the air force and navy began a costly program of flights along the perimeter of the Soviet Union and China.[xiii] These flights were, as would become characteristic of much of Cold War collection, numerous intelligence collection discipline (INT) efforts collecting SIGINT but also Measurement and Signature Intelligence (MASINT). These and many other collection efforts were designed to penetrate one of the great obstacles to U.S. (and later North Atlantic Treaty Organization [NATO]) intelligence on the Soviet Union: the very size of the Soviet landmass. Add to this massive problem the efficiency of Soviet information control—much more effective and sophisticated than the United States and its Allies had encountered in penetrating occupied Europe during the Second World War—and the Western allies faced major intelligence collection problems.

Technology also completed the full twentieth-century evolution of SIGINT, which emerged from the Second World War with COMINT and ELINT as well established, if not fully integrated, subdisciplines. The appearance of missiles, especially intercontinental ballistic missiles, as major weapons systems[xiv] made intelligence on their range, payload capacity, and other characteristics intelligence requirements of the highest priority. Data on these were of importance first of all to the nations developing the missiles, and the collection of these data required the placement of measuring

---

[xii] Historian Christopher Andrew has commented that the United States suffered strategic surprise at Pearl Harbor with only two cryptologic agencies but that the failure associated with the North Korean invasion of the South required four.

[xiii] Over the years, several of these aircraft were shot down with significant loss of aircrew memorialized in the National Cryptologic Museum and the National Reconnaissance Park, both at Fort Meade, Maryland.

[xiv] The mating of nuclear weapons with missiles were, in effect, the characteristic strategic weapons challenge of the Cold War. The Germans had achieved the first effective use of missiles late in the Second World War, but fortunately for the allies, these were armed with conventional warheads and represented an effective (because of the absence of counter measures), accurate, and deadly weapon but not one capable of having strategic effect, at least at that stage of the war.

devices—or telemetry devices—on the missile. The interception of those data by foreign services became telemetry intelligence or ELINT, later renamed as FISINT.

Over a relatively short period of time, the recognition that SIGINT existed as an evolved combination of COMINT, ELINT, and FISINT came to be understood within the world's technical intelligence services, especially those of the major powers. Cryptology remained (and remains) a core capability within these services but is incorporated into a much broader set of collection, processing, analysis, and reporting skills. The agencies responsible for this range of functions may be conveniently described as "cryptologic," but the reality is that by the late twentieth century, only a relatively small percentage of the workforce in any of them would have been employed in the actual process of making or breaking codes and ciphers. "Cryptologist" had by this time become a largely generalized term of convenience and professional identity for all those working in the field.

Writing the history of Cold War SIGINT in terms of which country best penetrated another, or which event of the period was most significantly affected by SIGINT success or failure, will be hard to do for many years to come. The Ultra and Magic secrets came out, after all, only thirty years after the German and Japanese surrenders. It is possible though not likely that the full—or even the greater part of—the SIGINT story of the Cold War will be opened by 2020, an equivalent distance in time from the collapse of the Soviet Union.

This is nevertheless an appropriate place to mark the intelligence process as applied to SIGINT during the last half of the twentieth century, from many perspectives a "golden age" in technical intelligence. This was, after all, the period in which SIGINT needed to adapt to at least one new national security domain—space—and begin the process of adapting to another—cyberspace. The latter process continues and will be discussed in detail next. One other development needs to be addressed in assessing the SIGINT process of this era; that is the information revolution (or more accurately several generations of information revolution), centered on the electronic computer and its applications, including, toward the end of the century, the Internet and all that has meant to world affairs.

At least through the Cold War, COMINT remained in many respects the core subdiscipline of the SIGINT process. The interception of communications—between two individuals, or among a party of individuals, or from a command center to subordinate units—remains a key intelligence objective for the obvious reason that communications in this form represent an essential method by which nations, military services, corporations, terrorist groups, and other entities pass information up (and down) their chain of operations and command. COMINT in this sense retains both a tactical and a strategic application, depending largely on whether the communications are taking place between heads of state or between platoon leaders. (This statement needs, it should be noted, to be taken as a general rule rather than as an absolute. Relatively low-level communications, for example, taking place at a "tactical" level, could have strategic implications if they signaled the start of a preemptive war or acknowledgment that an assassination of a major world figure had been approved.)

ELINT remains a significantly tactical subdiscipline, attempting to determine the location, composition, and activity of forces employing equipment that emits radar and other signals. At its most tactical, ELINT can alert aircrews not only that they have been spotted by an adversary's air defense system, but also that an air defense radar has gone from the operating mode that indicates it is still searching for a target to a mode that indicates it has located the target and is prepared to fire. In a more general sense, ELINT analysis can match an emitter with the platform on which the emitter is placed. This can be vital in developing electronic orders of battle, telling a force commander (or potential force commander) critical information on the capabilities of a potential opponent.

FISINT, as previously described, provides information intercepted from telemetry and other devices that measures performance characteristics of missiles and other weapons. Originally intended to monitor technical and operational developments for defense planning, the role of FISINT in late–Cold War and post–Cold War eras has proven important in monitoring arms reductions agreements. It is one of the disciplines that puts reality into the desire to "trust but verify" a rival's compliance with provisions of such agreements. Finally, FISINT remains important in following arms development and proliferation efforts, especially involving countries—for example, North Korea and Iran—that consider denial of information on such programs to be critical national security priorities.

Requirements

The development of requirements for SIGINT is a complex and difficult task. In part, as with Geospatial Intelligence (GEOINT) and MASINT, which are the two other forms of technical intelligence, the officials with an intelligence need are, in many cases, unfamiliar with the capabilities (and weaknesses) of such intelligence. Such limits do not exist as applied to HUMINT—especially in the case of the potential user who somehow believes in the omniscience of the intelligence process.[xv] But SIGINT requires a relatively elaborate requirements process to translate information needs that are often expressed in economic, political, or legal terms into the technical capabilities of the SIGINT system. Establishing and prioritizing

---

[xv]Consumers with such views often manage to alternate between the conviction that intelligence is cheap, easy, and unlimited in capability, as expressed in "I want everything on Fredonia" requirements, and the equally strong conviction that intelligence is miserably incapable in meeting their needs, expressed in something like "Why didn't you people warn about the Japanese earthquake?" judgments.

requirements—for SIGINT as for every other INT—is largely a bureaucratic rather than a technical process but with technical and other factors incorporated into requirement decisions.

Collection

Over the last half century, one of the extraordinary developments within the world's SIGINT systems has been in the range of collection platforms available to intelligence services. Tall antenna towers, sometimes covered with geodesic domes, remain a staple, even as the radio (or later, telecommunications environment) has changed and expanded. Over time, the set of collection "platforms" available, at least to the SIGINT organizations of the superpowers and a few other nations, have come to include almost any surface large enough to mount the equipment and capable of being placed in an advantageous location. Planes and ships of various sizes—some dedicated to collection purposes, others carrying out these duties in addition to a primary function—receive heavy use. Some platforms are either designed or adapted to a range of missions, with collection equipment—including cameras and technical collection gear—packaged in more or less modular form.

Within a very short period after the launch of the first artificial satellite, the Soviet Sputnik, in 1957, the possibility of using space for the interception of signals (and also the provision of photos or, in later technologies, images) was actively pursued by the powers able to afford such systems, initially the United States and the Soviet Union. For the United States, success meant an ultimate solution to the Soviet landmass problem. The brilliant U-2 program had provided an essentially temporary solution to the problem, ending with the shooting down of a U-2 in May 1960, to the great embarrassment of the United States. Within a few months, the first photographs from Corona, the U-2's satellite-based successor program,[xvi] would mark the beginning of a new era in the collection of information. First used for intelligence purposes, within a few decades, satellite imagery and SIGINT became an essential part of everything from treaty verification to the mapping of climate and demographic changes. Interception of signals broadcast "over the air" has been and will remain an important technique. Collection capabilities must cut across broad ranges of the radio spectrum and must match the operating frequencies of communications systems that provide options dependent on intended transmission distance, the medium through which a signal was supposed to pass (including water), and other considerations.

For much of the Cold War period, collection by SIGINT organizations focused on dedicated communications systems—that is, specific systems used by a single country's communications and carrying in some cases only

---

[xvi] At least for the purpose of overflying the Soviet Union. The U-2 remains in service to this day, a tribute to a remarkable aircraft program.

a single form (military or diplomatic, for example) of information. Knowing the existence of such systems provided collection engineers and analysts important clues as to the value of underlying communications, another instance of the way in which study of the externals of communications plays an ongoing role in the SIGINT process. Once collectors found a system of interest and isolated its signal or signals, those signals needed to be processed and exploited through a series of analytic steps that explain in part the expensive nature of modern SIGINT.

The relatively predictable Cold War environment is today much changed, as discussed later in this chapter.

Processing and Exploitation

Media accounts of the NSA or Britain's GCHQ always seem to note the size of the organizations. Among the reasons for this size (and the concomitant expense that goes with it) is that few signals (as with few images in the world of GEOINT) "speak for themselves." If the advantage of technical intelligence is its sheer capability, a disadvantage, at least in times of austere budgets, is that this capability is not cheap. Moreover, each generation of information technology (IT) seems, by some Malthusian law, to complicate the processes of technical intelligence, leading to generational changes in expense and complexity that at least appear to go beyond arithmetic increase. In the case of SIGINT, this involves a sequence of processes that involve analyzing the signal itself (or on networks rather than on individual signals) or the various processes that place the information on a carrier signal and on the encryption system used to conceal the underlying plaintext. If the encryption system cannot be "broken" immediately or in time to provide useful information, traffic analysis (and later network analysis) fills its historic role of providing usable information in the absence of plaintext. Finally, of course, even if the plaintext is recovered, there is the issue of translating it from its original language into, in the U.S. case, English. SIGINT may, in the end, be described as a form of "technical intelligence," but the techniques involved are not exclusively mathematical or scientific. At any given time, a large and important part of the workforce in any SIGINT organization will be language analysts. As in any other form of language work, translation can only be an approximation of the original. Cryptologic linguists and their organizations work continuously on the tension between "exact" translation of the words and full communication of their meaning. Cultural meaning is also important. Communications between the ambassador and his or her chief of state may seem, to American ears, for example, to be fawning or even sycophantic. But some effort to convey a traditional, even class-based, deference central to the culture and politics of the country involved may be a requirement for the language analyst. For decades, machine translation has been something of a holy grail for technologists working on the language issue. Significant progress has been made in this area but, for now, language remains a human construct best, if imperfectly, rendered by humans.

In the whole range of processing and exploitation disciplines, the past twenty years or so have been marked by three troubling considerations: volume, variety, and velocity.[xvii] This brings us, not for the last time, to the information revolution and its effects. As recently as the early 1990s, directors of the NSA could testify to Congress about the magnitude of the agency's task by speaking of the agency's need to collect information "equivalent to the holdings of the Library of Congress." This was impressive in its time, even if the period required for such collection was months—and then weeks. As we move through the second decade of the twenty-first century, information equivalent to the holdings of the library enter the Internet faster than you can read this paragraph. Or so it seems.

As if volume were not enough, the variety of information of consequence in national security issues has expanded. In the Cold War, the United States expended probably at least 50 percent of every national security dollar on programs focused on the Soviet Union and its allies and surrogates. Then, of course, the Soviet Union went away. Even during the immediate post–9/11 period, it is clear that terrorism occupied nothing approaching an equal proportion of national security spending. Globalization has brought with it an astonishing breadth to what we now consider national security issues, including terrorism, climate and energy issues, health and food security issues, and so on. To make matters even more complex, these issues tend to link in significant and often unpredictable ways. Finally, of course, even with the emergence of cyber security (which will be dealt with on its own in more detail), terrorism is not following the Soviet Union into history—at least not yet.

The information involving this mass of data on a broad range of issues creates its own velocity dimension—at least metaphorically. The speed of light remains, after all, the speed of light. But the velocity at issue here is as much that of the speed at which information needs to be acted upon. A World War II Ultra handler may have had hours, even days, to react to information on the coming rendezvous of a concentrated German U-boat wolf pack. Questions of how to intercept them, how to build a cover story designed to protect the information source, and so on, could be dealt with in what must seem to twenty-first-century decision makers (if not the Ultra handlers themselves) as a leisurely time period. Volume, variety, and velocity will remain important pressures on the SIGINT process—especially its processing and exploitation—for a long time to come.

[xvii] In the case of SIGINT, processing and exploitation extends from analyzing the signal intercepted to separating text from carrier signal, decrypting the text (where possible), analyzing the externals associated with the communication, and in the event the text is recoverable, translating it from its original language into English. At that point, the "plaintext" intercept may be forwarded to a consumer, alone or analyzed along with other intercepted text.

Analysis and Dissemination

One factor in SIGINT has not changed since the Ultra experience—at least not completely. That is the fundamental question: Now that we have the plaintext, what do we do with it? More precisely, how do we place it in the hands of persons needing the information (often if not always the person requiring the information in the first place) while, first, ensuring that the information, which may be partial and fragmentary, is intelligible to the reader, and second, ensuring that the methods by which the information was obtained remain secure? On that last point, the availability of similar information will surely depend.

Several considerations play into this. First, how much analysis is the SIGINT organization prepared and permitted to do? Should the role of the SIGINT analyst be limited to the accurate processing and translating of the intercepted message or messages? Should he or she be permitted to make the intercepted communication more meaningful by making reference to another source of information (HUMINT, imagery, or open source information)? Or is that the role of the "all-source" or "finished" intelligence analyst? It is still common in some quarters to speak of organizations such as NSA and the National Geospatial-Intelligence Agency (NGA) as "collection agencies." This is to suggest that signals and images not only speak for themselves but also that they are, in all cases, fully contextual. This issue will not be resolved here; it is one of the continuing tensions in intelligence that is revisited in other chapters of this book. As for protecting the SIGINT source, some of this is done by limiting access to persons specially indoctrinated to know the fragility of SIGINT. These persons are continually alerted to the sensitivity of the material they are reading by the presence of prominent marking on the material indicating that the information is "compartmented"—that is, from a sensitive source not to be communicated to persons not indoctrinated for SIGINT.[xviii]

At some point, however, SIGINT must be communicated to persons who can use it. "The battle is the payoff," after all, and somehow ways must be found to overcome the issue of sensitivity. The Second World War's Ultra handling system remains a classic example. Other techniques include releasing SIGINT information to broader channels, with any reference to the source of the information deleted or concealed by a phrase such

---

[xviii] Years ago, the author visited the Truman Library in Independence, Missouri, to review NSA documents stored in the library's security vault. On one State Department note, suggesting a dire outcome for the contest for dominance in Western Europe in the early Cold War period, President Truman had written to an aide, "This is the sort of top secret malarkey" that sometimes came to his desk. I was so struck by the note I asked the National Security Council (NSC) to approve my obtaining a copy of the memo. In due time, the memo was forwarded to NSA's policy office, but I never received my copy. Finally, I called and was told they were still researching it. They could find no evidence that NSA had ever used the phrase *top secret malarkey* to compartment information.

as "according to sensitive information" or "based on a reliable source," with other details (the names and positions of the communicants) deleted or obscured. Details such as precise dates and times that could indicate if not reveal communications as the source may also be obscured.

In recent years, especially since 9/11 and in response to the issue of velocity noted previously, "tear line" reports have become commonplace. In this format, the sensitive portion of the information appears only above the tear line, with a sanitized version appearing below. The use of the term *tear line* is increasingly metaphorical, with electronic portioning supplanting the tearing off of pieces of a hard copy report.

Signals Intelligence: An Assessment

Even a brief review of the intelligence process as it pertains to SIGINT makes clear that it is a complex, multidisciplinary, and expensive discipline. At each stage of the process, an advanced technology (or perhaps a rare language) must be stripped from an intercepted communication. The steps, from collection analysis to the compilation of a report on the intercept, generally act as links in a chain. Identify the signal but fail to penetrate the encryption and the SIGINT process fails—at least in terms of the ultimate goal of plaintext. Penetrate both the signal and the encryption but fail at translation and the result is the same.

In assessing SIGINT strengths and weaknesses, one of the obvious strengths is that being able to read or hear of an adversary's plans, intentions, or capabilities—from the source—is a powerful information tool. In ELINT, the ability to associate a signal with the particular type of vehicle carrying the equipment producing the signal remains an important, even lifesaving capability. For diplomats and other policymakers, the ability to "read an adversary's mail," leaving aside Stimson's concerns, can provide enormous insight into not just the plans of a counterpart, but also of his or her character and personality.

As with the other INTs, SIGINT has its weaknesses. A change in systems or patterns of communication can lead to a target "going dark," sometimes at inopportune times. This happened several times to the cryptanalysts working the Enigma during the Second World War. It is at these times that traffic analysis can maintain some level of continuity on a target, providing useful information about the volume of communications and perhaps the source and recipient, even during periods when plaintext is unavailable.

A reality of COMINT is that the most a cryptologic organization can hope to do is to collect, process, and analyze accurately what the intercepted communications said. The SIGINT analyst cannot prevent a diplomatic or military official from reporting inaccurately—or from being incompetent. Analysts need also to be alert to the idea that some communications are deceptive in intent. The persons communicating may be involved in a conscious plan to deceive an intercepting organization. Or they may be attempting to deceive a superior. Providing bad news to Adolf Hitler or Saddam Hussein could not have been looked upon by their subordinates as either career or life enhancing. Finally, the official doing the communicating may not be deceptive so much as incompetent. In all of these cases, as in any intelligence analysis, either by professional analysts or by the "customers" of intelligence, a measure of skepticism is not unwarranted. Any official who says an act is going to occur because NSA or GCHQ or any other SIGINT organization "says it's going to happen," needs to realize that those organizations have as their mission the accurate transmission of what they intercept and process. They cannot necessarily vouch for the truthfulness or the competence of the person whose communications they intercept.

Finally, of course, the complexity of the SIGINT process, essential to its being in its mature form, is in itself a potential weakness. SIGINT (like imagery) is a very expensive INT. For smaller nations, and even for great powers dealing with economic or fiscal crises, the price tag for SIGINT is very high and makes SIGINT an attractive target when "belt tightening" comes along.

The Information Revolutions and Signals Intelligence: Computers, the Internet, and Cyber

Some decades ago, an IBM official predicted a world market for computers limited to a very small number of special purpose machines. More accurately, in 1965, Gordon Moore wrote his four-page essay "Cramming More Components onto Integrated Circuits,"[8] predicting that integrated electronics would "make electronic techniques more generally available throughout all of society." If anything, Moore underestimated the speed and impact of the information revolution—or a series of continuing information revolutions on late-twentieth- and early-twenty-first-century society. Intelligence, and especially technical intelligence, has been both at the forefront of these revolutions and at times struggling to keep pace with them.

The use of computing technology in cryptanalysis precedes the advent of the all-electric computing device, most prominently in the *bombes* (the early "super computers" of their day) that supported decryption of the German Enigma. After the Second World War, some of the technologists involved in the IT of the period stayed in government service; others left for the emerging corporate computing industry. In the two decades after the Second World War, companies such as IBM, UNIVAC, and others built "special purpose" computers for NSA, a process followed for other cryptologic or SIGINT organizations in other countries. Whether these computers were one-of-a-kind creations or variations on commercially available machines, the goal was to provide greater, faster computing power than was available on the commercial market. NSA had one of the most famous machines of this era; it was the IBM-built Harvest, an enhanced version of a commercially available IBM model. NSA began operations with Harvest in 1962, retiring it from service in 1976. Harvest continued to operate effectively to the end—its deactivation related more to the difficulty of replacing parts than to operational obsolescence.

Computers soon became foundational in the SIGINT business, in roles including but not limited to cryptanalytic attack against very complex encryption systems. They soon became commonplace in a range of other functions—administrative as well as operational. In fact, the range of public uses for computers, even in the early 1970s, had totally confounded any predictions measuring the ultimate computing market as being able to support only dozens of machines. Computers were getting faster, more powerful, cheaper, and more common at a rapid pace. Then, in the late 1970s, the Tandy Corporation introduced, through its Radio Shack stores, the first practical personal computer. For many SIGINT professionals, these were little more than toys, markedly inferior to the mainframe computers available to them. Suffice it to say, any employee of any SIGINT organization in the world had access to computing power beyond that imaginable, let alone available, to the general public. This was about to change.[xix] Another tide of fundamental change in the information environment was rising.

By the late 1990s, the Internet Society could proclaim "the internet is for everyone." This proclamation could not have been issued two decades before—first, because there was no Internet, and second, because the world had not passed the point where computers were few and operated by skilled personnel trained, among other specializations, in unique programming languages. The latter consideration disappeared quickly in the concurrent appearance of the personal computer and the MS-DOS operating system. At first, as could have been predicted, the old-line (though they would have barely been finishing their third decade of operation) companies—and the government entities they supported—held to the view that the superior performance of larger computers would forever eclipse the limited speed, power, and storage of the desktop computers.

Within a few years, however, several of the old-line companies were out of business or on the ropes, and Microsoft and other "new" firms were kings of the IT hill. In an earlier era, it had been the connection of nuclear weapons and ballistic missiles that created a fundamental alteration in the world's strategic environment. In the 1980s and 1990s, it was the linkage of cheap personal computers with the networking capabilities of the Internet and its web of hypertext documents (aka the World Wide Web) that changed the information environment. As this happened, and social function after social function from education, to banking, and on and on converted to electronic form, other technologies followed.

[xix] This was not lost on everyone in the SIGINT professions. See Lawrence C. Tarbell Jr., "The Technology of Future Personal Powerful Computers," *NSA Technical Journal* (Summer 1980): 1–27.

Among these was encryption. If the only information moving across the Internet was e-mail, recipes, and the like, the market for encryption remained small. But once financial and corporate records followed suit, encryption—long the preserve of government documents of the greatest sensitivity—became a global phenomenon.

Together, these changes in the environment produced enormous stresses on the SIGINT system. As in auto manufacturing and other industries, the "startup costs" to be a major player in protected communications had been very high. By the 1990s, however, costs of entry to the Internet, by everyone from students, to small companies, to terrorists, and to drug lords, had become extremely low. The same dramatic changes in computing were also striking telecommunications with similar effects. In the late 1970s, one's phone was an instrument wired into the kitchen wall or on a desk in an office. Movies that showed characters speaking on a mobile telephone usually portrayed wealthy characters speaking into something the size of a paving brick. Here, too, the information environment was changing and, roughly speaking, at Moore's Law pace or *better*.

Coincident with the end of the Cold War, SIGINT organizations were placed in a difficult position. They had been designed to work against a conventional adversary (and a somewhat slow and cumbersome one) that built large, complex hierarchies to deal with the business of state. For communications, these adversaries created large, powerful, worldwide systems used only for their own communications and consequently vulnerable to analysis that would reveal the type of information on each.

Suddenly, a new set of adversaries, including some that were not even nation-states, were on the scene and communicating on the same global networks used by average, ordinary citizens. As if this were not enough, the former point-to-point nature of communications, including telephone communications, was being replaced by a global network in which packets of information—that is, segments of formerly intact communications—moved about the globe at the speed of light, with the promise they would be reassembled at the receiving end. Finally, for nations such as the United States, with significant (after the 1970s) clarity in the distinction between foreign intelligence and interception (legal but under oversight) and domestic intelligence or interception (largely prohibited), the nature of the communications world had changed. No longer could it be presumed that a phone call between Philadelphia to Houston went directly from Philadelphia to Houston. Nor could it be presumed that the only phone traffic moving between Philadelphia and Houston originated in one of those cities and was intended for receipt in the other. The networks may well have moved a message from a drug lord in Colombia to his banker in Lisbon through one or more American cities.

For the United States, at least, this was a disturbing and difficult shift in environment—even before September 2001. From that time, however, it became a major policy issue that threatened to alter if not destroy long-standing arrangements that permitted national security issues to be segregated from law enforcement issues and, even more importantly, one that permitted legal and regulatory barriers between "foreign" and "domestic" security arrangements and organizations. The United States, along with the other democracies to varying degrees, faced serious issues in sorting out static laws versus shifting technology. Managing the tension created by concurrently held public desires for both security and the protection of privacy and other civil liberties promises to be an enduring and difficult process.[xx] At moments in the period since 9/11, these competing objectives could easily be placed in an either/or context, an undesirable (and arguably unnecessary) option.

For SIGINT professionals, the convergence of transnational terrorism, a global network that provided easy access to virtually any individual or group, with limited costs of entry onto the network, created an enormous challenge. Determining al-Qaida's "order of battle" would require techniques unlike those needed to determine the structure of the Red Army in an earlier period. (This is not to say, it should be noted, that lessons could not be drawn from that experience. They could.)

Well before September 2001, the growing importance of IT in national security—with national security being defined ever more broadly than in its use through most of the twentieth century—had led to the use of the term *information warfare*. In some sense, of course all warfare has a significant information basis. One must locate and target the enemy before applying force to the enemy. But without question, the emphasis on the information weapon as compared with kinetic weapons has changed as the information revolution has progressed. Instead of sending fleets of bombers over targets, armed with (in retrospect) grossly inaccurate ordnance, as was the case in the Second World War, the United States took a quantum step on the deployment of precision weapons in the First Gulf War, a trend that has continued in Iraq and Afghanistan. The reality is, even at the tactical level, there can be no precision weapons without precise information loaded onto them.

Beyond the use of such data for guidance purposes, by the late 1990s, theorists were noting both the world's growing reliance on electronic data and the vulnerabilities of those systems.[9] In future wars, should one attack an adversary's navy with bombs or torpedoes? Or could you disable the adversary's ability operate his navy? Or control his banking system? When the Japanese attacked Pearl Harbor in 1941, the markings on the aircraft (among other evidence) left no doubt as to the source of the attack. Will that be true in a future war fought between adversaries attempting to attack or defend information systems in cyberspace?

[xx] Nondemocratic states face the same environmental issues but do so without the additional tension created by conducting intelligence under considerable public oversight.

To some degree, the problem with what was first called "information warfare" and now "cyber security," results from the nature of the global network that dominates much of the world's commerce, communication, and public life. Cyber security experts work on a network of networks not designed with security as a first consideration. Moreover, the legal and bureaucratic complications of this new national security domain contain all manner of complexities. Is cyber security a criminal justice issue? Or is it a national security issue?

As of this writing, most of the world has made some provision for cyberspace in both its security and legal domains. These efforts are largely provisional, attempting to deal with an issue that continues to develop at a rapid pace. In the United States, this has led to an arrangement in which a "cyber tsar" operates from the office of the president, while the DHS, the Justice Department, the DoD, and other agencies attempt to (a) protect their own systems while (b) developing tools to defeat if not destroy the capabilities of attacking states, groups, and individuals.[xxi] For those in the SIGINT professions, the simultaneous need to protect on the one hand and exploit and attack on the other is surely reminiscent of the code making and code breaking nature of cryptology from its earliest time.

Where does this new environment place SIGINT? In one sense, it places SIGINT organizations and their skills at the center of a major national security debate. It also raises issues regarding the authorities under which SIGINT organizations must operate. If the arrangements in place in the 1950s or 1960s made it clear that intercepting an adversary's battle plan as it was communicated over the air was a SIGINT function, while stealing it in its physical form was a human intelligence responsibility, how does this arrangement work in the cyber world? If "a reliable source" reports that the plan is stored in a certain location on a computer in some government building, who goes after the plan while it resides on the computer?

In the United States, this and other questions have led to a number of decisions assigning responsibility for the cyber issue, or as we will call it here, the cyber domain. The NSA remains the center of U.S. cryptology (and SIGINT), but substantial concerns exist within the Congress and the public on how much influence they want an intelligence agency to have on issues, such as cyber, that clearly cross not only foreign and domestic lines but also into the private sector. Since 2010, NSA and the newly created U.S. Cyber Command have been headed by the same individual.[xxii] Will this arrangement be permanent? That's hard to answer. Along similar lines, NSA leads the U.S. IA effort. Even in an earlier period, some members of Congress felt it was inappropriate for a "defense intelligence" agency to handle

---

[xxi] Many corporations operate in a similar set of circumstances, providing security technology to governmental and other entities, while having to invest substantial resources to protecting their own information and information systems.

[xxii] Currently, General Keith Alexander, United States.

so much of the nation's assurance concerns. This became especially true after encryption began to penetrate the information systems of banks, hospitals, the electrical grid, and so on. Would civil and corporate IA be more appropriately housed in some organization outside the DoD? What impact would such an arrangement have on the cryptologic portion of SIGINT core skills, which have, if anything, seen the technologies of the last decade or so bring their offensive and defensive professionals into closer alignment than existed, for example, in the Cold War?

What, then, of SIGINT itself? How does it relate to the new issue of cyber issues? While conceding that cyber issues as a national security issue will be in a period of definition for some time, it is possible to make several observations. First, the conceptual and organizational issues raised by this new phenomenon, while unique in some particulars, bear resemblance to several periods in twentieth-century national security history. For centuries, national security included diplomacy, security of trade and other economic activity, and the military dimensions of security, themselves divided into warfare on the ground and war at sea. The twentieth century gave rise to the consideration of air as a possible third military dimension. But knowing the dimension was out there did not define it or provide immediate organizational responses to it. Was it a unique domain? Or an extension of the previous domains? Was it important enough to consider it separate from army and navy organization? Or should it be handled within those "senior" services?[xxiii]

One important consideration, as it applies to the air in the early twentieth century, nuclear weapons (mid-century), or space (a bit later), is the flexibility of the concept of the national security domain. As with the others, the cyberspace domain operates across a number of dimensions from the purely technological, to the applied processes, to legal and political constructs. Within a given domain, it can be understood that the technological dimension is the foundation for much if not all change but that, especially in democracies, the legal, political, and even public dimensions require attention.

SIGINT as it evolved in the twentieth century represented an extraordinarily rich national security endeavor, still linked to its roots in an ancient desire to communicate as needed for reasons of state, commerce, or personal privacy in a way that ensures security, along with an equally ancient need, at least on occasion, to penetrate an adversary's security arrangements. Whether the term *SIGINT* remains in use ten or twenty years from now is anyone's guess. Perhaps it becomes a component of a defined cyber domain. Perhaps experience and technology leave it related to cyberspace but somehow apart from it.

However this conceptual issue is resolved, the very power of SIGINT makes it a controversial capability—especially in democratic societies, the

---

[xxiii] Once again, these did not not necessarily resolve themselves into "either-or" solutions. The U.S. solution to the air domain in the late 1940s was to "unify" the armed services by creating a separate air force, while leaving the army, navy, and marines with significant air assets.

United States perhaps above all others. Americans are little more than a generation from believing that intelligence, apart from military intelligence in time of war, is somehow an alien, "Old World" practice. The American public has made its peace with a permanent and powerful intelligence establishment, subject to history-making legislative oversight and an understanding—partly explicit, partly implicit—that American intelligence will conduct itself in ways consistent with American law and values. As one would expect in a democratic society, disagreement as to what constitutes a violation of those laws is part of the political process.

In the cyber-based, homeland security–focused environment of the early twenty-first century, accusations of unauthorized surveillance on a nation's citizens or even abuse of the SIGINT service by political masters will always attract attention and, to one degree or another, generate mistrust. Those difficulties notwithstanding, SIGINT power makes it a key element in the modern national security process, reflecting the centrality of information and information technologies in the modern world. Perhaps Henry Stimson was right: gentlemen do not read one another's mail. Until, however, leadership in the world is limited to ladies and gentlemen, the democracies will, one hopes under law and with some measure of public confidence, make use of that power.

References

1. David Kahn, *The Codebreakers: The Story of Secret Writing* (New York: Macmillan, 1967), 79–80.
2. J. C. Masterman, *The Double Cross System* (New Haven, CT: Yale University Press, 1972).
3. Frederick W. Winterbotham, *The Ultra Secret* (New York: Harper and Row, 1974).
4. Reginald V. Jones, *Most Secret War* (London: Hamish Hamilton, 1971).
5. Jozef Garlinski, *The Enigma War* (New York: Scribner's, 1979).
6. Ibid.
7. National Security Agency, "The Venona Story," www.nsa.gov/about/_files/cryptologic_heritage/publications/coldwar/venonastory.pdf.
8. Gordon E. Moore, "Cramming More Components onto Integrated Circuits," *Electronics Magazine* 38, no. 8 (April 19, 1965): 114–117.
9. See, for example, Thomas A. Stewart, *Intellectual Capital: The New Wealth of Organizations* (New York: Crown Business, 1998).

5

Geospatial Intelligence

Darryl Murdock and Robert M. Clark

Geospatial Intelligence, commonly known as GEOINT, is a relatively new intelligence field, founded by definition in 2003. However, its roots date back to the creation of the earliest maps and the first use of aerial photography—balloons used for reconnaissance purposes.[1] Historically, maps were used for military and intelligence activities as well as for commerce. Those rulers with accurate maps of friendly and enemy dispositions and ideal trade routes gained a major advantage over those who did not. Accurate and timely maps were highly coveted articles of intelligence. During the twentieth century, aerial reconnaissance photos were routinely used beginning in World War I. In World War II modern photogrammetric and image interpretation techniques were developed.[2] The launch of the Earth-Observation Landsat 1 satellite in 1972 started an entirely new era of commercial remote sensing and arguably was the beginning of the GEOINT era as we now know it. For the first time in history, non-defense scientists around the globe were able to look at images of the earth on a regular, repeated basis. Changes in land use and land cover could be measured and human impacts on the globe assessed. These developments also had and continue to have a direct influence on national security and defense decisions.

Geospatial Intelligence Defined

There are two main definitions of GEOINT—one that has its roots in U.S. defense and intelligence and one that is derived from more recent developments in both computing capability and non-intelligence related businesses. The current and most widely recognized definition of GEOINT stems from United States Code, Title 10, section 467 (10 U.S.C. §467), which states:

> The term "geospatial intelligence" means the exploitation and analysis of imagery and geospatial information to describe, assess, and visually depict physical features and geographically referenced activities on the earth. Geospatial intelligence consists of imagery, imagery intelligence, and geospatial information.[3]

It is the final sentence of this statutory definition that is most often cited and that forms the basis for most discussions about the functional authority of the National Geospatial-Intelligence Agency, commonly called NGA. NGA has functional authority over GEOINT for the National System for Geospatial Intelligence (NSG) and the Allied System for Geospatial Intelligence.[4] The NGA definition of GEOINT is identical to the statutory definition. However, within NGA Publication 1.0, the definition of GEOINT is made both clearer and broader.[5] Chapter 1 of the NGA publication has four sections:

- Section A describes GEOINT as a "discipline" or, more commonly with the U.S. Intelligence Community (IC), GEOINT Tradecraft.
- Section B outlines data used in the performance of GEOINT as an analytic intelligence collection discipline (INT), namely imagery, Imagery Intelligence (IMINT), and geospatial information. Because geospatial information has such a broad definition and widespread use, we will discuss later on in this chapter how this broadening of GEOINT data sources has and will continue to impact the U.S. IC.
- Section C explains the idea of Geospatial-Intelligence Preparation of the Environment (GPE), which parallels the military concept called Intelligence Preparation of the Battlefield (IPB).
- Section D describes GEOINT products, which are in reality ever-changing.

Since the publication of this document in 2004, much of what is contained therein remains unchanged in practice. Department of Defense Directive (DoDD) 5105.60, dated July 29, 2009, and with the subject line "National Geospatial-Intelligence Agency (NGA)," outlines all of the NGA functional authorities under 10 U.S.C., and 50 U.S.C. DoDD 5143.01 (along with DoDD 5105.60 itself) reaffirms the NGA responsibilities as a U.S. Combat Support Agency.[6]

All of these statutory and functional legal documents produced by the U.S. defense community and IC underscore and highlight the importance of the *where* and *when* in the formulation and execution of national security policy. The very fact that NGA exists today is a testament to the importance we place on knowing what is happening, where it has happened, where it is happening, and what will happen next. Mapping, charting, and geodesy all are disciplines that help depict the earth in a way that can be readily shared. The NGA motto is "Map the earth, show the way, understand the world." NGA's stated mission is: "NGA provides timely, relevant and accurate geospatial intelligence in support of national security."

The practice of GEOINT is undergoing a significant and, one can easily argue, constant role change. The nature of the change is summed up in a recent modification to the NGA mission statement: NGA Director Letitia A. Long (2010–2014) summarized the mission as "Putting the power of GEOINT in your hands." Director Long's statement reflects the huge role that mobile and web technologies play in our daily lives and highlights

NGA's desire to transform itself into an organization capable of integrating the most modern of analytic tools and technology. Consider these statistics: In May 2013, 91 percent of American adults had a cell phone and 6 percent of American adults had a smartphone.[7] In December 2012, 65 percent of American adults had a high-speed broadband connection at home.[8] Global use of cell phones is approaching 100 percent, with several markets in excess of 100 percent (many people prefer to keep a personal line and a separate business line).[9]

"In 2013, over 2.7 billion people were using the Internet, which corresponds to 39% of the world's population.

In the developing world, 31% of the population is online, compared with 77% in the developed world"[10]

It is clear that we have embraced the notion of ubiquitous and mobile computing and near instantaneous communications. The lightning speed at which ideas, ideologies, pictures, photographs, videos, treaties, and treatises can be shared globally has resulted in a need to revamp and revisit what GEOINT means and how it is conducted as a tradecraft within U.S. national security constructs. Outside of the U.S IC, GEOINT is being used in a wide variety of business applications, perhaps most notably within the field called location-based intelligence (LBI). One could easily show that Global Positioning System (GPS) technology, funded by the U.S. Department of Defense (DoD), has enabled an entire market centered on LBI. In developed countries, use of GPS in automobiles and smartphones allows us to quickly, and usually accurately, figure out how to navigate from point A to point B. We no longer use paper maps to plot our trips. Rather, we use online tools such as Google Maps, Yahoo! Maps, and MapQuest to create our own best route for vacations and for trips across town. This ubiquitous routing capability used to be the sole domain of the intelligence or defense analyst, where layers of Mylar were used to help the intelligence analyst identify "go, slow go, and no go" terrain. What we now take for granted as readily available decision tools were once custom analytic products taking hours to days to compile. It is this trend of speed to decision and available (and expected) speed of analysis that is at the core of the new GEOINT discipline. Location is now an assumed part of how global business is conducted and is a routine part of business analytics and business intelligence activities.

The definition of GEOINT, therefore, is far from static and is likely to remain dynamic for some time. GEOINT can be seen, first and foremost, as part of the intelligence process and an aid to decision-making. Decision makers within the IC, Congress, and global business leaders regularly use intelligence products created by GEOINT practitioners. One attempt at a wider GEOINT definition is "actionable knowledge, a process, and a profession."[11] These three components are certainly part of the overall construct of today's GEOINT professional. But they fall short in describing the breadth and depth of critical thinking needed or already taking place, and they fail to take into account the types of data used; they also ignore the temporal element, which is a central part of today's GEOINT environment. A more comprehensive definition of GEOINT might be this: GEOINT is the professional practice of integrating and interpreting all forms of geospatial data to create historical and anticipatory intelligence products used for planning or that answer questions posed by decision-makers.

This simple expansion of the discipline definition is inclusive of the U.S. IC idea of GEOINT and also allows business leaders to understand GEOINT fully in the context of doing business. It has been posited that over 80 percent of all data has a geospatial component.[12] For this reason alone, most business and governmental leaders have considered or have already created a strong GEOINT staff, assuming they do not already have robust in-house GEOINT capability. The senior or "c-level" position—which in the corporate world is the Geospatial Information Officer and within the U.S. government is the Geospatial Intelligence Officer—is a rising trend, further underscoring the importance of place in all decisions.

This GEOINT chapter concentrates primarily on the traditional U.S. DoD and IC definition and application. And it also provides examples of GEOINT as it applies to activities performed beyond the standard IC treatment of GEOINT as a discipline or profession and suggests future trends. To understand how GEOINT has changed over many centuries and continues to evolve, it is worth taking a close look at its history.

A History of Geospatial Intelligence

This is a history of three distinct disciplines—two ancient, one relatively modern—and their convergence into what is now known as GEOINT. The oldest of these disciplines probably is terrain knowledge.

The value of terrain knowledge—both of physical terrain and of what is often described today as the human terrain or, more broadly, human geography—was recognized in ancient times for both military purposes and commerce. Sun Tzu's *The Art of War* discusses six different types of physical terrain and the combat tactics appropriate to each. The Israelites' attempt to scout the land of Canaan (an early example of assessing the human terrain) is documented in the Bible (Numbers 13). And traders from the earliest times had to plan trade routes, taking into account terrain, climate, season, time of day, known friendly ports and oasis locations to make travel easier and to avoid bandits and tariffs.

The importance of physical terrain (topography) in war is well documented. One of the best examples was the battle of Thermopylae in 480 BCE. The Greeks had a very good understanding of the Persian army. They knew that it could not stay in one place for long because of logistics. It had to attack or retreat. They knew how effectively the Persians used cavalry. They knew Persian battle tactics.

The Greeks also had great geospatial knowledge and applied it to their tactics. The pass at Thermopylae was the only way into Greece by land. The Greek infantry would be able to block the narrow pass with ease, with no risk of being outflanked by cavalry. In the pass, the Greek hoplites would be very difficult to assault for the more lightly armed Persian infantry. And as the story is told in many books and in the movie *300,* King Leonidas and a force of 300 men held the pass against far superior forces—until the Persians got a geospatial advantage in the form of a Greek Human Intelligence (HUMINT) source. A shepherd told the Persian king Xerxes of a separate path through Thermopylae, which the Persians then used to outflank the Greeks.

These historical examples illustrate a pattern: GEOINT long has relied on HUMINT and continues to do so even given the rich set of sensors and computational tools that are used today. The original product of these collection efforts took the form of maps and charts, discussed next.

A Short History of Maps and Cartography

The oldest known land maps are preserved on Babylonian clay tablets from about 2300 BCE. Cartography—the art or technique of creating maps and charts—was a well-developed skill in ancient Greece.

Planning a course at sea requires knowing the direction and distance between departure and destination points, along with some understanding of the hazards enroute. So sea navigation long relied on mariners' accumulated knowledge acquired during their experience at sea. The Greeks, admittedly, preferred to sail in sight of land, having little means of navigating on the open seas. When acquired, navigational information gave a definite commercial advantage, making mariners loath to share it, especially with potential competitors. Fifteenth century Portuguese mariners kept secret the sailing directions to the East Indies for nearly a century.

Over time, sailing directions were written down in handbooks, which the English called rutters. They contained a wealth of additional information such as detailed physical descriptions of shorelines, harbors, islands, channels, landmarks, and tidal patterns as well as the locations of reefs and shoals. By the fourteenth century, marine navigators were capturing this knowledge in the form of nautical charts.

Maps and nautical charts were especially critical assets from the very beginning of the settlements in the New World. Numerous examples exist of the development of mapping in the Americas, but the mapping of the Louisiana Purchase is probably the most ambitious of these efforts. In 1803, Captains Meriwether Lewis and William Clark began an expedition to explore this new territory and to record what they found. Traveling west from St. Louis to the Pacific Ocean, Lewis and Clark brought back maps and detailed first-person knowledge about the activities of Indian tribes and potential rival European powers in the region.[13] The expedition is another example of the value of combining mapping and HUMINT reporting.

Although maps of North America were important in the settlement and defense of U.S. territory, before 1917 there was not much demand in the United States for maps of foreign countries. In 1917, the United States entered World War I, and the U.S. perspective on global mapping permanently changed.

Proliferation of Mapping Organizations

The fifty-year period that began with World War I is characterized by the proliferation of governmental and commercial organizations that produced maps and charts to serve specialized purposes. The map scales used, and the features displayed, are quite different depending on whether the map is to be used for naval, aerial, or land navigation. Different features are required for military, intelligence, other governmental, or commercial use. Where such separate organizations did not already exist, a number of military, governmental, and commercial units stepped up to serve these specialized needs.

Nautical Charts and Surveys

The U.S. Navy has a long history of producing charts to meet navigational needs. In 1830, the navy created a Depot of Charts and Instruments. In 1854, the depot was renamed as the U.S. Naval Observatory and Hydrographical Office, which subsequently was divided into two separate activities in 1866.

Prior to the establishment of a separate hydrographic office in 1866, U.S. navigators were almost entirely dependent on British charts. The hydrographic office was responsible for conducting marine surveys and providing charts, sailing directions, and navigation manuals for the use of all seafarers—but primarily for international and foreign waters. A separate organization, the Coast and Geodetic Survey of the Treasury Department, was given responsibility for the systematic hydrographic survey of the coasts of the United States.

The hydrographic office provided nautical charts and survey products for the U.S. Navy in every war thereafter. Some of the most difficult and dangerous of such surveys were those conducted to support coastal operations against hostile territory, especially combat force landings. Two examples from two different wars illustrate some of the challenges inherent in such surveys.

Prior to the Normandy invasion during World War II, the allies needed detailed hydrography of the planned invasion site, including sounding data to support both the landings of troops and the placement of large floating docks (code named "mulberries") after the beach was secured. They also needed information on the beach condition. The U.K. Hydrographic Office created a special team of hydrographic surveyors to gather the needed soundings off the Normandy shore. Between November 1943 and January 1944, the team conducted six soundings and gathered beach samples.

They relied on personnel landing craft that were modified for survey work by an underwater exhaust to silence the engine, an echo sounder to obtain water depth, and a navigational radio to get locational data.[14]

The second example comes from the Korean War. In July 1950, invading North Korean forces pushed South Korean and U.S. forces into the southeast corner of the Korean peninsula. General Douglas MacArthur, commanding general of the allied forces, decided on a counterstrike that required U.S. naval forces to land at Inchon, a major port on Korea's Yellow Sea coast. From Inchon, MacArthur reasoned, the allies could mount a major ground offensive to cut off North Korean forces in the south.

The North Koreans, and many U.S. planners, considered the Inchon area unsuitable for a major amphibious operation. Tides rose and fell an average of thirty-two feet daily, producing strong currents in the narrow, winding waterways; the harbor approaches were easy to mine, lined by defensible islands and marked by extensive mud flats, high seawalls, and dominating hills. The harbor facilities had little room for logistical shipping to support an invasion.

The allied planning effort was a model of GEOINT analysis. It made good use of overhead imagery from aircraft (IMINT), debriefings of former inhabitants (HUMINT), and on-the-ground reconnaissance by naval special warfare teams (mapping). The use of this combination of geospatial intelligence sources allowed planners to select the best water approach and to select the best time for the amphibious assaults.

The amphibious landing on September 15, 1950, took the North Koreans completely by surprise. As a result, a large portion of the North Korean forces to the south were isolated and caught in a trap.[15]

Army Mapping

The U.S. Army uses different types of maps than the charts used by the U.S. Navy. Ground forces require large-scale, highly detailed maps that show terrain features, topography, population centers, and roads. In mapping, scale refers to the proportional depiction of objects relative to their true dimensions. A 1:1 scale would be a full-scale model. A 1:24,000 scale means 1" = 24,000" or 1" measured on a map = 0.38 statute miles. Large-scale maps generally contain more detail than small-scale maps.

The Army Corps of Engineers in 1910 had set up the Central Map Reproduction Plant. With the advent of World War I in 1917, the unit was reorganized and expanded by Major Charles H. Ruth in anticipation of a map supply crisis. During the course of the conflict, the unit produced some nine million maps. Under Major Ruth's initial direction, the map unit became one of the major military topographic organizations in the world. Near the end of World War I, Sherman Fairchild solved a problem that had hindered the use of aerial cameras for mapmaking: The photographs were distorted because the relatively slow shutter speeds could not keep up with the aircraft movement. Fairchild's camera placed the shutter inside the lens, increasing shutter speed and reducing the distortion.[16] For several decades thereafter, the Fairchild camera was the best available source of material for mapmaking.

After World War I, the Central Map Reproduction Plant was renamed the Engineer Reproduction Plant, where extensive research and experiments in cartographic and photolithographic processes and aerial photogrammetry—the science of making measurements from photos—were conducted. During these interwar years, the major advances in mapmaking came from the use of aerial cameras as a source, relying on the Fairchild camera.

The Army Map Service was created in 1942 by consolidating the Engineer Reproduction Plant and the Cartographic Section of the War Department General Staff. At first, the maps were produced by revising existing maps. By the middle of World War II, the service was producing small and medium-scale maps, using the available large-scale maps as source materials. By the end of the war, considerable effort was being applied to large-scale mapping by stereo-photogrammetric methods.

Aerial Charts

Aircraft navigation requires a different type of chart than those used by either the army or the navy. Aerial charts typically are medium to large scale and need to show hazards to flight. After World War I, as airplane capacity and range improved, the need for such charts grew.

To meet this specialized need, the Army Air Corps had set up a map unit in 1928. World War II produced a demand for aerial charts spanning the globe. In response, the Army Air Force in 1943 commissioned an Aeronautical Chart Plant in St. Louis, Missouri. It was transferred to the U.S. Air Force in 1947 and subsequently renamed the U.S. Air Force Aeronautical Chart and Information Center (ACIC).[17]

Governmental and Commercial Mapping

After the end of World War I, Sherman Fairchild focused his attention on nonmilitary uses of his camera system that had been developed during the war. Recognizing the commercial potential of photography-based mapping, in 1921 Fairchild created a company called Fairchild Aerial Surveys. It quickly became the largest and most commercially successful aerial photography company in the United States. Fairchild Aerial Surveys in rapid succession produced maps of Manhattan Island, Newark, New Jersey, and other towns and cities in the United States. Another Fairchild company mapped large regions of Canada.[18]

By the late 1930s, two-thirds of the continental United States had been mapped using aerial photography. Much of this mapping was done by federal government agencies such as the U.S. Forest Service, Soil Conservation Service, Agricultural Adjustment Administration, U.S. Coast and Geodetic Survey, and the U.S. Geological Survey.[19]

Specialized Intelligence Maps

While the military services were developing and expanding their mapping units during World War II, a separate effort focused on mapping for intelligence purposes. Soon after its creation in 1942, the Office of Strategic Services (OSS) established the Map Division, which assembled an extensive collection of maps on paper and microfilm. It collected maps through its HUMINT sources, from the navy, the Army Map Service, the State Department, and several other government sources. The Map Division created a cartographic section responsible for producing maps that were used in OSS intelligence studies. It also produced relief models that were used by the U.S. Army and U.S. Navy for strategic planning.[20]

The foundation for producing maps specifically for intelligence established by the OSS Map Division continues today. A mapping unit was part of the Foreign Broadcast Information Service (FBIS), formed when the Central Intelligence Agency (CIA) was established in 1947. It now is a part of the CIA Open Source Center (OSC). CIA describes the unit in these terms:

> Open Source Center (OSC) geographers are the intelligence community's experts on foreign mapping, geographic information and geospatial technologies. They combine skills in geography and allied disciplines (i.e., cartography, geology, remote sensing, photogrammetry, imagery analysis, urban planning, etc.) with area knowledge to review and assess all sources of geographic information in all its varied forms (paper, digital, internet, etc.). OSC geographers provide maps, data, information, analytical products, training and a host of related geographic services to those on the front lines of intelligence today.[21]

Consolidation: Vietnam and the Stand-up of the Defense Mapping Agency

In the years just before the Vietnam War (1965–1975), the service mapping units had been working more closely together, sharing both mapping data and knowledge of cartographic techniques. Even before the United States became involved in Vietnam, the Army Mapping Service, ACIC, National Photographic Interpretation Center (NPIC), and the Navy Hydrographic Office had developed aeronautical and maritime charts, maps, and analyses for the region.[22]

During that war, it became apparent that the existing coastal charts (based largely upon World War II data) were inadequate. The army, in particular, needed detailed topography of Vietnam's river deltas to conduct riverine operations. The Naval Oceanographic Office conducted comprehensive geodetic, coastal, and harbor surveys of that complex coastline using a series of survey vessels. The product of the effort was an extensive set of updated maritime charts and publications that were used by the army and by local fleet and Marine Corps units in their blockade and interdiction operations. [23]

The cooperation during the Vietnam conflict foreshadowed what was to come next: the consolidation of all defense mapping into a single agency. In 1972, DoD created the Defense Mapping Agency (DMA), bringing into a single organization the mapping, charting, and geodesy (also referred to as MC&G) activities of all the three major services. The formation of DMA coincided with the emergence of a new concept in cartography—that of geographic information systems (GIS). Traditional cartography relied on a paper map to be both the database and the display of geographic information. GIS treats the database, spatial analysis, cartographic representation and display as being physically and conceptually separate aspects of handling geographic data. GIS, though, requires information to be in digital form. DMA, therefore, began a major effort in the 1980s to convert its mapping capabilities to digital format. By the mid-1990s, DMA had created a new system for generating maps, called the Digital Production System. Beginning in 1989, DMA used GIS techniques to produce a global database at a 1:1 meter scale, called the Digital Chart of the World.[24]

When Iraq invaded Kuwait in August 1990, DMA found that it did not have current detailed mapping of the combat region. DMA mapping and production systems were still focused on Cold War needs, emphasizing Eastern Europe rather than the Middle East.

Especially critical to combat requirements during the Gulf War that followed was detailed terrain elevation data. But the DMA digital terrain elevation data measured elevations only at roughly hundred meter intervals, which resulted in very rough elevation surfaces and inexact maps. Extensive areas of critical terrain were uncharted. DMA was forced to rely on images of the terrain available commercially through the National Aeronautics and Space Administration (NASA) Landsat program. The Landsat image maps filled the needs of theater commanders while DMA worked on a longer-term solution.

The long-term solution involved using the NASA space shuttle to take radar interferometry readings that provided detailed elevation and relief maps of the earth. Interferometry uses two images of the same area taken simultaneously from two different vantage points to provide a 3-D image. The space shuttle *Endeavour* in early 2000 completed an eight-day mission that recorded the needed topographic data.

After the Gulf War, DMA mapping skills were used for nonmilitary purposes on a number of occasions. During November 1995, representatives from the warring factions in Yugoslavia met in Dayton, Ohio, to negotiate what would become the Dayton Peace Accords. The U.S. participants were supported by a team from DMA and the U.S. Army Topographic Engineering Center. The team provided, in near real time, maps of the disputed Balkans areas that included cultural and economic data (the "human terrain").

Three-dimensional imagery of the disputed areas permitted cartographers to guide negotiators on a virtual tour of disputed terrain.[25]

History of Aerial Observation and Photography

One of the reasons that military units have always wanted to control the high ground was that it gave the possessor an observational advantage. From that perspective, aerial observation (and later, observation from space) was the ultimate high ground.

At first, balloons provided such an advantage. Observation from a balloon gave the French a critical edge in the battle of Fleurus in 1794. During the first half of the U.S. Civil War, the Union army made regular use of balloon observations. They were used to monitor Confederate encampments and movements in the first battle of Bull Run and in the battles of Fair Oaks, Sharpsburg, Vicksburg, and Fredericksburg. Balloons were subsequently used for assessing terrain in Cuba during the Spanish-American War in 1898. Being tethered, the balloons provided observational coverage over a relatively limited area.

The airplane had no such area limitation. The first use of airplanes for reconnaissance was by the Italians during their war with the Turks over what is now Libya (1911-1912). During World War I, all participants made use of aircraft for visual observation of enemy deployments and movements, though observation balloons also saw use. U.S. units such as the 91st Reconnaissance Squadron flew observation missions using a variety of aircraft in support of campaigns of Lorraine, St. Mihiel, and the Meuse-Argonne.

Visual observation and reporting was valuable, but observers often missed important details. Photography could capture details, which photo interpreters could then assess and report on more accurately than could an airborne observer, who would be working from memory or rough sketches created in flight or immediately upon landing. It was because of the tremendous amount of information available in the aerial photos that the use of aerial cameras and photointerpretation quickly became the preferred method of conducting aerial reconnaissance.

Several techniques had been tried for aerial photography—the first being from a kite in 1897. In 1903, Germans succeeded in putting a lightweight camera on a pigeon; during World War I, pigeon cameras were used to obtain pictures of the enemy lines. But the aircraft provided a means for precise targeting of photography.

The French, British, Germans, and Americans all conducted photography from aircraft during World War I. The U.S. Signal Corps' aerial photographers performed photoreconnaissance and aerial mapping that provided valuable intelligence about enemy forces and their disposition. Edward J. Steichen, who later became one of the world's most famous photographers, served as an officer in the Photographic Section of the Air Service in the American Expeditionary Forces.[26] Steichen advised the army on the best way to use large, aircraft-mounted cameras, significantly improving photographic quality.[27]

Aerial photos were important for cartography and military mapping, as noted earlier. But in addition to improving cartography, aerial photos were used to provide reliable battle damage assessments (BDAs) by comparing the images captured before and after bombing runs.

Between the two world wars, the Army Air Corps developed doctrine and tactics for the collection and use of aerial photography. Aerial photographs were recognized as valuable for targeting enemy units and for BDAs. The period in between wars allowed the military to develop a number of photo exploitation techniques.

World War II saw an explosive growth in the use of photo intelligence for military purposes. Long-range reconnaissance and widespread stereo photo coverage were essential for strategic planning and conducting combat operations. During the war, fighters such as the British Spitfire and Mosquito and the American P-38 Lightning and P-51 Mustang were adapted for photoreconnaissance. Such craft were stripped of weaponry, which made them defenseless against fighter attacks. For protection, the aircraft were camouflaged to blend into a sky background and typically had their engines modified to perform at very high altitudes (well over 40,000 feet). The premier photoreconnaissance aircraft of the war was the de Havilland Mosquito, a converted bomber that had three cameras installed in what had been the bomb bay. It could fly faster than most fighters at altitudes above 40,000 feet. The U.S. equivalent was a modification of the P-38 fighter, fitted with as many as five cameras in its nose. Nearly 1,000 P-38s were built or converted to photoreconnaissance aircraft during the war.

During the Korean War (1950–1953), the main workload of aerial photography was carried by the U.S. Air Force. The missions supported targeting and bomb damage assessments, and some of the RB-36 missions overflew Manchuria. Other squadrons flew tactical photoreconnaissance missions over Korea initially using RF-51Ds. Later in the war, a modification of the P-80 jet fighter, the RF-80A, flew photoreconnaissance along the Yalu River border between North Korea and China.

The Cold War and the Founding of NPIC

U.S. intelligence requirements during the Cold War drove IMINT to the strategic domain. At first, strategic photography was needed for indications and warning intelligence and for strategic targeting of the USSR and China. Subsequently, it became important for arms limitation and treaty verification.

CIA had created a Photographic Information Division to interpret sensitive photography in 1952. The U-2 program was then in its early stages; it subsequently would provide photographic surveillance of the USSR and China. Even then, it was apparent that both the military services and the national leadership needed the strategic intelligence that the U-2 would provide. The new CIA division was designed to handle both jobs.

In 1953, Arthur C. Lundahl became head of the division and remained its chief for the next twenty years, in the process becoming a legend in the imagery IC. Lundahl had been a photo interpreter during World War ll and the chief of the navy's Photogrammetry Division after the war.

Lundahl soon broached with senior DoD officials the idea of a joint photo interpretation center. In 1958, the Photographic Intelligence Center was established; the army and navy participated by contributing personnel, funding, and equipment, and the air force followed suit several years later. The center was renamed as the NPIC (or National Photographic Interpretation Center) in 1961.

Lundahl intended for imagery analysis to form a major component of intelligence reporting and initiated the publication of a memo series to advise analysts about photography related to their INTs. He organized the specialized fields of photo intelligence under a single management structure that had training programs, photo interpretation, photogrammetry, graphics, technical analysis, and a publications staff.[28]

The Cuban Missile Crisis provided an early test of NPIC photo interpretation skills. In August 1962, NPIC photo interpreters identified the construction of Soviet missile sites in Cuba. On October 14, U-2s obtained photography of six long, canvas-covered objects that were initially called "unidentified military equipment." NPIC photo interpreters identified the objects as having the unique signatures of Soviet medium-range ballistic missiles. Other photographs showed missile installations with supporting transporters, launch erectors, and command and control quarters.[29]

Vietnam provided another opportunity for NPIC to demonstrate its capability. In 1959, President Eisenhower had requested U-2 photographic missions over Vietnam to support U.S. policy decisions and tasked NPIC with an evaluation of the results. By 1962, NPIC analysts had already conducted bomb-damage assessments, identified possible targets, and produced valuable intelligence products.[30] NPIC support continued throughout the U.S. involvement in Vietnam, making use of both U-2 and SR-71 Blackbird photography.

The U-2—any reconnaissance aircraft, in fact—is vulnerable to anti-aircraft fire, so overflying hostile territory can be a problem. The most famous example was the Soviet shoot-down of Francis Gary Powers' U-2 over Sverdlovsk in May 1960, which happened just as space-borne reconnaissance was coming on line. The obvious solution to avoiding anti-aircraft fire was to send cameras into space. In 1961, the newly created National Reconnaissance Office (NRO) began to develop reconnaissance satellite programs, with NPIC having primary responsibility for exploiting the imagery product. In August 1960, the Corona program provided the first photographs taken from space. Corona imagery, especially of the Soviet Union, was retrieved from space once a month. It proved to be valuable in policy decisions, strategic planning, and cartography. In the late 1960s, the Gambit (KH-8) was launched and provided much improved imagery resolution over Corona.[31] Throughout the 1970s, the Hexagon (KH-9) provided even wider area coverage.[32] This was the beginning of the era of high-volume imagery. With an increasing deluge of both aircraft and satellite imagery, it was no longer possible for imagery analysts to look closely at all images returned, thus beginning the gap between collection and processing and exploitation.

Management of Imagery

With a rapidly expanding base of national and military imagery assets and of customers for imagery and imagery products, managing the collection, exploitation, analysis, and dissemination of imagery became a challenge. On July 1, 1967, the Committee on Imagery Requirements and Exploitation (COMIREX) was established to coordinate these functions for overhead imagery across the military and national intelligence communities. COMIREX replaced the Committee on Overhead Reconnaissance, which had managed overhead reconnaissance requirements (both SIGINT and IMINT) since 1960.[33] COMIREX in 1992 became Central Imagery Office within DoD. It was the focal point for managing imagery collection, analysis, exploitation, production, and dissemination.

Formed at about the same time as the Central Imagery Office, the Defense Airborne Reconnaissance Office was created to manage military intelligence requirements. It developed, acquired, and managed a system of manned and unmanned aerial reconnaissance aircraft, sensors, data links, data relays, and ground stations.

Increasingly, it also became apparent that overhead imagery had domestic value for disaster relief management and environmental monitoring. In 1975, the Civil Applications Committee, or CAC as it is known, was created within the Department of the Interior to fill this need. It was chaired by the director of the U.S. Geological Survey, with representatives from eleven departments and independent agencies of the U.S. government.[34] Today, the CAC continues to serve all U.S. government civil agencies, including DHS and HHS, which were both formed after the creation of the CAC.

Merging Imagery and Mapping

The organizational separation of creating maps of the land surface, aeronautical charts, and nautical charts, at least for military purposes, ended with the creation of DMA. But an organizational and functional separation still existed between mapping and imaging, though the two communities worked closely together. By the mid-1980s the separation was increasingly difficult to justify. Several agencies now were producing similar imagery or geospatial information products and delivering them in separate distribution channels. During the first Gulf War, NPIC, the Defense Dissemination Program Office, and the Defense Intelligence Agency (DIA) all provided imagery or intelligence based on imagery.

The close relationship between imagery and mapping that had developed since World War I made plausible a merger of the two functions. But a number of technical, cultural, and bureaucratic hurdles made such a merger very difficult.

Imagery analysts and cartographers operated on two quite different time frames. For imagery analysts, getting actionable intelligence out to customers was paramount. Speed in processing and analysis took precedence. For cartographers, precision was more important; they needed carefully calibrated mapping cameras that would provide geodetically fixed points as references for exact measurement. Mapping required cameras that could compensate for image motion, deviation from a vertical camera orientation at the time of exposure, and optical irregularities present in photographic lenses. Because of these two very different use cases the intelligence and mapping communities used images of the earth taken from aircraft or satellites but processed the information with different priorities. As a result, the processing systems used for imagery production and for mapping were technically incompatible.[35]

Also, a number of different agencies with different administrative structures and different customers existed in the 1990s. Both the intelligence and mapping communities independently used satellite images and their overlapping missions resulted in some duplication of effort. But customers of the various agency products were concerned that any merger might affect the imagery or mapping support that they were getting. For the military, this was an especially serious issue. The Defense Intelligence Agency (DIA), the service intelligence chiefs, and the joint command staff intelligence officers of the unified commands had one overriding concern: any combined imagery and mapping organization had to support the war fighter.[36]

National Imagery and Mapping Agency Stand-Up

The merger of imagery and mapping into a single agency required the concurrence of both defense and intelligence leaders, and that happened in 1995. Secretary of Defense William Perry, Director of Central Intelligence (DCI) John Deutch, and the Joint Chiefs of Staff (JCS) Chairman, General John Shalikashvili, proposed to Congress that a single agency be created within DoD and designated as the National Imagery and Mapping Agency (NIMA). Although Congress agreed, some members and staff voiced concerns about CIA willingly giving up its IMINT assets and about the support that non-DoD customers would receive from the new agency. Deutch subsequently appointed Rear Admiral Joseph Dantone to implement the merger and named him director designate of NIMA. NIMA came into existence on October 1, 1996, after a year of study and planning.

The NIMA stand-up had to overcome a number of challenges. Budget issues were an early problem. The components of the new agency operated under different funding lines. Intelligence and defense operated under different budgetary authorities, and thirteen different congressional committees had oversight of the budgets of NIMA components.

Incompatible systems presented a challenge from the beginning. The eight organizations that composed NIMA had different personnel systems, electronic office systems, procurement practices, and systems for creating and distributing products to customers.[37]

But merging cultures was the greatest challenge. Each of the components had its own history and corporate culture. NIMA absorbed four of those organizations entirely: CIA's NPIC, DMA, the Defense Dissemination Program Office, and the Central Imagery Office, along with parts of the Defense Airborne Reconnaissance Office. So NIMA continued for years to experience "legacy" problems, both in systems and in staff. Admittedly, these problems were not of the making of NIMA but rather a holdover from inheriting several disparate cultures, an expanding mission, and having been provided with inadequate resources.[38]

The stand-up was made more difficult because some of the managers involved did not prepare employees for the merger. The resistance of managers in all of the merged organizations was so great that for years afterward, the merger was referred to by many senior NIMA managers as "the sewer of standup."[39] The creation of NIMA remains a textbook example of how not to merge independent organizations.

The Transition to the National Geospatial-Intelligence Agency

The events after 9/11 reshaped NIMA. Two days after the 9/11 attack, Lt. General James R. Clapper Jr. (USAF, Ret.) took over as Director. Clapper pointedly did not resume his military rank to make the point that a civilian could run a Defense intelligence organization. The new director had to deal immediately with the imagery and mapping support demands of Operation Enduring Freedom, the U.S. intervention in Afghanistan. In that operation and later in Operation Iraqi Freedom, imagery from commercial satellites supplemented the agency's collection assets and provided imagery for coalition operations, in support of diplomatic initiatives, in humanitarian relief, and for reconstruction efforts.

Clapper also began laying the foundation for a different type of organization, promoting a number of initiatives to change the shape of NIMA. The most significant of these initiatives was the implementation of GEOINT as a guiding principle for the agency. As the GEOINT functional manager, Clapper implemented plans to manage GEOINT resources, including a new system to be known as the NSG. Believing that the right name also was an important factor in the agency's future, Clapper pushed for a new one. Clapper believed that NIMA stressed the two legacy cultures, imagery and mapping. He wanted a single, new culture.

Thus, NIMA officially became NGA[i] with the November 24, 2003, signing of the fiscal 2004 Defense Authorization Bill.

General Clapper moved the NGA focus from that of producing maps and pictures to an emphasis on combining multiple data sets to produce GEOINT, as IMINT was now renamed. NIMA had been in the business of producing two-dimensional maps with supporting text. NGA was now in the business of supporting customers with a wide range of products that enabled visualization as well as continuing production of a wide variety of maps and mapping products.

Geospatial Intelligence's Main Attributes and Components

Geospatial Intelligence Sources

The INTs discussed in this book vary significantly in their level of dependence on each other. At one extreme, it is possible to produce finished intelligence based solely on OSINT. HUMINT, SIGINT, and MASINT all depend to some extent on open source and GEOINT and upon each other. GEOINT is at the other extreme; it cannot function independently. By its nature, it draws from a rich set of sources, including data and information products from all of the other INTs. And as the preceding section illustrates, it has done so throughout history. The primary source of GEOINT for almost a century, though, has been visible imagery—first produced by photographic film cameras and for the last several decades produced by electro-optical (EO) imagers. The vast majority of imagery collections are now performed using these imagers that produce digital imagery. But film remains a viable collection medium—especially for developing nations that lack sufficient infrastructure to take advantage of digital images.

Imagery Platforms

Satellite Imagery. Within the IC, there are two main categories of satellite collection: commercial satellites and national technical means (NTM). Current NTM sensors and methods are classified and, therefore, beyond the scope of our discussion. Since 2002, the U.S. government has staged a public debate around the need for NTM sensors. The U.S. Congress funded over 50 percent of the cost of building four major 0.5 meter resolution (meaning the ability to spot an object that is at least 0.5 meters or 18 inches in size) commercial collection satellite systems for the companies GeoEye and Digital Globe. Both U.S. companies were given sole-source contracts to build these satellites and provide imagery at a set annual fee under the NextView and subsequently Enhanced View contracts. In 2013, Digital Globe acquired GeoEye. The

---

[i] Although the agency's name is National Geospatial-Intelligence Agency, the acronym is the three letter NGA—hence the use of the hyphen in the formal name. Clapper wanted NGA to be consistent with other national intelligence agencies, which also use three letter acronyms.

GeoEye-2 satellite development continues, but it may be used as a spare rather than launched.[40] In recent discussions between the authors and Digital Globe, there is revived interest in launching GeoEye-2 as a soon to be reinvigorated active program. WorldView-3, a satellite covering the visible spectrum to short wave infrared (panchromatic, 8 EO bands and 8 SWIR bands), is Digital Globe's most recently launched satellite. In June 2014, the U.S. Department of Commerce relaxed their 50cm ground sample distance resolution restriction, allowing Digital Globe to sell imagery at better resolutions. This decision will allow U.S. Commercial imagery to be sold and distributed to businesses within and outside the United States for use in their GEOINT applications. For Digital Globe, an NGA contract called "Enhanced View" and its companion "Enhanced GEOINT Delivery" allows NGA to acquire unlimited images from the Digital Globe collection constellation as well as allowing the creation of value-added imagery products for U.S. government use.

Airborne Imagery. Airborne surveillance, once the exclusive province of manned aircraft, now is being routinely conducted through the use of Unmanned Aircraft Systems (UAS), sometimes called unmanned aerial vehicles (UAVs). As of 2014, the U.S. Federal Aviation Administration has limited domestic use of UAS to uncontrolled airspace (defined as being above 65,000 feet altitude). This constrains the use of UAS for imagery within the United States. But regular UAS use continues to expand outside the United States, where such use is a normal way of performing operations that are considered dull, dirty, or dangerous. A long-awaited FAA ruling on commercial use of UAS within U.S. airspace is scheduled to be issued during 2015. However, as of this writing indications are that this ruling may be postponed. In the meantime, government and commercial GEOINT uses of UAS proliferate throughout the globe outside of the United States.

Sensor Spectral Bands

A number of different types of data (imagery) can be collected by sensors. The primary division of these types is based on the portion of the electromagnetic spectrum in which the sensor operates. Sensors have energy splitters and filters that allow collection of electromagnetic energy in discrete ranges, or bands. The science and art of interpreting imagery and data derived from various portions of the electromagnetic spectrum for specific missions and applications is at the heart of GEOINT as a discipline. This interpretation is often referred to as phenomenology. For EO imagery, it is also referred to as "read out," where analysts will "read" the imagery, identifying objects, establishing or verifying positions, establishing baseline activities and determining changes between images or data collected by the same or similar sensor system(s) but at different times.

Passive optical sensors divide their collection realms into visible (400–700 nm), panchromatic (0.4–0.9 um), near-infrared (NIR; 0.7–2.4 um), mid-infrared (2.5–5.5 um), and thermal infrared (8–12 um). Those collection realms are further divided into usable bands. Optical sensors have collected images from single spectral bands in these realms for years. Panchromatic imagery remains a primary GEOINT source because of the high resolution, image clarity and contrast this type of collection system provides to the analyst.

The growing trend, though, is to make use of commercial multispectral collection systems that have a single collection platform containing instruments with two or more separate sensors, each being sensitive to a different portion of the electromagnetic spectrum. Several commercial airborne multispectral collection systems passively collect from visible through near and even mid-infrared (IR). Perhaps the most well-known passive multispectral program is Landsat. The most recent satellite in this program, Landsat 8, contains two main sensors. One of the two, the Operational Land Imagery sensor, collects from 0.433 um through 2.29 um in nine separate bands. A separate thermal collection system, the Thermal Infrared Sensor, collects two thermal bands.[41] Hyperspectral collection systems expand the number of bands to several hundred using this same concept. Companies such as SpecTIR routinely use airborne hyperspectral imagers that provide detailed spectral and synoptic[ii] looks at large geographic areas. Primary commercial GEOINT customers for high spatial resolution hyperspectral data and analysis are oil and gas and mining and mineral exploration companies and scientific studies.

An important category of passive sensors which rose to prominence during U.S. military activities in the mid-2000s in the Middle East, primarily in the visible band, are those that provide video, usually from aircraft, helicopters, UAVs, or aerostats. Airborne video imagery is characterized by its rapidly changing technical nature and by the resultant proliferation of systems used by military, intelligence, and commercial organizations. One use of airborne video that is growing in worldwide use is for border and port surveillance using UAS, helping countries track movement of ships into and out of ports of entry. Combination multi-camera still and video systems allow synoptic views of large areas while maintaining the ability to leverage existing analyst tradecraft. UAS, while generally being safer to operate because the operator can remotely pilot the vehicle, nonetheless require access to the airspace in which they operate. A strong plus is that most U.S. UAS platforms are controlled by theatre-level commanders, shortening the time required to task and target these systems.

During Middle East operations the U.S. had complete freedom of movement and unlimited airspace access. For future military operations, this may not be the case. Therefore there is a healthy debate within the U.S. Intelligence Community about the balance between airborne and spaceborne assets to assure information flow in the case of denied airspace. It is generally accepted that various combinations of airborne and spaceborne collection systems, video and still imagery, active and passive systems, and commercial and NTM assets will be used for future overt and covert operations, the use and tasking of which will depend upon the specific mission at hand.

[ii] Synoptic coverage, in imagery, refers to the ability to obtain nearly simultaneous imagery of an entire region of interest.

Partly as a result of the proliferation of collection systems, airborne video is also noted for the proliferation of names for the product. Often simply described as full motion video (FMV), the category includes derivatives such as wide-area motion imagery, wide-area surveillance, and wide-area persistent surveillance. Persistent surveillance is defined as the following: "An Intelligence, Surveillance, and Reconnaissance (ISR) strategy to achieve surveillance of a priority target that is constant or of sufficient duration and frequency to provide the joint force commander the information to act in a timely manner."[42] Note that "persistence" in this context does not mean continuous surveillance. That fact is usually lost on most casual observers as well as those who create these video systems.

Passive Versus Active Sensors

Sensors are also categorized as either active or passive. The preceding section discussed passive sensors. Some important GEOINT collectors rely on active sensing, meaning that the sensor emits and subsequently receives energy. There are two main types of active remote sensing systems.

Radar (RAdio Detection And Ranging) systems emit and collect reflections of radio or microwave energy. Most radars can determine the range to a target. The synthetic aperture radars that are primarily used for imaging today have some unique characteristics. An important characteristic is signal coherence. Repeated collection with the same sensor over the same geography results in an analytic change detection process being possible, the analysis of which highlights very small changes in elevation. Radar products are used to determine change detection—what is new or different when comparing an initial and subsequent data collection—create elevation services, study changes in glaciers and ice packs, determine subsidence in locations where water is being pumped from the ground, as well as observe changes in mountainous areas where geologically young mountains are rising. Unlike passive systems, radar also is an all-weather collection system, capable of collecting usable data during severe weather conditions as well as through full cloud cover.

LiDAR (Light Detection And Ranging) uses coherent light (visible through near-IR and even into mid-IR) rather than radio or microwaves. Some specific LiDAR wavelengths have been chosen that penetrate water as well as allowing highly accurate terrain mapping. Airborne LiDAR systems send out a series of pulses which bounce or "reflect" off the earth's surface. The energy reflections are returned to an onboard receiver. The time delay between the transmission of the pulse and the returned energy for each pulse is used to calculate the distance from the sensor and the earth, creating a series of spot elevations in a swath, with each elevation also having a known location. Multiple swaths are stitched together, the result of which is an elevation map. Multispectral LiDAR systems allow the creation of near-photographic as well as elevation results. The primary use of LiDAR remains mapping ground elevation and bathymetric surfaces.

Other GEOINT Sources

Although imaging systems are the dominant source of GEOINT, nontraditional sources are changing the nature of mapping and analysis. Social media have become an important GEOINT source. In the aftermath of the tsunami in the Indian Ocean in 2004 and the typhoon that hit the Philippines in November 2013, normally reliable maps became almost useless. Both events had changed the landscape so dramatically that existing maps were rendered useless. In the case of the tsunami, NGA quickly replotted hydrographic and geodesic charts. In the Philippines, digital online mapping technology, coupled with programs that accessed and filtered social media, allowed the creation and constant update of the OpenStreetMap. More than a million tweets and Facebook status updates, combined with digital aerial imagery, allowed relief workers to identify and locate hazards, what roads were closed, and where people had congregated.[43]

GEOINT Products

All INT practitioners tailor their products to meet the needs of specific customer sets. GEOINT analysts do so routinely, providing several levels of products to meet different customer needs. Some products are time critical; speed is of the essence. Some require detailed analysis. Some depend on inputs from collateral INTs. Here are some examples:

- *Imagery.* In combat or crisis situations, it is essential to provide imagery to customers immediately. In this case, the processed image may go to customers at the same time that it goes to the imagery analyst.
- *Imagery Intelligence (IMINT).* Where detail and analysis are more important than timeliness, imagery may go through several levels of analysis to produce IMINT, as discussed in the next section on GEOINT analysis.
- *Geospatial information.* Maps are the foundation of geospatial information. Marine and hydrographic charts, aeronautical charts, and topographic maps all are produced to meet specific customer needs. Digital maps and charts mostly have replaced the paper form, allowing a quicker delivery process. Some geospatial information products are time-critical; notices about hazards to aircraft and marine navigation must be delivered quickly, for example.

Increasingly, GEOINT is being provided online, on-demand. The concept is for customers to have on-demand discovery of, and access to, GEOINT content, services, expertise, and support online. This on-demand concept is also true in the commercial sector, where location-based applications and services proliferate.

GEOINT products can be viewed in two distinct ways: as a physical product and conceptually—that is, in terms of the results achieved. Let's first examine GEOINT as a physical product.

Physical Products

GEOINT typically takes one of two product forms:

- *Standard products.* Organizations such as NGA and its counterparts in other countries provide a wide range of standard products to their customers. These take the form of maps, charts, and imagery, often supplemented with geographic or intelligence information. Standard products are designed for wide distribution to a large customer set, including military, intelligence and civil agencies.
- *Specialized products.* These are customized for a specific purpose and typically for a select, narrowly defined customer set. They often draw on special sensors such as spectral imagers and tend to rely more heavily on inputs from other INTs.

There are too many types of specialized products to illustrate them, but typical examples of standard products include the following:

- Aeronautical charts and graphics and flight information publications,
- Nautical and hydrographic charts and notices to mariners,
- Topographical and terrestrial maps, charts, and databases such as digital terrain information data,
- Geodesy and geophysical data, and
- GEOINT analytic reporting such as intelligence briefs, highlight cables, and imagery reports.

Conceptual Product: Situational Awareness

The most important result of GEOINT, viewed from an intelligence perspective, is not a physical product; it is captured in the term *situational awareness*. GEOINT provides intelligence to support situational awareness by providing terrain mapping, detecting movement and physical changes within a geographical area, monitoring illicit activity such as narcotics and gray arms shipments, detecting illegal immigration, and monitoring international trade activity. Several different terms are used to describe situational awareness, as discussed next.

Battlespace awareness is the term used to describe situational awareness within a combat area. Battlefield commanders rely on GEOINT to monitor the activity of friendly and hostile forces within their areas of responsibility. Such situational awareness is provided by imagery, radar, and electronic intelligence (ELINT).

Closely related to the idea of battlespace awareness is *maritime domain awareness* (MDA). Such awareness is important for ensuring port security and for enforcing national sovereignty over an exclusive economic zone. Ships, once beyond the range of shore-based surveillance systems, can become invisible to shoreside authorities. So ships can essentially disappear until they reappear shortly before the next scheduled port call.

A combination of sensors is used to provide MDA. All ships over a certain size conducting international voyages, and all registered passenger ships, must carry an automatic identification system, a transponder that allows other ships and satellites to identify and track a ship.[44] Ocean surveillance is also conducted using ELINT satellites and radar-equipped aircraft.

Safety of Navigation: Safe travel in the air and on the water depends on aircraft and ships having two types of geospatial information. One is the location of fixed hazards such as submerged objects (for ships and submarines) and high-terrain features or towers (for aircraft). The other is location and movement information about other aircraft or ships in the immediate area. Fixed hazards can be handled by maps and charts, updated as the need arises. Moving objects require a system for real-time situational awareness.

Activity-based intelligence (ABI) has been described as "a discipline of intelligence where the analysis and subsequent collection is focused on the activity and transactions associated with an entity, population, or area of interest."[45] It is a form of situational awareness that focuses on interactions over time.

Closely related to the idea of ABI is the concept of *movement intelligence,* often called MOVEINT. Both rely heavily on FMV. Take, for example, the video being downlinked from a Predator UAS. Intelligence officers are prone to call the product MOVEINT, while operational staff simply call it FMV.

Location-based intelligence (mentioned earlier in the chapter) might best be described as "situational awareness in the commercial world." All business transactions and operations are performed in physical locations. Providing real-time data about these transactions and operations in geospatial form—and allowing users to contribute their own data—permits organizations to quickly become aware of situations that affect them. So armed, they are able to act more quickly and effectively.

Handheld and vehicle-equipped GPS devices are driving a growing awareness of the LBI concept of "location" and its value in attaining operational efficiencies, revenue growth, and more effective management. It includes the following:

- Using geospatial information to interpret marketing and operations data,
- Analyzing customer demographic information, and
- Answering the question "Where is this happening?" when looking at sales data.

For example, the transport and logistics industries are pioneering the use of mapping technology, using GPS to track the routes that drivers take, as well as metrics like speed and traffic, in order to accurately schedule deliveries and economize on fuel.

Response to Natural Disasters: The Department of Homeland Security (DHS) and NGA have an increasingly important situational awareness mission: to support disaster response and mitigation activities both within the United States (e.g., Hurricane Katrina in 2005 and Hurricane Sandy in 2012) and outside the United States, as noted above. These natural disasters have highlighted the importance of timely, accurate, relevant GEOINT data and analysis. Images taken before and after natural disasters, geospatial data that pinpointed locations of structures (such as hospitals, police, and municipal government buildings and roads), and subsequent analysis of best ad hoc shipping ports and airfield locations all helped relief workers rapidly respond to these disasters in the most effective manner possible and also allowed lawmakers and the global community to better understand the full impacts of these natural disasters.

Geospatial Intelligence Analysis

The production of GEOINT typically requires much more than imagery and maps. It requires geospatial information, which can come from any intelligence source as well as many non-intelligence sources. The question then becomes this: Just what *type* of analysis is needed to produce GEOINT? It is a question that has caused some controversy within the U.S. IC and has led to the introduction of competing terms for analysis.

National intelligence collection organizations perform what is called *single-source analysis*. NGA, for example, is tasked to do single-source analysis based on imagery. Its job is to process, exploit, and analyze material collected from their primary sources (imagery, in the case of NGA). As explained in Chapter 1, collection agencies often make use of material from other INTs and refer to such material as collateral intelligence. So if an imagery analyst makes use of communications intelligence (COMINT), she would refer to the COMINT as "collateral." And a COMINT analyst making use of imagery would call the imagery "collateral."

A number of national agencies and military service units are charged with producing all-source analysis: the CIA, DIA, and the State Department all have the responsibility to provide all-source analysis at the national level.

Supposedly, a functional boundary exists between GEOINT and all-source analysis. It is an artificial boundary that, in practice, is often ignored. Single-source analysis groups want to produce all-source intelligence, and because intelligence is shared among collection organizations, they usually are able to do so. British author Michael Herman has observed that "the single-source agencies now are not pure collectors of 'raw intelligence'; they are also institutionalized analysts, selectors, and interpreters" and on the distinction between the two, that it is "intellectually artificial to chop up into parts what is in reality a continuous search for the truth."[46]

The boundary between single-source and all-source analysis has therefore become blurred, and that is unlikely to change. Single-source analysts who rely on other collection sources in their analysis call the product "multi-INT fusion" in an attempt to distinguish the product from that of all-source analysts. Whatever the name, the result can be a better intelligence product. The single-source analyst can take some of the workload off of the heavily loaded all-source analyst. Also, the whole idea of competitive analysis is built around the idea of a fresh and different perspective looking at the raw material. A different set of eyes on the material can often surface something important. The potential problem is that the single-source analyst does not have the same breadth of access to sources and usually does not have the same depth of experience or expertise in dealing with the topic, nor the close access to the customer, that the all-source analyst has. So the single-source analyst producing multi-source or all-source intelligence can provide a poor assessment (which the customer might just use).

GEOINT analysis must deal not only with the artificial boundary issue of all-source versus single-source analysis but also with the blurred boundary between GEOINT and Measurements and Signatures Intelligence (MASINT). The collection and analysis of infrared, spectral, or synthetic aperture radar intelligence often involves both imagery and signature measurements. So either INT could claim the field as its responsibility. As a result, NGA and DIA have created different terms for the intelligence. NGA has defined a special type of GEOINT called "full-spectrum GEOINT," formerly known as Advanced Geospatial Intelligence (AGI). The definition calls full-spectrum GEOINT "technical, geospatial, and intelligence information derived through interpretation or analysis using advanced processing of all data collected by imagery or imagery-related collection systems." Presumably, this refers to infrared, spectral, and radar imagery. DIA, with functional responsibility for MASINT, prefers to call it "imagery-derived MASINT."

How Geospatial Intelligence Is Managed

Of necessity, GEOINT management is decentralized. GEOINT is produced by a number of government agencies, military and civilian, and by commercial entities on behalf of and unrelated to the U.S. government. Within the U.S. government, DHS, U.S. Department of Energy (DOE), State Department, Treasury Department, Health and Human Services, U.S. Department of Agriculture (including the Forest Service) and the Federal Bureau of Investigation (FBI) all have significant GEOINT-related missions that are outside the purview of U.S. National Intelligence.

The director of NGA serves as the DoD GEOINT manager and the functional manager for the IC. Functional responsibility includes the processes for tasking imagery, geospatial information, and technical collection; processing raw geospatial data; exploiting geospatial information and IMINT; and analyzing and disseminating information and GEOINT to consumers.

The Requirements and Tasking System

A number of organizations, governmental and commercial, manage the requirements and tasking for imagery and geospatial information. Distinct systems exist at the national and military command levels.

Collections and collection management are functions performed by a variety of NSG personnel. At the time of this writing, national-level imaging assets and commercial imagers are tasked by NGA through the Source Operations and Management Directorate. Each mission's tasking requirements are submitted to NGA, which are then considered together with all requests for imagery. NGA then establishes overall collection priorities. From this combined tasking priority list, NGA maintains a prioritized requirements database that is used to plan collection tasking.

The maintenance and steering or pointing of NTM collection sensors is handled by the NRO. For such collection, the prioritized requirements are passed to NRO for execution using NTM sources and to DigitalGlobe for collection using U.S. commercial collection systems. A list of U.S. commercial collection systems is found in the table.

DigitalGlobe Imaging Satellites

Satellite	GSD	Revisit Times	Description
IKONOS	.8 m	3 days	Collects panchromatic and multispectral imagery for map creation, change detection, and imagery analysis
Quickbird	.61 m	2.4 days	Collects panchromatic and multispectral imagery
GeoEye-1	.41 m	< 3 days	Collects panchromatic and multispectral imagery with wide area coverage
Worldview-1	.5 m	1.7 days	Collects panchromatic imagery with wide area coverage
Worldview-2	.46 m	1.1 days	Collects panchromatic and multispectral imagery with wide area coverage
Worldview-3	.31 m	< 1 day	Collects panchromatic and multispectral imagery with wide area coverage

From the DigitalGlobe website[47]

DIA is responsible for coordinating requirements between the national-level organizations and theater users for the collection of both national and airborne GEOINT. Within combat commands, a GEOINT cell has the responsibility for requirements management and tasking theater collection assets.[48]

For U.S. science-related and international GEOINT, the U.S. Geological Survey (USGS) is the mission manager and the proponent agency for all of the NASA Landsat missions, and as such handles requirements and tasking.

Because of the wide variety of collection systems and the increasingly rapid collection rate for commercial sources, some collection requests may already be fulfilled by the time a collection manager receives the initial tasking request. It is not unusual for multiple collections to occur over the same geography using different collection systems, as differences in the end-use of the imagery or imagery product often dictate which systems can be used and which systems are inadequate for the task. For example, it is not possible to identify vehicles using 30m Landsat data (nominally thirty meters by thirty meters per pixel, or picture element—the smallest collection unit available on digital sensors), but it is possible in most cases to distinguish between a sedan and a utility truck using WorldView-2 imagery.

Collection

The development and operation of imagery collection systems has been driven primarily by three customer needs:

- *Better resolution.* No matter how good the imagery quality is, customers always seem to need that extra bit of detail that just isn't quite there.
- *Synoptic coverage.* The simultaneous (or almost simultaneous) coverage of a very large area of the earth helps assure the customer that important features haven't been left out.
- *Surveillance.* Aircraft and satellites provided reconnaissance, or periodic coverage of a target area. Aerostats and UAVs have provided surveillance, or continuous coverage; and both MOVEINT and ABI require surveillance.

Trade-offs usually have to be made among these needs—especially the first two. Improving one often makes another worse. A major challenge of collection management is to adjudicate these trade-offs.

The acquisition of collection systems frequently is managed separately from the operation of those systems because the two activities require different skills and processes. Building systems requires engineering and program management expertise. Operating the systems requires expertise in mission planning, targeting, and dealing with a large customer base.

A large number of collection resources feed into U.S. GEOINT:

- *U.S. government.* The NRO designs, builds, and operates the nation's reconnaissance satellites, which compose one of the primary collection sources for GEOINT data. These classified satellites (along with some airborne systems) are referred to as NTM within the IC. All of the military services acquire and operate airborne Intelligence, Surveillance, and Reconnaissance (ISR) platforms (aircraft, UAVs, and aerostats) that collect imagery. The U.S. Navy acquires and operates systems for undersea acoustic geolocation. NASA builds and operates a series of remote sensing satellites.

- *Commercial collectors.* The U.S. and several countries operate commercial imaging satellites that operate in the visible and infrared bands. Canada, Italy, and Germany currently provide commercial Synthetic Aperture Radar (SAR) imaging satellites.
- *International and coalition collection.* Increasingly, GEOINT collection systems are being developed and operated by international or coalition groups. The International Monitoring System operates a network of seismic and hydroacoustic monitoring stations worldwide that detect seismic and underwater acoustic signatures of earthquakes and subsurface explosions. The United States shares imagery collection with its "Five Eyes" partners (the United Kingdom, Canada, Australia, and New Zealand). Coalition partners in combat areas such as Afghanistan share GEOINT products.

Management of collection operations typically is further divided into sub-INTs. Specifically, visible imaging, spectral imaging, and radar imaging are often managed by separate organizations because of the type of handling required. Visible imagery, for example, can be time-critical; therefore, it has to be structured for rapid dissemination of the product. Radar imaging requires more extensive processing and exploitation to be usable by customers, so the entire process is managed differently. Spectral imaging (often dozens to hundreds of bands) also requires extensive processing and exploitation, and the products created are often not time-critical.

The collection of material for maps and charts is managed quite differently from that for imagery. It draws from a much wider range of sources, many of which are openly available. And geospatial information can be drawn from any of the INTs, requiring that a GEOINT organization develop close working relationships with all collection INTs.

Processing, Exploitation, and Analysis

GEOINT processing, exploitation, and analysis of necessity draws on a wide range of expertise and specialized professional disciplines. These occupations are often described as tradecraft specialties. Some of the most prominent specialties (generally called "jobs" or "work roles") are as follows:

- *GEOINT analysis.* This field involves deriving meaning from geospatial data and geospatial information systems to answer intelligence questions.

- *Targeting analysis.* Often called "source analysis," this specialty requires working with mission partners and other collection INTs to develop integrated collection strategies and plan collection against high-priority targets.
- *Regional analysis.* This field requires understanding of the political, economic, military, social, and infrastructure factors in a country or specific geographical area.
- *Imagery analysis.* These practitioners specialize in extracting intelligence from imagery.
- *Marine analysis.* It involves translating hydrographic, oceanographic, and bathymetric data into maritime navigation and pilotage information, usually in the form of maps and charts.
- *Cartography.* This is the specialty of producing maps and charts.
- *Imagery science.* Skills here are applied in the development of imagery collection systems and their application in providing imagery.
- *Geodetic science.* This is the application of geodesy and geophysical expertise to the measurement and representation of the earth, including its gravitational field. Geodesists also measure phenomena such as motion of the earth's crust and tides.

The combination of commercial and NTM imagery creates a baseline of data available to the GEOINT analyst. However, the volume of data being collected throughout the IC containing location and time information continues to increase. All geographic information can be used within the GEOINT enterprise. Since 2004, Open Source Intelligence (OSINT) information has become an important data source for the GEOINT analyst. Persistent video has emerged as an ABI source. Improvements in computing power and storage have allowed ever-increasing availability to the analyst of all imagery sources. However, simply creating a "ready to be viewed" image is only one part of the process. Search and discovery of the appropriate image for analysis is needed, as is search and discovery of all other available, appropriate data for a specific geography. Adding available OSINT to the mix creates an enormous volume of data for GEOINT analysts and imagery analysts. For the imagery analyst, NTM and commercial source imagery are the primary sources used during analysis. In practice, most first phase analysis is performed by forward deployed GEOINT analysts, both NGA Support Team (NST) and service members, while second and third phase analysis (discussed next) is performed by NGA and the services usually at U.S. locations.

National-level GEOINT products are mostly produced by NGA. Two NGA directorates manage the production:

- The Source Operations and Management Directorate is responsible for acquiring data used for imagery analysis and geospatial information production.

- The Analysis Directorate provides GEOINT and services to policymakers, military decision makers, and war fighters, and tailored support to civilian federal agencies and international organizations.

Other U.S. government organizations also provide GEOINT as open source information. The U.S. Geological Survey, for example, processes, exploits, delivers, and archives imagery from the NASA Landsat program.

Exploitation and analysis of imagery can go through as many as three phases, depending on the conflicting demands of timeliness and analytic detail. The nature of these three phases, the time each takes, and the quality of the product have been dramatically improved as a result of the shift from an analog product (a photo) to a digital product (an electronic image) that took place during the 1970s and 1980s.

- *First phase exploitation.* Where timeliness is the dominant factor, an imagery product is delivered to customers within twenty-four hours, often much faster. Usually, the product is highly perishable intelligence, such as meeting Indications and Warning (I&W) needs. Annotations to the imagery identify changes or activities that are immediately significant.
- *Second phase exploitation.* This imagery product typically is delivered to customers within a week after the imagery is obtained and provides a more organized and in-depth look at the target.
- *Third phase analysis.* Often called third phase exploitation, this is really a form of all-source analysis. It provides detailed and complete reports, especially strategic studies of facilities and activities. There is no specified time frame for these in-depth studies, but they seldom take less than a week to complete.

Third phase analysis requires access to intelligence from, and often close coordination with, the other INTs. NGA GEOINT analysis depends on having close ties with the National Security Agency (NSA), and a partnership between the two organizations benefits the product of both. COMINT and ELINT collectors provide geolocation of target emitters, for example. HUMINT and OSINT provide insights, especially about activities that result in ABI, while MASINT provides details on physical and geophysical phenomena.

Increasingly, because of the high velocity and volume of so many GEOINT sources, ABI has become a critically important organizing principle for analysis. Living globes, where the "best available" imagery, geospatial information, and analytic products are shown as they are made available to the GEOINT analyst, are emerging. As communications networks become more ubiquitous, data kept in what were previously data silos are now used routinely by an increasing number of analysts from a wide variety of disciplines. Therefore, the line between the all-source analyst and the GEOINT analyst continues to blur, lessening the need to define the various phases of analysis. Requirements are stated; products are delivered; analysis is conducted; and results are posted for others to use, review, and add to the analytic picture. The biggest GEOINT trends are this compression of time between request and fulfillment and the convergence of formerly disparate disciplines (e.g., imagery analyst and all-source analyst).

Dissemination, Storage, and Access

Dissemination

GEOINT dissemination for military purposes has to deal with two criteria: a need for speed and a need to share the product. The intelligence in imagery is especially perishable in the battlefield, and the product often must be shared with coalition partners who have relatively low security accesses. Material has to be released at an unclassified or (at most) secret level.

Dealing with these criteria has long been a management challenge. In several Mideast coalition operations, imagery products did not reach coalition partners in a timely fashion. The availability of unclassified commercial imagery has helped ease the sharing problem, and the availability of imagery from UAV and aerostat platforms has helped with the timeliness issue. In many operations, especially those where indigenous forces are part of the coaltion, commercial GEOINT sources are uniquely used to allow for complete intelligence sharing among all friendly forces.

Like requirements and tasking, GEOINT dissemination operates through multiple channels.

- The NGA Enterprise Operations Directorate manages the NSG. That system delivers GEOINT products to a wide range of government customers (military and civilian) and to coalition partners.
- The Defense Logistics Agency provides worldwide logistics support for military departments and combat commands, and other DoD components and federal agencies. In this role, the agency serves as the integrated material manager for all standard geospatial information and services products.[49]
- Within U.S. combatant commands, the GEOINT cell coordinates the procedures and manages the tasks to search for, find, access, and gather GEOINT information and data from existing holdings, databases, and libraries. [50]

Storage

Storage of GEOINT source and products is a perpetual challenge. The main system used to search for and view individually collected images in the IC is WARP (Web Access and Retrieval Portal). This is a web-based search-and-discover capability where the analyst or user fills out a form and sends a request to a centralized search server. The appropriate images matching the search description are returned for either further sifting, viewing, or selecting. Additionally, Image Product Libraries allow local access to portions of the available IC collected imagery, depending on location, storage, and network availability. The replacement being fielded as of this writing is iSToRE, which will improve and simplify analysts' access to stored data at multiple locations.

The flood of FMV from the Afghanistan–Pakistan theater during the decade-long deployment created both a lag in analysis—too many pixels requiring not enough available analysts—and a need to store, find, and retrieve relevant video. Semi-automated methods of feature identification and extraction are used, but manual viewing remains the main method of analyzing FMV. Petabytes of video are collected, yet only a small fraction of the data collected is viewed by analysts.

Open source data is another enormous data source, dwarfing all imagery types combined. Not all data is stored forever. Each classified source collected is automatically tagged with a specific time of collection, source, and "expiration date" (the date when it becomes unclassified). Unclassified sources used by analysts are assessed for content and tagged appropriately, as some of the material becomes classified when it is used to support part of a larger analysis. All reports are saved. Metadata (data about data) is used extensively throughout the GEOINT enterprise to catalog each and every piece of data, with varying effectiveness.

Access

Customers, including all-source intelligence analysts, have to be able to access the stored GEOINT product—which means that a robust search capability must exist.

Search is a key component of the GEOINT enterprise. If an analyst cannot find adequate data (source) then it may not be possible to perform the requested analysis. There are a number of search capabilities within the IC. Some are web-based. Some use proprietary technology. Some are stand-alone or legacy (no longer upgraded but maintained for mission continuity). The primary imagery and imagery product search engine within NGA is called WARP. WARP is used to find relevant NTM and commercial imagery and image product holdings. Enhanced GEOINT Delivery (EGD) is the follow-on effort from the Rapid Delivery of Online GEOINT contract under the EnhancedView contract. EGD provides value-added products, including best available imagery for specific areas over the globe. Search for EGD (commercial) is performed using the EGD search engine, which is a web-based front end. However, individual images used to create the EGD "skins" are also available via WARP.

Multiple search pathways allow analysts from varied backgrounds to discover appropriate source data.

Geospatial Intelligence Standards

All of the collection disciplines require standards to facilitate the sharing of intelligence, or as it is often described, *interoperability*. We will define interoperability as the ability to share data and information products on a variety of systems, regardless of infrastructure or domain. Standards that permit interoperability have several aspects. Communications systems must be compatible with each other. There must be an agreed-upon system for quickly sharing classified material, especially in coalition operations—a problem that is common to all INTs.

For GEOINT, agreed-upon standards are especially important. It is unlike all of the other INTs in one respect: much of the collection and much use of the product is done outside the IC and outside the government. So GEOINT has to be shared widely, and that requires some standard data formats for sharing. The exchange of maps and imagery (radar, visible, and spectral) in digital forms is not possible without a shared standard for formatting the maps and imagery.

Achieving interoperability, though, is a challenge for the GEOINT analyst. Metadata, or data describing data, is the key to successful interoperability. In the decade since 2004, there has been a strong push to standardize metadata and allow access to data and intelligence (information) products. The objective is to create open consensus-based standards that are accepted throughout the U.S. government as well as by international, industry, and academic partners. GEOINT standards come from a variety of private sector and government standards bodies, as discussed next.[51]

The U.S. government has its own set of standards for NTM sources where other standards are not applicable. In addition to metadata, data, and intelligence product standards, there are several main networks within the IC. Those networks, by design, do not contact one another, partly for security reasons, partly to limit access to a specific agency or mission partner. As a result, there exists a web of networks and a matrix of available data with a variety of metadata and standards that create a maze for the analyst to navigate to search for, find, obtain, create, use, and share GEOINT data and intelligence products.

Organizations such as the International Organization for Standardization (ISO), the Federal Geospatial Data Committee (FGDC), and the NGA Geospatial Intelligence Standards Working Group have set metadata and data-sharing standards for the geospatial community. Private organizations such as Open Geospatial Consortium (OGC) have attempted to create standards for a small subset of data and web-based services. Some of these niche standards have been adopted by governments, typically within a specific agency.

Technical Standards

Several international organizations are working to establish agreed-upon standards for GEOINT data:

- The ISO Technical Committee 211 on Geographic information/Geomatics began working in 1994 to address the standardization of digital geographic information.
- The Defence Geospatial Information Working Group is an international coalition standards forum, comprising defense organizations of member nations, that deals with the standards to allow the exchange and exploitation of geospatial data between defense communities and is specifically concerned with interoperability for North Atlantic Treaty Organization (NATO) and coalition forces.
- The International Committee for Information Technology Standards (L1—Geographic Information Systems) develops and adopts digital geographic data standards that apply to the unique requirements of GIS.
- The OGC is an international industry consortium of 369 companies, government agencies, and universities participating in a consensus process to develop publicly available interface standards. OGC contributes standards and specifications that promote the interoperability of geospatial data and systems. OGC develops and tests open (publicly available) interface standards that can be supported by standards-based commercial off-the-shelf software packages.

Training Standards

The development of GEOINT professionals depends on the existence of standards for training and tradecraft. NGA is responsible for developing these standards and applying a certification program.

International Geospatial Intelligence

Many countries produce GEOINT for their commercial, intelligence, and other purposes. They often combine the management of both GEOINT and MASINT in the same organization. Some maintain separate GEOINT entities for military and civilian purposes; others combine both missions in a single unit.

Approximately thirty-two countries participate in the Multinational Geospatial Co-production Program, which is aimed at producing digitized geospatial data at 1:50,000 or 1:100,000 scale of the entire world. Member nations contribute data to the International Geospatial Warehouse and have unlimited access to all of the data in the program. The program is designed to reduce duplication of effort while increasing availability of geospatial data. Almost all European and North and South American countries are participants.

China

China operates a number of independent but seemingly overlapping programs for earth imaging and mapping, both for military and civilian purposes. The Ziyuan program is designed to provide earth observation to support both military and civilian needs. One part of the program addresses People's Liberation Army (PLA) needs. Reportedly, the Ziyuan-2 program conducts aerial surveillance for the PLA.[52]

The Tian Hui-1 series of satellites are part of the Ziyuan program and are used for the evaluation of ground resources and mapping.[53] The PLA appears to be the primary customer. The satellites are equipped with two different camera systems that operate in the visible and infrared light ranges. The visible light camera is able to produce 3-D earth imaging.[54]

On the civil side, the Ministry of Land and Resources operates imaging satellites to monitor resources, land use, and ecology and for use in urban planning and disaster management. The ministry includes the Ministry of Geology and Mining, State Administration of National Land, State Administration of National Oceans, and State Bureau of Surveying and Mapping. The ZiYuan-3, launched in January 2012, is a high-resolution imaging satellite. ZiYuan-3 satellites are operated by the State Bureau of Surveying and Mapping.

Separately, China's National Committee for Disaster Reduction and State Environmental Protection Administration manages a series of environmental monitoring and disaster management satellites. The Huanjing series of satellites provides visible, infrared, and multispectral imaging of the earth. In 2012, the committee added a synthetic aperture radar satellite, the Huanjing-1C, to the mix.[55]

Russia

Russia (and the Soviet Union previously) has been orbiting satellites for both military and civilian GEOINT purposes almost as long as the United States has. During the Cold War, Soviet satellites tended to be of shorter lifespans than U.S. systems. During crises, the Soviets would launch additional sensors. In the period after the collapse of the Soviet Union, Russia was "blind" for a period, having no operational imagery satellites. Some observers thought this was dangerous and suggested that the United States share necessary imagery with Russia. Russian capabilities have since recovered.

In 2013, Russia's space agency (Roscosmos) put in orbit the Resurs-P1 imaging satellite, the first in a new generation of high-resolution remote sensing satellites. Users include the Russian government's ministries responsible for agriculture, the environment, emergency situations, fisheries, meteorology, and cartography. The satellite is intended to monitor natural resources and to support response to natural disasters. The satellite can also collect hyperspectral data.[56]

During 2013, Russia also put into orbit its Kondor synthetic aperture radar satellite. The satellite was under development at NPO Mashinostroenia (known as NPO Mash) for nearly twenty years prior to launch. Kondor was planned as a dual-purpose (military and civilian use) program.

Roscosmos is currently developing its own radar satellite, the Obzor-O. The new satellite is intended for supporting cartography, seafaring safety, monitoring natural and man-made disasters, and observing natural resources.

North Atlantic Treaty Organization

NATO has a GEOINT effort that is intended to do the following:

Ensure the provision of seamless, consistent and timely geospatial information, services and advice to the NATO military authorities, NATO nations, forces deployed in support of NATO missions, and where appropriate to other non-military bodies and organizations, to achieve mission success.[57]

The NATO Intelligence Fusion Center at RAF Molesworth, United Kingdom, carries out this mission by creating databases and intelligence support products and by providing situation awareness on designated groups, persons of interest, terrain, population, demographics, and infrastructures. It creates an adversary order of battle and performs exploitation of commercial and tactical imagery to support NATO intelligence requirements.

United Kingdom

The United Kingdom has a long history of worldwide economic and political interests and a history of mapping and imaging to support those interests.

Oversight of the military part of GEOINT is the responsibility of the Defence Intelligence Joint Environment (DIJE). DIJE develops GEOINT policy. It also provides overall guidance to the Defence Geographic and Imagery Intelligence Agency, the U.K. Hydrographic Office, the Meteorological Office, and the No. 1 Aeronautical Information and Documents Unit. The DIJE is the focal point for bilateral and international arrangements that involve the sharing of IMINT and MASINT.[58]

The U.K. functional lead for GEOINT is the Defence Geospatial Intelligence Fusion Centre, based at RAF Wyton in Cambridgeshire. It was created in 2012 from the staff of the National Imagery Exploitation Centre, formerly known as the Joint Air Reconnaissance Intelligence Centre (JARIC). JARIC traces its history back to clandestine airborne reconnaissance operations at the beginning of World War II.[59]

Canada

Canada has merged the defense geospatial, imagery, meteorology, and oceanography support functions into a single GEOINT organization. Called the Directorate of Geospatial Intelligence (D Geo Int), it is responsible for planning and policy. Units within D Geo Int handle MASINT, mapping and charting, imagery exploitation, and meteorological and oceanographic services. D Geo Int manages international and national partnerships with its counterpart organizations such as NGA.[60]

Canada operates a number of airborne imagery collection assets to support its GEOINT program, but its RADARSAT constellation is probably the most important contributor. The three satellites in the RADARSAT constellation mission are responsible for maritime surveillance (ice, wind, oil pollution, and ship monitoring), disaster management (mitigation, warning, response, and recovery), and ecosystem monitoring (forestry, agriculture, wetlands, and coastal change monitoring). The constellation provides extensive coverage of Canada's arctic regions.

Australia

GEOINT in Australia is managed by the Defence Imagery and Geospatial Organization (DIGO). DIGO is responsible for the collection, processing, analysis, and dissemination of imagery and geospatial products and for determining the standards for imagery and geospatial information. DIGO depends on the Australian Hydrographic Service and the Royal Australian Air Force Aeronautical Information Service for maritime and aeronautical geospatial information. DIGO's primary customers are Australia's defense and intelligence organizations, and it provides GEOINT support in response to natural disasters.[61, 62]

DIGO also operates a web-based system called Palanterra. It provides spatial representation of information. Users can view and share near-real-time information and can ingest data from multiple web-accessible sources, including weather feeds, live cameras, and event information, allowing any user to view an updated common operating picture instantly.[63]

DIGO has a close working relationship with Geoscience Australia, the Australian government onshore mapping agency. Geoscience Australia and DIGO cooperate to provide mapping support for the Australian Defense Forces.[64]

Israel

Israel maintains a Central IMINT Center that processes aerial imagery products and disseminates reports to combat units. The center is able to provide analyzed imagery to military units in very near real time. The Israelis also have a national GEOINT database that merges the product collected by imaging and Signals Intelligence (SIGINT) assets (ground and air based) with existing GIS information from other sources. The database combines GEOINT with human terrain information; it includes an image of each village, with infrastructures, educational and administrative institutions, and religious sites, along with population data and details about village or regional leaders.[65]

Israel has a UAV program for aerial surveillance and imaging that dates back to 1978 with the introduction of the Scout UAV for military intelligence use. Since then, their UAVs have taken on a number of critical missions including strategic intelligence, reconnaissance, and maritime surveillance. The Israeli fleet, one of the most advanced in the world, includes the Hermes 450, Hermes 900, and Heron.[66]

Since 1988, Israel also has operated a fleet of imagery satellites to support its GEOINT efforts. The oldest and best known is Ofeq, in part because of its unique orbit. Ofeq satellites are launched westward in what is called a retrograde orbit over the Mediterranean so that the launch does not overfly populated areas in Israel and neighboring Arab countries. The resulting orbit is intended to give good daylight coverage, with several passes each day, of the Middle East. Israel also since 2008 has operated the TecSAR, a synthetic aperture radar satellite, to provide radar imagery for defense and intelligence purposes.

Japan

Japan's Geospatial Information Authority is responsible for surveying and mapping Japanese territory. Formerly called the Geographical Survey Institute, it is part of the Ministry of Land, Infrastructure, Transport and Tourism.

The Japan Aerospace Exploration Agency operates satellites for Earth observation. Japan's first Earth observation satellites were MOS 1A and MOS 1B, launched in 1987 and 1990 respectively. In January 2006, the agency launched the Advanced Land Observation Satellite. Its next satellite will carry a synthetic aperture radar to provide disaster monitoring, land use and infrastructure information, and global monitoring of tropical rain forests to identify carbon sinks.

Germany

The Bundeswehr Geoinformation Service provides GEOINT for the German Armed Forces. Its job is to ensure that geospatial and environmental information is available and useful for planning and conducting military operations. The service provides a geopolitical atlas, satellite data, regional maps, and navigational maps, available through a web portal.[67]

The German military makes use of photoreconnaissance UAVs and has operated Israeli-made Herons for reconnaissance in Afghanistan. The Bundeswehr's Strategic Reconnaissance Command operates the SAR-Lupe, a military satellite reconnaissance system. SAR-Lupe is a constellation of five identical synthetic aperture radar satellites, controlled by a ground station that is responsible for controlling the system and analyzing the imagery product.[68]

India

India is active in both military and civilian GEOINT. The military side is managed by the Defence Image Processing and Analysis Centre, a component of the Indian Army's Defence Intelligence Agency. The Centre controls India's satellite-based imagery programs. The army also has an unmanned aerial vehicle (UAV) program to provide battlefield surveillance. The Nishant, a short-range field mobile UAV, is used by Indian army units for video reconnaissance. The Indian Army relies heavily on GEOINT in combating insurgency and in countering terrorist attacks.

The Indian Space Research Organisation (ISRO) manages the civilian side of GEOINT, though it also supports military needs. India Remote Sensing (IRS) satellites are a series of earth observation satellites, built, launched, and maintained by ISRO. The names of the satellites indicate their purposes: OceanSat, CartoSat, and ResourceSat, all in polar sun-synchronous orbit. ISRO also operates two radar imaging satellites. RISAT-1 was launched on April 26, 2012, carrying a sophisticated C-band SAR payload; it can provide images with either coarse resolution for wide area coverage or high spatial resolution that is useful for intelligence purposes. A similar satellite, RISAT-2, was launched in 2009. Both satellites were built by Israel for India.[69]

Italy

The Italian Space Agency operates the COSMO-SkyMed constellation earth observation satellites. The program is jointly funded by the Italian Ministry of Research and Ministry of Defence for both military and civilian use. The space segment includes four satellites equipped with synthetic aperture radars. The imagery is used for defense purposes, seismic hazard analysis, environmental disaster monitoring, and agricultural mapping.[70]

France

France has a Joint Geospatial-Information Office that is developing the GEODE 4D program to maintain permanently a complete updated GEOINT database that will include regional, local, urban and 3-D mission specific data.[71]

Since the 1980s, France has operated a number of optical imaging satellites, beginning with the SPOT series, first launched in 1986. In 2011 and 2012, France launched the Pléiades high-resolution imaging satellites that are dual-use (military and civilian).

The Types of Intelligence Targets against Which It Works Best

In general, GEOINT is used to determine what is physically present, where it is located, and its physical condition. (When he was the Director of NGA, Gen. Clapper used to point out that everybody and everything has to be somewhere on the face of the Earth.) It is of increasingly greater value in tracking the movement of people and vehicles.

GEOINT does not provide access to human thought processes. So it usually cannot provide intent, or predictive intelligence. It may be able to state what has happened, but not what will happen. An important exception is ABI that shows intent.

Following are three general categories that describe the intelligence value of GEOINT. It is the primary source for a number of important intelligence issues. For others, it usually is not the primary source but contributes to the intelligence picture and on occasion becomes a critical source. And for some issues, it is seldom a contributor but may occasionally provide insights.

Geospatial Intelligence as a Primary Source

Situational awareness. GEOINT provides situational awareness to support political, military, and law enforcement operations. It is especially valued for providing battlespace situational awareness—that is, locating friendly and hostile units, and monitoring force movements and for battle damage assessment.

Arms control and treaty monitoring. The use of imagery for treaty monitoring became important during the Strategic Arms Limitation Talks (SALT) negotiations in 1972 and 1979. Without the ability to verify missile and aircraft numbers and deployments that overhead imagery provided, the sides would not have been able to conclude an arms limitation treaty. Overhead imagery has continued to be the primary means of verifying treaty compliance in a number of treaties since then, one of the most recent being the Strategic Arms Reduction Treaty (START) between the United States and Russia that went into effect in 2011. An important aspect of these treaties was the obligation of both parties not to interfere with each other's NTM.

Environment and natural resources. GEOINT is best suited to provide warning of environmental problems such as desertification, climate change, and industrial pollution. It may provide the first indication of natural or man-made water diversion.

Humanitarian disaster and relief operations. GEOINT is the main source of information about on-the-ground conditions after natural and man-made disasters overseas. It was critical in planning for U.S. responses subsequent to the 2004 tsunami that struck Indonesia and the 2010 earthquakes in Haiti and Chile. Domestically, information is more likely to be available from first responders than is the case overseas. But when Hurricane Katrina struck the Gulf Coast in 2005, GEOINT played a major role in planning for relief operations.

Geospatial Intelligence as a Major Contributor

Military and civilian infrastructure.

Agriculture and food security. Imagery can support crop forecasts and so provide advance warning of food production shortfalls. It allowed the CIA in 1981 to forecast a wheat shortage in the USSR that would require the Soviets to purchase wheat on the international market.[72]

Terrorism. It provides locations and movements of key terrorist leaders, typically relying on COMINT or HUMINT tip-off. The takedown of Osama bin Laden is the most dramatic example.

Transnational organized crime. GEOINT has been a valuable source of intelligence in combating piracy and illicit weapons shipments.

Demographics, migration, and population movements. Imagery can identify massive shifts in population, such as refugee movements. It provided valuable intelligence on refugee movements during the Libyan crisis in 2011 and during the 2012–present conflict in Syria.

Chemical warfare development and proliferation.

Missile development and proliferation.

Nuclear weapons development and proliferation. The manufacture, movement, and storage of nuclear materials can often be identified by the unique signatures associated with the materials. Nuclear fuel reprocessing facilities are large complexes with distinct signatures, sometimes emplaced in underground facilities.

Foreign military combat capabilities, operations, and intentions. Imagery provides intelligence about military exercises and force movements. This allows assessing likely battle tactics and inferring weapons capabilities.

Human rights and war crimes.

Energy security. Oil and gas drilling and damage to or disruption of existing extraction or refining facilities can usually be identified in imagery.

Advanced conventional weapons development and proliferation. The production, deployment, testing, and proliferation of conventional weapons can be monitored in imagery.

Geospatial Intelligence as an Ancillary Source

Leadership intentions. Except in cases where military or law enforcement force movements indicate intent, GEOINT rarely can help on leadership intentions.

Counterintelligence. The primary contribution of GEOINT here is in identifying imagery denial and deception efforts.

Cyber threats. GEOINT finds use, relying on information from cyber collection, in geolocating the sources of threats.

Political stability. GEOINT may help with demographic information.

Foreign policy objectives and international relations. Foreign policy planning concerns intent, where GEOINT usually does not contribute.

Infectious diseases and health. The origin and spread of disease is best understood and analyzed using a map display.

International trade. Intelligence to support negotiations on trade typically makes little use of GEOINT.

Economic stability and threat finance. Threats to economic stability, responses to sanctions, and similar assessments generally will not have a significant GEOINT contribution.

Emerging and disruptive technologies. These technologies generally are assessed using other INTs.

Prisoners of war and missing in action. GEOINT has contributed to intelligence about prisoners of war (POWs) by identifying possible holding cells; it did so during the Vietnam War.

Biological warfare development and proliferation.

Non-Traditional Intelligence Uses

This chapter is about the intelligence uses of GEOINT. Many of the most important contributions of GEOINT, as discussed earlier in the chapter, directly support commercial or governmental operations that do not involve the traditional definition of intelligence—air and ocean navigational safety being a significant example. Business intelligence activities are often GEOINT analyses, where the location of desired investment, competitor activities, supply chain management, and future markets all play critical roles in how resources are allocated.

Trends

Several emerging trends have already been mentioned. These include the increasing "democratization" of GEOINT, where GEOINT products and services are now widely available to a global commercial customer base at a moment's notice via mobile devices and the web where previously only the defense and intelligence community had access to these data and products. Additionally, the blending of imagery and GIS data has created new products and services for an expanding global business user base.

UAS use for GEOINT collections and real-time reconnaissance and surveillance will continue to rise, both in government and increasingly within the private sector for intelligence, security, and exploration uses. UAS are already being used to collect all types of data, including RADAR, LiDAR, panchromatic, multi-spectral, thermal, acoustic, magnetic, and hyperspectral data.

The satellite constellation will continue to expand, offering unprecedented global and temporal coverage at spatial resolutions of less than 1 meter. Users will be able order imagery and receive their image or data product within hours. Archived data will grow in use because it is less costly than tasking and collecting new data. Many countries that previously have had no satellite collection capabilities have planned launches within the next few years.

Add to this growing commercial capability the concept of small satellites (smallsats). This class of satellites is seen as a huge part of the future of commercial GEOINT as well as an increasingly important part of a back-up plan should the U.S. NTM constellation encounter problems. Smallsats range in size from near-automotive vehicle size down to the smallest current 10 cm cube sats and even smaller nano-sats, and typically have a 1–10 kg mass. More than 1,000 smallsats are scheduled be launched within the next 5 years.[73] While the resolution capability of smallsats cannot yet rival their larger, traditional sensor cousins, they can perform many synoptic (large area) collections at a fraction of the cost of putting the more capable sensor collection systems into orbit and operations.

Location-based Intelligence (LBI) data and intelligence, including the Internet of Things (IOT), will continue its dramatic increase as more machines are made location aware. Volunteered Geographic Information (VGI) is also an increasing trend, especially for disaster relief. Local residents and people from around the globe can quickly update a disaster recovery crew on what is happening on the ground immediately following a hurricane, tsunami, tornado, or other severe storm. Because of the tremendous increase in the availability of commercial source imagery and data smallsats, LBI, VGI, and IOT, NTM use will continue to decline as a proportion of the overall use of GEOINT data products and services while maintaining its role as primary source of the highest quality available imagery and products.

References

1. Paul R. Baumann, "History of Remote Sensing, Aerial Photography," 2001, http://www.oneonta.edu/faculty/baumanpr/geosat2/RS%20History%20I/RS-History-Part-1.htm.
2. National Geospatial-Intelligence Agency, "The Advent of the National Geospatial-Intelligence Agency," Office of the NGA Historian, September 2011, 8, https://www.nga.mil/About/History/Pages/default.aspx.
3. United States Code, Title 10, section 467 (10 U.S.C. §467), http://uscode.house.gov/download/pls/10c22.txt.
4. "Geospatial Intelligence in Joint Operations," *JCS Joint Publication 2–03* (October 31, 2012), http://www.dtic.mil/doctrine/new_pubs/jp2_03.pdf.
5. National System for Geospatial Intelligence, "Geospatial Intelligence (GEOINT) Basic Doctrine," *GEOINT Publication 1.0* (September 2006).
6. Department of Defense Directive 5105.60, "National Geospatial-Intelligence Agency (NGA)," July 29, 2009, http://www.dtic.mil/whs/directives/corres/pdf/510560p.pdf.
7. Pew Research Internet Project, "Mobile Technology Fact Sheet," January 2014, http://pewinternet.org/Commentary/2012/February/Pew-Internet-Mobile.aspx.
8. Pew Research Internet Project, "Three Technology Revolutions," 2014, http://pewinternet.org/Static-Pages/Trend-Data-%28Adults%29/Home-Broadband-Adoption.aspx.
9. International Telecommunications Union, "ITU releases latest global technology development figures," February 27, 2013, http://www.itu.int/net/pressoffice/press_releases/2013/05.aspx#.U_tlsE0g8rQ.
10. Ibid.
11. Todd S. Bacastow and Dennis J. Bellafiore, "Redefining Geospatial Intelligence," *American Intelligence Journal* (Fall 2009): 38–40.
12. Carl Franklin and Paula Hane, "An Introduction to GIS: Linking Maps to Databases," *Database 15*, no. 2 (April 1992): 17–22.
13. National Geospatial-Intelligence Agency, "The Advent of the National Geospatial-Intelligence Agency," 5.
14. Alan Gordon, "Mapping and Charting for the Greatest Collaborative Project Ever," *The American Surveyor*, June 2005, http://www.amerisurv.com/PDF/TheAmericanSurveyor_D-DayMapping_June2005.pdf.

15. U.S. Navy, *Naval Doctrine Publication 2: Naval Intelligence*, n.d, http://www .dtic.mil/doctrine/jel/service_pubs/ndp2.pdf.

16. Baumann, "History of Remote Sensing, Aerial Photography."

17. "History of the Aeronautical Chart Service," 2008, http://www.escape-maps .com/escape_maps/history_aeronautical_chart_service.htm.

18. Baumann, "History of Remote Sensing, Aerial Photography."

19. Ibid.

20. Office of Strategic Services, "Office of Strategic Services (OSS) Organization and Functions," June 1945, http://www.ibiblio.org/hyperwar/USG/JCS/OSS/ OSS-Functions.

21. Central Intelligence Agency, "Careers and Internships," 2007, https://www.cia .gov/careers/opportunities/support-professional/geographer.html.

22. National Geospatial-Intelligence Agency, "The Advent of the National Geospatial-Intelligence Agency," 10.

23. Ibid.

24. Esri, *GIS in the Defense and Intelligence Communities* 3 (2008): 3, http://www .esri.com/library/brochures/pdfs/gis-in-defense-vol3.pdf.

25. National Geospatial-Intelligence Agency, "The Advent of the National Geospatial-Intelligence Agency," 29.

26. James Warren Bagley, "The Use of the Panoramic Camera in Topographic Surveying: With Notes on the Application of Photogrammetry to Aerial Surveys," *U.S. Geological Survey Bulletin #657,* (Washington, DC: Government Printing Office, 1917).

27. National Geospatial-Intelligence Agency, "The Advent of the National Geospatial-Intelligence Agency," 6.

28. CIA, "CIA History & Heritage," 18 January 1961, http://www.foia.cia.gov/ sites/default/files/document_conversions/18/1961–01–18.pdf.

29. National Geospatial-Intelligence Agency, "The Advent of the National Geospatial-Intelligence Agency," 13.

30. Ibid., 6.

31. National Reconnaissance Office, "Gambit 3 (KH-8) Fact Sheet," September 2011, http://www.nro.gov/history/csnr/gambhex/Docs/GAM_3_Fact_sheet .pdf.

32. National Reconnaissance Office, "Hexagon (KH-9) Fact Sheet," September 2011, http://www.nro.gov/history/csnr/gambhex/Docs/Hex_fact_sheet.pdf.

33. National Reconnaissance Office, "The HEXAGON Story," December 1992, http://www2.gwu.edu/~nsarchiv/NSAEBB/NSAEBB54/docs/doc_44.pdf.

34. Jeffrey Richelson, "U.S. Reconnaissance Satellites: Domestic Targets," *The National Security Archive,* April 11, 2008, http://www2.gwu.edu/~nsarchiv/ NSAEBB/NSAEBB229.

35. National Geospatial-Intelligence Agency, "The Advent of the National Geospatial-Intelligence Agency," 14.

36. Ibid., 14.

37. Ibid., 26.

38. Peter Marino, chairman of the commission, "The Information Edge: Imagery Intelligence and Geospatial Information in an Evolving National Security Environment," *Report of the Independent Commission on the National Imagery and Mapping Agency, Final Report,* December 2000, viii.

39. Personal communication to the author by former NGA director of R&D Rob Zitz, 2003.

40. Satellite Imaging Corporation, "GEOEYE-2 Satellite Sensor," http://www
.satimagingcorp.com/satellite-sensors/geoeye-2.html.

41. United States Geological Survey, "Frequently Asked Questions about the Landsat Missions," http://landsat.usgs.gov/band_designations_landsat_satellites
.php.

42. U.S. Joint Forces Command, "Commander's Handbook for Persistent Surveillance," Vol. I-3, June 30, 2011, http://info.publicintelligence.net/USJFCOM
-PersistentSurveillance.pdf.

43. "Evolving Digital Maps Play Key Role in Philippines Relief Efforts," *IEEE
Spectrum Tech Alert* (November 14, 2013).

44. John W. Allan, "Redefining Maritime Security," *Geo Intelligence,* March-April
2011, http://www.wbresearch.com/uploadedFiles/Events/UK/2012/10980_006/
Download_Center_Content/18–22%20John%20article%20low%20res.pdf.

45. Gabriel Miller, "Activity-Based Intelligence Uses Metadata to Map Adversary Networks," *Defense News,* July 8, 2013, http://www.defensenews
.com/article/20130708/C4ISR02/307010020/Activity-based-intelligence-uses-
metadata-map-adversary-networks?odyssey=nav|head.

46. Michael Herman, *Intelligence Services in the Information Age* (London: Frank
Cass Publishers, 2001), 192–193.

47. DigitalGlobe, http://www.digitalglobe.com/resources/satellite-information.

48. "Geospatial Intelligence in Joint Operations," *JCS Joint Publication 2–03*
(October 31, 2012): IV–2.

49. Ibid., II–3.

50. Ibid., IV–2.

51. National Geospatial-Intelligence Agency, "Geospatial Intelligence Standards
Working Group," http://www.gwg.nga.mil/guide.php.

52. Rui C. Barbosa, "China Launches Tianhui-1B via Long March 2D," NASA
Spaceflight.com, May 6, 2012, http://www.nasaspaceflight.com/2012/05/
china-launches-tianhui-1b-long-march-2d/.

53. Ibid.

54. Ibid.

55. Rui C. Barbosa, "Chinese Long March 2C Lofts Huanjing-1C into Orbit,"
NASA Spaceflight.com, November 18, 2012, http://www.nasaspaceflight
.com/2012/11/chinese-long-march-2c-huanjing-1c-into-orbit/.

56. Stephen Clark, "Russian Imaging Satellite in Orbit After Soyuz Launch," *Spaceflight Now,* June 25, 2013, http://spaceflightnow.com/news/n1306/25soyuz/#
.UhoFULrD-JA.

57. Patrick Fryer, "Overcoming the Challenges of Providing Geospatial Services to
NATO," http://www.wbresearch.com/uploadedFiles/Events/UK/2011/10980_005/
Info_for_Attendees/presentations/Pat%20Fryer.pdf.

58. National Geospatial-Intelligence Agency, "Mission Partners," https://www1
.nga.mil/Partners/InternationalActivities/Pages/default.aspx.

59. Group Captain Ian Wood, Commander, JARIC, "Transition or Transformation?
Defence Intelligence 2010," http://www.wbresearch.com/uploadedFiles/Events/
UK/2011/10980_005/Info_for_Attendees/presentations/Ian%20Wood%20
Updated.pdf.

60. Col. DHN Thompson, "Meet Canada's Directorate of Geospatial Intelligence,"
Pathfinder, March/April 2009, 3–4, http://www.hsdl.org/? view&did=19385.

61. National Geospatial-Intelligence Agency, "Mission Partners."

62. Frank Colley, "Providing Strategic GIS Support to Australian Defence and National Security Operations Presentation, http://www.wbresearch .com/uploadedFiles/Events/UK/2012/10980_006/Info_for_Attendees/ presentations/10.10%20Frank%20Colley%20day1.pdf.

63. Australian Department of Defence, "Defence Imagery and Geospatial Organisation," http://www.defence.gov.au/digo/geoint-palanterra.htm.

64. Ibid.

65. Ammon Sofin, head of the Intelligence Directorate, Israeli Intelligence Service, "Strategically Positioning & Using GIS in Intelligence," http://www .wbresearch.com/uploadedFiles/Events/UK/2012/10980_006/Info_for_ Attendees/presentations/15.10%20Brig%20Gen%20Amnon%20Sofrin.pdf.

66. Barbara Opall-Rome, "International ISR: Israel Tackles The Last Frontier of UAV Technology," *Defense News*, June 3, 2013, http://www.defensenews.com/ article/20130603/C4ISR01/306030015/International-ISR-Israel- Tackles-Last- Frontier-UAV-Technology.

67. University of Munich, "GeoInfoPortal for the Geoinformation Service of the Bundeswehr," 2005, http://www.unibw.de/inf4/professuren/geoinformatik/ geoinformatik-en/forschung/projekte/geoinfo-en.

68. OHB, "OHB-System AG: SAR-Lupe Now Officially Handed Over to Strategic Reconnaissance Command," December 4, 2008, http://www.ohb.de/ press-releases-details/items/ohb-pr_sl_%C3%BCbergabe.html.

69. Rajeev Sharma, "India's Spy Satellite Launch?" *The Diplomat*, April 30, 2012, http://thediplomat.com/indian-decade/2012/04/30/indias-spy-satellite-launch.

70. Italian Space Agency, "COSMO-SkyMed Mission," 2007, http://www .cosmo-skymed.it/en/index.htm.

71. Colonel Jean-Armel Hubault, Head of the Joint Geospatial-information Office, Tri-Services General Staff, "How French Geo Organization Is Supporting Operations, Some Current Challenges . . . and Moving to Future . . .," DGI Europe, 2009, http://www.wbresearch.com/uploadedFiles/Events/UK/2010/10980_004/ Info_for_Attendees/10980_004_misc_hubault.pdf.

72. CIA Intelligence Memorandum, "USSR: A Third Consecutive Crop Failure," August 1981, http://www.foia.cia.gov/sites/default/files/document_conversions/ 89801/DOC_0000498196.pdf.

73. "Nanosats Are Go! Small Satellites: Taking Advantage of Smartphones and Other Consumer Technologies, Tiny Satellites Are Changing the Space Business," *The Economist,* June 7, 2014, http://www.economist.com/news/technology- quarterly/21603240-small-satellites-taking-advantage-smartphones-and-other- consumer-technologies.

6

Measurement and Signature Intelligence

John L. Morris and Robert M. Clark

The term *Measurement and Signature Intelligence* (MASINT) to describe this intelligence discipline is of relatively recent origin. It dates from the late 1970s. The discipline comprises different techniques that are much older.

Until shortly after World War II, the techniques that are now considered part of MASINT were almost exclusively applied to support military operations (SMO). Underwater sound collection to identify and locate submerged submarines dates from World War I, as does the use of acoustic sensors to locate enemy field artillery. The use of radar to detect, identify, and track aircraft and ships blossomed during World War II. Chemical detectors to identify chemical warfare agents were in wide use by the end of World War II. Even unattended acoustic and seismic sensors, under the Igloo White Program, were first introduced by the United States in the late 1960s during the Vietnamese conflict to monitor infiltrating enemy soldiers and supplies entering South Vietnam from the North along the Ho Chi Minh trail at night.

It was not until the USSR began nuclear weapons testing that MASINT was rapidly refocused to national-level strategic needs. This was particularly significant since the timelines for supporting military operations were shrinking at the same time, making it less useful for SMO. The strength of MASINT was in its scientific core, answering the really hard intelligence questions where the speed of reporting was secondary to the accuracy of reporting. Therefore, the discipline developed, grew, and evolved in response to the Cold War with the former Soviet Union. A strategic need to understand Soviet, and later Chinese, nuclear weapons capability drove the development of several MASINT subdisciplines. The stringent internal security measures that these two countries imposed made it difficult to get the needed intelligence from human intelligence (HUMINT), signals intelligence (SIGINT), and imagery intelligence (IMINT). Nuclear MASINT, in contrast, could provide accurate information on weapons types and yields from measurements taken during and after nuclear tests. Radar MASINT could provide intelligence on the range and accuracy of ballistic missiles as well as the number and design of their nuclear warheads. Acoustic MASINT could identify and track ballistic missile submarines on patrol. All these developments required the computing capability and the in-depth analysis expertise provided by engineers and scientists from research laboratories.

New technologies and analytical methods, along with heavy influence from the new space race with the Soviet Union, drove what could be described as the third major wave of MASINT development (tactical applications and the strategic weaponry shift being the first two). The old joke about needing to be a rocket scientist to understand something was actually true about MASINT in that era. This has been an ongoing process over the past five decades. Science and technology (S & T) principles were applied to extracting new types of intelligence from IMINT and signals intelligence (SIGINT) collectors using their unexploited sensor capabilities. HUMINT collectors were tapped for sampling missions and to emplace new types of MASINT sensors. At the same time, existing MASINT collection capabilities were being steadily improved by the application of technological advances.

Finally, in the last two decades, carefully focused MASINT innovation along with strengthened national-level oversight and war fighter advocacy have driven a fourth major wave of development and application. MASINT has returned to its origins in the battlespace. Although this coincided with the standup and operation of the Central MASINT Office (CMO), enabling innovation was a necessary factor. New levels of analytic expertise combined with more powerful computers and extensive communications networks, new sensors, signature-based processing and exploitation technologies, and diverse collection platforms all came together to allow real-time delivery of a variety of MASINT products to combat units. As a result, MASINT has become an integral and important part of military operations. In applications as diverse as weather prediction, search and rescue operations, battlefield terrain mapping, targeting battle damage assessment, theater warning and operations planning, MASINT has served the war fighter well.

This chapter follows the same general format as that of the other major intelligence collection disciplines (INTs) already discussed. After this introduction, the reader will see a discussion of the definition of MASINT—which is far and away the most difficult of all INTs to define. We then provide a short history of MASINT under that name, followed by a description of its six distinct subdisciplines. Then comes a discussion of how MASINT is managed and an overview of MASINT efforts in countries other than the United States. The chapter concludes with a section on the types of intelligence targets where MASINT is a contributor. For purposes of comparison among the INTs, similar if not identical intelligence issues will be used.

MASINT Defined

One of the more descriptive definitions of MASINT that the authors prefer came from the then newly formed Central MASINT Office of the mid 1990s:

> Measurement and Signature Intelligence (MASINT) is technically-derived intelligence that enables detection, location, tracking, identification, and description of unique characteristics of fixed and

dynamic target sources. MASINT embodies a set of sub-disciplines that operate across the electromagnetic, acoustic and seismic spectrums, and material sciences. MASINT capabilities include radar, laser, optical, infrared, acoustic, nuclear radiation, radio frequency, spectro-radiometric, and seismic sensing systems as well as gas, liquid, and solid materials sampling and analysis. MASINT is an integral part of the all-source collection environment and contributes both unique and complementary information on a wide range of intelligence requirements. MASINT is highly reliable since it is derived from the performance data and characteristics of actual targets.[1]

This definition provides some insight into what MASINT is and what it is used for, rather than what it is not—as many of the word-of-mouth definitions from the 1980s and early 1990s did.

The other INTs discussed in this book tend to be easily understood and often relate to the literal human senses—seeing and hearing, those primary senses used by most people for gathering information on a day-to-day basis. SIGINT is thought of as the "ears" of the U.S. Intelligence Community (IC); IMINT as the "eyes"; the new geospatial intelligence (GEOINT) gives geographic context to IMINT, now its subdiscipline; and everyone knows that HUMINT is "James Bond." In contrast, MASINT has no such core collection method tied to the literal senses with which it can readily be identified. Therefore, one might consider MASINT methods to be tied to the "nonliteral" senses—smell, taste, and touch.

Whereas many of the other intelligence disciplines are considered collection INTs, MASINT has always been considered to be more of an in-depth exploitation and analysis discipline, often taking its data from a different collection discipline and applying MASINT techniques in order to gain more information than would otherwise have been reported by the original collector. On the other hand, MASINT does offer some unique collection capabilities, thus adding to the inability to clearly type it as collection or exploitation. Nonetheless, MASINT has long since proven itself as an INT, co-equal with the others discussed in this book.

With its longstanding emphasis on in-depth exploitation and analysis, MASINT has long defined itself in terms of the underlying sciences and technologies it uses. But this view only tends to further mystify MASINT for its nontechnical customers.

Some of this mystery might be stripped away by looking at MASINT from different perspectives beginning with the U.S. government definition. The U.S. Department of Defense (DoD) defines MASINT more by *what it does* than by what it is, as in the following:

Information produced by quantitative and qualitative analysis of physical attributes of targets and events to characterize, locate, and identify them. MASINT exploits a variety of phenomenologies to support signature development and analysis, to perform technical analysis, and to detect, characterize, locate, and identify targets and events. MASINT is derived from specialized, technically-derived measurements of physical phenomenon intrinsic to an object or event and it includes the use of quantitative signatures to interpret the data.[2]

Beyond this general definition, MASINT is not easily defined. It evades a strict disciplinary definition. However, it might be instructive to explain "technically" how the name came about. This may provide more insight than any formal definition.

Origin of the Name

First, the word *measurement* refers to any data observed and recorded during a MASINT collection. It's that simple.

All of the sensors described in this chapter collect measurements of phenomenology unique to their particular sensor types. For example, radars transmit a radio frequency (RF) wave of a known strength and measure the return strength, or amplitude, from a target, along with the location and movement of the target. Normalizing this data set—removing the noise, sensor, motion, and atmospheric effects—and putting it into a signature-like format, such as a graph or spreadsheet, allows one to isolate the phenomenology being measured. We refer to this normalized, corrected data as *signature data*. Many erroneously think that this is a signature, but it is only normalized, corrected data at this point.

These normalized, corrected data do enable comparison with a known *reference signature,* which can yield information about the performance and/or characteristics of the target. If this data set yields more unique details about the characteristics of the target than the reference signature does, the new information can be used to update the reference signature as "the new validated signature" for that target. As this process continues, the "validated" or reference signature progresses in its utility—first being about to detect a particular target among other targets, noise, or clutter; next being able to classify the target; and ultimately being able to uniquely identify the target, just as a fingerprint uniquely identifies a specific individual.

Thus, a *signature* is a repeatable representation of data from a given collection phenomenology that is characteristic, sometimes uniquely so, of a specific target or class of targets. Not all collections will result in a new signature of that target; many collections will either be incomplete or even duplicative of previous signature data. But all will provide information on the characteristics of that particular target, to include performance, at the time of collection.

A second perspective is by analogy; think of it as a *methodology* perspective. MASINT involves obtaining signatures on targets of intelligence interest. These targets exhibit some phenomena or have some characteristics that can be measured by sensors, quantified, and compared to known values in databases for identification. In that sense, MASINT analysis is often described as being like a forensic examination: A technical specialist takes measurements from the crime scene, such as blood splatter patterns, bullet holes in a victim and elsewhere at the crime scene, biological samples such as saliva on a cigarette butt, etc. He or she derives signatures from the blood collection (typing) and biological samples (DNA) to determine the identity of the victim and/or perpetrator as well as, from analysis of the victim's position and the trajectory of the bullet, determine certain attributes of the perpetrator—all helping to solve the "intelligence problem." This perspective leads one to think of MASINT as the CSI of the U.S. IC and is the most popular perspective for those without intelligence training.

A third perspective is that of the scientific phenomenology being measured—that is, the science perspective. Reduced to its essentials, MASINT involves finding a defining characteristic, or fingerprint, for target identification. It typically includes observing physical or chemical features, measuring phenomena, and plotting signatures. This information can be derived from collecting many different types of emissions from target-related phenomenologies—nuclear radiation; electro-optical (EO) energy such as ultraviolet (UV), infrared, and visible light; radar waves; unintentional RF waves; geophysical elements such as acoustic, seismic, magnetic, and gravitational data; and material samples.

By comparing the signatures gained from these emissions or samples, MASINT professionals can detect, locate, and track targets. MASINT generates precise measurements that reveal unique characteristics of targets. The variety of these characteristics and the precision with which they are measured further reinforces the fingerprint analogy. Looking at these different views separately as most people did in the early days, one can understand why MASINT is the least understood of the INTs by both users and IC members. It is often perceived as a strategic collection INT with limited tactical application. But increasingly, MASINT is providing real-time warning, situational awareness, and targeting within timelines that make it operationally relevant to the military customer and more useful to the other INTs for tip-off and cueing of their collection assets.

To summarize, MASINT diversity has provided it with an inherent resiliency to operate in an increasingly complex world. For example, MASINT is now called upon to provide traditional Cold War treaty monitoring and strategic analysis simultaneously with reliable military applications such as real-time tactical warning, targeting, search and rescue and accurate weather predictions in addition to rapid support to asymmetric operations of counterterrorism, homeland defense, and environmental crises. MASINT has finally taken its place as one of the recognized INTs. In fact, in the next section, you will note that major intelligence agencies are now competing to incorporate MASINT technologies and capabilities into their tradecrafts.

A History of MASINT

It was pointed out in the introduction that many of the techniques used to collect MASINT predate the creation of that term. Acoustic collection and materials collection, for example, date back centuries. The use of radar for intelligence dates back to World War II. Prior to the 1970s, military services and other intelligence organizations used various scientific and technical methodologies to gather data for intelligence purposes. However, this section will relate how the policy was developed to bring modern technologies together as a coherent system to better serve the intelligence needs of the United States.

Developing Policy in the Beginning

As the U.S. intelligence organizations were being formed after World War II and focusing on strategic intelligence, they needed scientific and technical intelligence (S&TI) that could be gathered by an organization with global reach. Thus, the U.S. Air Force took on the mission as a natural complement to its mission of air defense of the homeland. In the early days of U.S. intelligence collection of MASINT information before MASINT was named, three players dominated the scene within the United States—the U.S. Air Force, the Central Intelligence Agency (CIA), and the Defense Intelligence Agency (DIA).

The National Security Agency (NSA) also took more than a casual interest, but as an agency they were committed to getting their arms around a diverse and globally separated U.S. SIGINT System. Thus there was no real commitment for NSA to pursue MASINT as a separate INT, only as yet another subdiscipline of SIGINT. CIA, on the other hand, was "the national agency" that looked more broadly at applying S & T principles to its own collection, exploitation, and all-source assessments. They fully supported it standing up as a separate INT to ensure the survival and growth of a capability that could enhance their strategic analysis which supported U.S. policymakers every day.

DIA did not have its own collection assets but did have strong influence within DoD circles, including a close relationship with the program manager of the General Defense Intelligence Program (GDIP), who funded all service-related intelligence activities. DIA was a firm believer in the value of MASINT as an independent INT and formed a solid partnership with the U.S. Air Force as their executive agent.

Although the assistant chief of staff of intelligence (ACSI, now the A2) for the Air Force was only a major general at the time, he had assigned full colonels as the intelligence program element monitors (PEMs) and had given them experienced Pentagon-savvy lieutenant colonels as their action officers (AOs). They were able to obtain approval for programs not only by doing outstanding staffing but even by attending to small details, such as the naming convention for newly proposed collection programs.

In one instance, the PEM for the Air Force technical sensor program named a proposed new mobile radar system after his wife and then proceeded to confide to key people in the Pentagon whose coordination he might need that he named it after their wife, girlfriend, daughter, etc., who had the same first name. Cobra Judy was one example of this strategy. Nonetheless, several key decision makers nonconcurred on the proposed Presidential Decision Directive (PDD) that went forward; however, President Gerald Ford was the one who counted, and he approved Cobra Judy, the new mobile precision radar program, anyway.

Early MASINT Radars

Beginning in the late 1950s, the U.S. Air Force developed and fielded very powerful (for that day) fixed-beam radars, the most mature of the modern MASINT technologies at that time, along the periphery of the Soviet Union in order to monitor the progress and performance of the Soviet ballistic missile program. Turkey and Alaska provided the closest access from which testing of Soviet intermediate-range ballistic missiles (IRBM) and intercontinental ballistic missiles (ICBM), respectively, could be observed and monitored. Since technology only allowed fixed-beam radar operations at that time, the AN/FPS-16 and the AN/FPS-17 were the appropriate radars to install in the late 1950s at Diyarbakir, Turkey, and at Shemya, Alaska, respectively.

The Air Force's newly established Air Defense Command (ADC, later dubbed ADCOM, and today titled the Air Force Space Command) was assigned the responsibility for operating these radar sites, and the Foreign Technology Division (FTD), now the National Air and Space Intelligence Center (NASIC), of the Air Force Systems Command (AFSC), was assigned the executive agency responsibility for analyzing and reporting the results to the DIA and the CIA as well as other national and defense agencies as well as military services that were concerned about the growing Cold War threat environment. AFSC acquired and deployed the radars to ADC and FTD specifications. These radars, however, only gave the most rudimentary of performance information as the ballistic missiles flew through the radio frequency fences that were established by the FPS-16 and FPS-17 radars.

With the successful launch of the Soviet Sputnik satellite capping off the 1950s, the United States now needed more precise performance information about the USSR space systems and their dual track space booster-ICBM development program. Thus, high-precision, single-beam tracking radars were developed and established at Diyarbakir and Shemya, the AN/FPS-79 and AN/FPS-80, respectively, in the mid-to-late 1960s. These radars enabled the first precision tracking of the growing USSR strategic missile program.

At the same time, the Air Force began developing advanced mobile MASINT sensors—film-based ballistic framing cameras for determining reentry vehicle (RV) terminal trajectory performance, optical spectrometers for warhead heat shield materials definition, and first generation phased array radars for determination of the size/shape/motion of the RVs as they approached reentry into the atmosphere and impacted on an instrumented ICBM range on the Kamchatka peninsula.

These sensor programs were developed by AFSC in the early 1960's and phased into airborne intelligence operation by the Strategic Air Command (SAC) later in the 1960's with such exotic program nicknames as Lisa Ann and Nancy Rae/Wanda Belle, which were later formalized to Rivet Amber and Rivet Ball, respectively.

According to the legendary former director of the BIG SAFARI Program Office, Colonel Bill Grimes (USAF, retired), the Lisa Ann development was initiated with Hughes Aircraft Co. in Aug 1963 and later renamed Rivet Amber (RC-135E) prior to delivery to SAC in Sep 1966—operations began immediately. On 5 Jun 1969, the aircraft was lost on a flight from Shemya AB to Eielson AFB, AK. No trace was ever found of the aircraft. "The 2 MW computer-controlled, phased array radar could track a target the size of a soccer ball at a distance of 300 NM," according to Colonel Grimes.

The first RC-135S, initially named Nancy Rae, then Wanda Belle, then Rivet Ball, was built in Oct 1960 and flown directly to Shemya AB, AK — where it crashed upon landing on 12 Jan 1969. A second fully capable Cobra Ball aircraft was delivered one year later to Shemya AB.

In addition, in the 1960s, AFSC began developing what was to become a patchwork global network of optical telescopes and space track radars to assist ADC in their evolving space object identification (SOI) and tracking mission. Although FTD had no responsibility in the space track mission, their all-source threat assessment analysts did have a directed charter from DIA to assess the capabilities of all foreign spacecraft as an integral part of their intelligence assessment mission.

Air Defense Command, now ADCOM, along with the global network of space track optics/radars, continued as the operator of the ground-based radars, whereas FTD continued as the intelligence processor and exploiter for all Air Force–collected radar intelligence (RADINT) and optical intelligence (OPTINT) data for the nation.

As the nuclear arms race heated up in the early 1970s, both the United States and the USSR escalated their testing of ICBM delivery systems. Growing alarmed, the leaders on both sides decided that diplomacy might be a wise course or the race might yield a winner—with dire consequences to the losing side. Therefore, two key treaties limiting these weapons of mass destruction (WMDs) were negotiated and signed within a matter of just two and one half years of intense negotiation. The first treaty (Anti-Ballistic Missile Treaty, or ABM Treaty) limited the number and placement of anti-ballistic missile (ABM) systems. The second treaty (Strategic Arms Limitations Talks, or SALT I) was an interim agreement on limiting strategic offensive arms. Both the ABM Treaty and the interim agreement stipulate that compliance is to be assured by "national technical means (NTM) of verification," and were signed in May 1972 in Moscow.

The United States took this opportunity to replace the AN/FPS-17 and AN/FPS-80 radars with a modern L-band phased array radar at Shemya, Alaska—referred to as Cobra Dane and shown in Figure 6.1. This radar was declared a "national technical means of verification" for the SALT Treaty between the United States and the Soviet Union. The specifications were provided to the Soviet Union to emphasize the U.S. capability to monitor the SALT Treaty. The FTD had provided the specifications for the technical capabilities of the radar and provided onsite performance monitoring and support to contractors who operated the radar.

Earlier in the late 1960s, the FTD had developed a tasking plan for the Advanced Range Instrumentation Ships (ARIS) to support the U.S. IC, although the ships were primarily developed to support the U.S. manned space flight program at that time. The ships' mobile C-band radar gave the U.S. Air Force the capability to quickly move to broad ocean areas and dwell for long periods where the USSR announced closures to international maritime traffic due to impending ICBM testing.

Unfortunately, the ARIS radar ships were not capable of providing the precision radar data needed to support the more stringent protocol of monitoring the SALT Treaty. Therefore, the ARIS mobile radar capability was eventually upgraded in the late 1970s with a dedicated intelligence-gathering

Figure 6-1   Cobra Dane Radar

Source: U.S. Air Force Space Command. Source: Public domain, from Air Force Space Command website, accessed at http://www.afspc.af.mil/news/story.asp? id=123343230

platform that employed a state-of-the-art S-band phased array radar that could track multiple objects the size of a soccer ball at 1,000 km range. This new capability was named Cobra Judy. Cobra Judy's acquisition coincided with the signing of the final protocol of the Strategic Arms Limitation Treaty (SALT II) after several years of intense negotiation in 1979. Several years later, the Missile Defense Agency added a single beam X-band precision signature capability to the Cobra Judy platform.

Real-Time Missile Warning from MASINT

In the 1960s, the Air Force had fielded an operational ICBM launch detection system to give as much early warning against an attack to the nation as possible—an over-the-horizon forward scatter radar system (OTH-F) known as Project 440L. The AN/FRT-80 transmitters in Europe established a high-frequency curtain at low grazing angles across the top of the Sino-Soviet landmass from Europe to multiple AN/FSQ-76 receivers along the eastern periphery of the USSR to close the curtain. When ballistic missiles disrupted the electron density of the ionosphere within this curtain directly above the landmass, the receivers would detect the missile movement via a Doppler shift in the observed frequency. This "disturbance" to the ionosphere was designed to detect only a mass missile raid and "ring the alarm bell" but could not provide much definitively about individual missiles. There were numerous false alarms—both positive as well as negative. A new, more reliable phenomenology was desperately needed to handle individual missile warning and ultimately targeting information, since there was clearly a growing threat in the aftermath of a successful Soviet Sputnik I satellite launch in 1957.

Therefore, the newly created Advanced Research Projects Agency (ARPA) assumed responsibility for experiments begun by the Air Force in the late 1950s on a new missile detection phenomenology—infrared detection—dubbed Project 461 or Project MIDAS. Project 461 was a special access program that developed and launched a small infrared sensor, shown in Figure 6.2, in conjunction with a series of Discoverer satellites over a period of several years. Responsibility for the program was transitioned back to the Air Force by 1960 after successful tests. The most striking detection successes of two Polaris missiles, one Minuteman, and one Titan II were reported immediately to the White House via a supplement to the president's weekly report in May 1963. As a result of this series of successful experiments, the decision was made to develop and deploy an operational infrared missile detection network, starting in 1970; that network is still fully operational today as the Defense Support Program (DSP). DSP satellites—shown in Figure 6.3—are slowly being phased out by their replacement capabilities, called the Space-Based Infrared System (SBIRS). More will be discussed in the EO MASINT section of this chapter.

Figure 6-2   MIDAS Satellite

Source: Wikipedia/Flickr/Cliff. Source: Public domain image, accessed at http://en.wikipedia.org/wiki/
Missile_Defense_Alarm_System

Intelligence application of this new technology initially was referred to as infrared intelligence (IRINT) but today is known as overhead persistent infrared (OPIR). At the time that this initial IRINT feasibility success was being reported to the president in 1963, it was considered critical to demonstrate that ICBMs could be reliably and repeatedly detected and tracked in order to provide accurate and timely early warning of nuclear-tipped strategic missile attacks. As a result, the 440L OTH network was deactivated as soon as the DSP system became fully operational.

MASINT Analysis and Tradecraft

This explosion in precision RADINT and OPTINT collection in the 1960s and early 1970s gave rise to closer coordination and collaboration among the key data providers and producers of "national intelligence"—the Air Force as data provider, and the CIA and DIA as national and defense, respectively, intelligence producers. As a result, seniors at the air staff, the DIA, and the CIA signed several bilateral and trilateral agreements of cooperation and data sharing, including (1) an analyst exchange program between CIA and FTD and (2) chartering a peer-level analytic group for sharing exploitation techniques and debating data analysis results in the

Figure 6-3   Defense Support Program Satellite

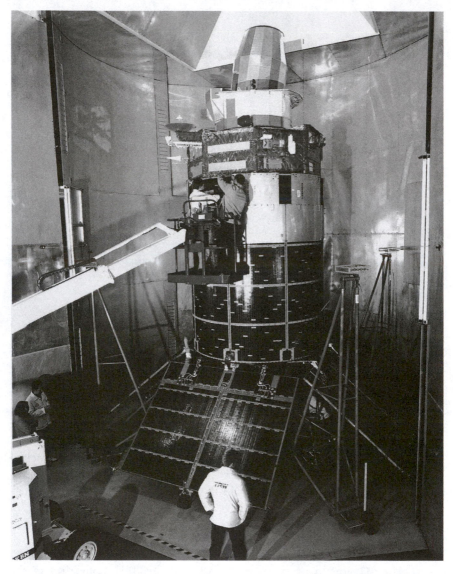

Source: United States Air Force/Courtesy of TRW. Source: Public domain image, accessed at USAF web site: http://www.au.af.mil/au/awc/awcgate/smc-fs/dsp_fs.htm

early 1970s to the late 1980s—the RADINT and OPTINT Working Group (ROWG). Both programs were highly successful in sharing data, exploitation technology, and common tradecraft but especially in creating a collaborative relationship. The ROWG experience was most likely the first identifiable starting point for developing a "MASINT culture."

Analytic representatives from every U.S. intelligence organization participated in the ROWG. This Air Force-, CIA-, and DIA-chartered and FTD-chaired technical working group was the forerunner to the DCI-chartered MASINT Committee (MASCOM) technical working groups more than a decade later. Quarterly meetings were normally held at FTD, Wright-Patterson Air Force Base in Ohio, since the CIA headquarters at Langley, Virginia, was still considered a covert location.

Under a separate agreement in the early 1970s, FTD's Engineering Directorate, CIA's Directorate of Science and Technology, and NSA's Directorate of Advanced Weapons and Space Systems merged their analytic tools for performing ballistic missile flight reconstruction into a common program. All three organizations funded the development of the Modularized Vehicle Simulation (MVS) program, which was originally designed as a diagnostic tool for the Titan missile program that accepted external sensor observations as well as telemetry. The missile profile-driven MVS program was updated, observables from all relevant U.S. intelligence sensors (especially MASINT) were included as individual optional modules, and all three organizations validated the results against known standards. FTD maintained the missile profile database for all to access, in coordination with the DIA all-source S&TI assessment centers. This arrangement allowed trajectory analysis comparisons to be made based upon analytic differences and not tool differences and thus enabled development of a common tradecraft for ballistic missile analysis that has stood the test of time. An abbreviated version of this trajectory analysis program, dubbed the Trajectory Reconstruction Program (TRP), was developed in the late 1970s in order to host on smaller general-purpose computers, such as the Hewlett-Packard VAX. Some versions of these common tools are still used today, especially by NASIC, NSA, CIA, and the National Geospatial-Intelligence Agency (NGA).

Finalizing MASINT Policy

Over the course of the 1970s, a number of different (but somewhat related by scientific principles) disciplines that were unaligned within the IC began to coordinate and collaborate with more urgency: RADINT, OPTINT, IRINT, electro-optical intelligence (EOINT), acoustic intelligence (ACINT/ACOUSTINT), nuclear intelligence (NUCINT), laser intelligence (LASINT), and unintentional radiation intelligence (RINT).

In the early 1980s, there was significant discussion over both IRINT (renamed as overhead non-imaging infrared, or ONIR), and directed energy weapons intelligence within the U.S. intelligence Community. NSA made the case for including them as a SIGINT subdiscipline. However, the Air Force suggested a simple test to determine whether a given subdiscipline was SIGINT or MASINT: If the observable carried information content, it was SIGINT. If it did not and was unintentional or observed from a weapon system, it was to be MASINT. The observables from directed energy weapons (DEW)—RF or high-powered microwave (HPMW) weapons, particle beams, electromagnetic pulse (EMP), and high-energy lasers—were deemed by the director of Central Intelligence (DCI) to be MASINT. However, certain low-energy lasers that carried information, such as laser communications, were clearly SIGINT. Deciding which intelligence discipline that IRINT (later renamed ONIR), fit into became a much more highly debated political decision, but it remained with the Air Force as MASINT.

In the mid 1970s during a series of policy meetings among Air Force, CIA, and DIA seniors, consensus was finally reached on naming this bundle of overlapping yet separate capabilities under a single unifying nomenclature—MASINT. And the recommendation was approved by the DCI in about 1977, although DIA had already begun to use the name informally.

DIA had already leaned forward and developed a defense requirements process in order to provide specific guidance to collectors with respect to analytic needs. Shortly after the official "naming" of MASINT, this process was formalized around the name of the new collection requirements—Measurement and Signature Data Requirements (MASDRs). Among the first to actively use the new process were the DIA-chartered U.S. Air Force, U.S. Army, and U.S. Navy S&TI centers and the Defense Special Missile and Astronautics Center (DEFSMAC), jointly chartered and manned by DIA and NSA.

Formalizing MASINT Management

In 1983, the DCI formed the MASINT Subcommittee from key DIA and Air Force individuals and assigned it under the SIGINT Committee solely for its administrative support until the community could evaluate the MASINT management experiment. The MASINT Subcommittee recommended policy directly to the DCI, established national collection priorities, advocated for MASINT programs, and collaborated with the ROWG to assure a forum for technical exchange.

In 1986, the experiment in national MASINT management was deemed a success; therefore, the DCI approved the establishment of a full MASCOM. The committee provided policy and guidance for developing future MASINT capabilities; validated and prioritized current collection and exploitation requirements; evaluated MASINT programs; defended MASINT programs as appropriate in the budget cycle; advocated for new MASINT programs as appropriate; and provided structured technical working groups to foster information exchange and collaboration and to advise the MASCOM chairman as required. The committee continued as the sole IC body for overseeing MASINT until the Central MASINT Office (CMO) was established in 1992.

In 1992, the CMO was formed under DIA as a joint DoD and IC organization overseeing all MASINT activities, including both national and theater budgets. The DCI signed a DCI Directive 2/11 (DCID 2/11) naming the director of CMO as the MASINT functional manager; this DCID was a carbon copy of that for the new Central Imagery Office (CIO), except that the CMO was also given authority to plan and execute research, development, test, and evaluation (RDT&E) projects and the funding to support the function. The deputy secretary of Defense signed a DoD Instruction (DODI) paralleling the DCID authorities. The DCI and the secretary of Defense funded CMO with both national and Defense line items, to include RDT&E. This allowed CMO legitimacy in operating with both the strategic and the tactical communities as the functional manager for MASINT in both the National Foreign Intelligence Program (NFIP) and the Tactical Intelligence and Related Activities (TIARA) programs. MASCOM was physically co-located with CMO as an advisory forum for both the IC and the DoD; the MASCOM chairman was dual-hatted as the deputy director of CMO, reporting to the director of CMO. However, CMO stood up as a very lean organization, with only thirty-eight funded manpower slots, and received a multiagency, multiservice budget and execution oversight responsibility of several billions across the entire Defense and national ICs that rivaled that of many larger agencies.

Initially the director of CMO reported directly to the director of DIA; however, within the first year, the CMO was placed within the DIA National Military Intelligence Collection Center (NMICC) and under the DIA director of Operations, who became dual-hatted as the director of CMO. In 1993, an agreement between CMO and the Air Force created the Central MASINT Technology Coordination Office (CMTCO) to help plan and to execute the CMO RDT&E budget. The purpose of this RDT&E budget was (1) to give CMO leverage with other research and development (R & D) agencies, and (2) to allow CMO to initiate new technologies and processes quickly in a new "INT" that was known for fast-moving innovation.

In 1997, after some maturing of its processes, CMO regained a director unencumbered with other responsibilities when the principal deputy director was redesignated as the director. This organizational placement remained until later in the year when a DCI Principals' Committee review of MASINT management recommended more community transparency, greater authority for the director of CMO with a standing expectation to 'sit at the table' with the other three INT functional managers for IC planning and decision making, and a larger management structure for MASINT functional management and customer outreach.

At the same time, in late 1997 the CMO Director suggested to industry that they organize and form a MASINT trade association so that he could deal with industry in a more organized and efficient manner. Industrial leaders agreed and formed the Measurement and Signature Technology (MAST) Association, a non-profit 501(c)6 trade association that was incorporated in January 1999. MAST soon was renamed as the MASINT Association and in 2008 reorganized as the Advanced Technical Intelligence Association. Its mission is to provide education and training, in addition to awareness of MASINT and other advanced technologies that support the U.S. defense community.

In early 1998, the director of DIA elevated CMO to become a key component of DIA, on the same level as the Directorate for Intelligence (J2) of the Joint Staff, the director of Operations, and the director of Intelligence Production. The director of CMO was invited to all community-level decision meetings, communicated directly with the DCI and the Congress, and the DCI made additional manpower and funding investments to expand the CMO functional manager's effectiveness and community outreach functions. CMO expanded the CMTCO authority to bypass execution year inefficiencies in the DIA comptroller process and created several new outreach functions.

The CMO Director, with the support of the DIA Director and the DCI, initiated several organizational changes that significantly expanded CMO's capability to operate as the MASINT functional manager. Several new oversight and outreach functions were extended or created:

- The CMTCO execution authority was expanded to bypass execution year inefficiencies in the DIA comptroller process.
- The Central MASINT Processing and Exploitation Coordination Office was established and collocated with NASIC at Wright Patterson AFB OH.
- The Central MASINT Training and Education Coordination Office was established and collocated with the Joint Military Intelligence Training Center at Bolling AFB MD.
- The MASINT Operations Center was collocated with the Defense Collection Coordination Center in the Pentagon.
- Recognizing that the military customers needed a jump start on tasking for relevant MASINT support, CMO placed the MASINT liaison officers in all combatant commands (COCOMs), the Joint Staff, and key national agencies to include the State Department.
- The CMO Director established "MASINT chairs" at the two service graduate schools, the Air Force Institute of Technology (AFIT), Wright-Patterson Air Force Base in Ohio, and the Naval Postgraduate School in Monterey, California.

By 1999, this organizational structure was fully in place and operating effectively. CMO was recognized as a co-equal by the other INT functional managers, agency directors, military services, and the COCOM customers, to include signing agreements independent of DIA. After almost five years of leading MASINT, the outgoing director of CMO was assigned to the Office of the DCI in mid-2000 to help transition MASINT more comprehensively into the intelligence analytic processes and products.

In 2003, the CMO organization was completely integrated into DIA to become the Directorate for MASINT and Technical Collection, thus considered by the IC as solely a DIA organization. The director of DIA assumed the authority of the MASINT functional manager. Once again, MASINT national priorities had difficulty competing with those of DIA mainstream programs, since DIA was primarily an all-source agency with heavy manpower bills to pay. MASINT technical sensors that were in most need of modernization had difficulty competing with the priorities of critical manpower salaries within DIA and its S&TI centers, many of which were associated with ongoing conflicts in the Middle East. While most other agencies were on a steady resource curve upward after 9/11, CMO was struggling to maintain the modernization program that was initiated prior to 9/11.

Late in 2002, the Deputy DCI for Community Management and the Assistant Secretary of Defense for Command, Control, Communications and Intelligence jointly reassigned responsibility for tasking, processing, exploitation, and dissemination (TPED) of certain types of imagery-derived MASINT from DIA to NGA. After no consensus on responsibility for ONIR (now OPIR) was achieved, that decision was deferred pending the outcome of an in-depth evaluation by the assistant DCI for collection. The in-depth evaluation was tasked late in 2003; however, it was slowed by the stand-up of the newly formed DNI organization and the complexity of the issues involved. Successfully completed in 2005, the results of the ONIR Management Evaluation Study were documented in the July 22, 2005, decision memorandum referenced next. As a result, ONIR responsibilities were transferred to NGA, as originally proposed.

In 2005, the director of National Intelligence (DNI) and the director of NGA agreed to an expanded definition of GEOINT that incorporated what had previously been considered MASINT—the subdisciplines of overhead non-imaging infrared (now OPIR) and EO, infrared, and Synthetic Aperture Radar (SAR) MASINT. That agreement redefined GEOINT so as to do the following:

> To incorporate all Overhead Non-Imaging Infrared (ONIR) and space-borne Imagery Derived MASINT. This definition is in keeping with the DNI memo of 22 July 2005 transferring responsibility for tasking, processing, exploitation [and] dissemination of all overhead electro-optical and radar MASINT phenomenologies, including overhead non-imaging infrared.[3]

Notice that this action removed only "space-borne Imagery Derived MASINT" from the MASINT definition, thus leaving airborne imagery-derived MASINT where it remains today with the MASINT discipline.

As with all sudden organizational changes in direction, there was good news and there were challenges.

Here was the good news:

- NGA had a faster growing budget, with a smaller percentage of civilians on the payroll and thus more flexibility to address MASINT funding issues.
- NGA was inherently a collection and exploitation agency rather than an all-source agency.
- NGA had ready access and the delivery means to a much larger set of customers.

- NGA had acquisition authority and thus understood how to execute more effectively.
- NGA had an RDT&E organization, the InnoVision Directorate.
- NGA was happy to now claim some collection capability of their own.

The challenges were mostly cultural:

- NGA was accustomed to scientific personnel being support people, not mainstream data producers and intelligence producers.
- NGA middle managers had little time, patience, or motivation to support insertion of low spatial resolution product lines into their processes.
- NGA products did not usually require the higher level of characterization and calibration of their sensors that MASINT requires.
- The ONIR National Imagery Interpretability Rating Scale (NIIRS) rating was less than 1.0 in an agency that valued imagery with very high NIIRS ratings over everything else.

To overcome some of these challenges, the director of NGA did the following:

- Required specialized familiarization training for all deputy directors and for all senior personnel seeking promotions
- Established a flag-rank civilian manager co-located at NASIC to stand up an NGA Geospatial Intelligence Advancement Testbed to leverage the NASIC MASINT experience as now an integral part of the National System for Geospatial Intelligence (NSG), as well as to lead the integrated NGA Support Team already in place at NASIC
- Renamed ONIR to OPIR, which emphasized 'persistence', the trait that was considered a strength within NGA, even by those imagery analysts who favored high resolution over all else
- Normalized Advanced Geospatial Intelligence (AGI), a transition term which included OPIR, into all NGA processes and functions as quickly as possible to emphasize that middle managers were now accountable for treating it just like all other forms of GEOINT, including using it in all products and reports.

Unfortunately, it is not clear that enough visibility remained to allow for an unbiased evaluation of organizational performance, other than anecdotal.

MASINT Primary Subdisciplines

MASINT has six distinct components, or subdisciplines, as shown in Figure 6.4. Though shown as separate, they often overlap with each other and with other INTs, especially with GEOINT and SIGINT. Some of them are

Figure 6-4   The MASINT Subdisciplines

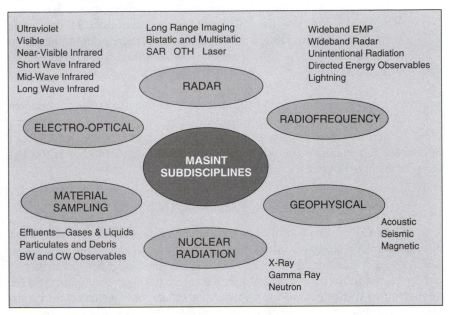

associated with measurements made in the electromagnetic spectrum, others with specific collection devices, and yet others with scientific measurements of phenomenology.

The goal of this section is to familiarize the reader with the different subdisciplines that make up MASINT, what might give rise to their observables, and some representative signatures to demonstrate how MASINT information might be used. In general, most intelligence agencies treat MASINT as one of their most closely guarded sources of information. Without violating those confidences, this section will also provide some insight into the utility of each of these subdisciplines, either separately or in combination with other subdisciplines.

Most of the signatures derived from MASINT are the result of collection in some part of the electromagnetic spectrum. The signatures are representative of electromagnetic energy being either emitted by an object or reflected from it. Three of the MASINT subdisciplines depend on these phenomena:

- EO MASINT relies on natural emissions, solar reflections, or emissions from artificially heated objects or events, such as explosives or rocket engine exhausts (often observable in the infrared region of the EM spectrum) that produce a characteristic signature.

- Radar MASINT depends on obtaining a signature from the energy reflected or retransmitted by a target toward the radar receiver.
- RF MASINT obtains its signature from unintentional RF emissions from man-made objects, from natural events such as lightning, or in some cases from very broadband emissions of highly energetic explosive events.

Once signatures have been validated, they can be used to either analyze a newly collected data set to determine its deviation from the norm or can often be automated to classify or even uniquely identify the specific target or event. Let's examine these three first and then discuss the MASINT signatures that are not electromagnetic in nature.

Electro-optical MASINT

EO MASINT involves measuring all physical phenomena associated with a target or scene—spatial, spectral, radiometric, polarimetric, phase (for active sources), temporal—and then analyzing those optical or infrared emissions to determine operating characteristics, material composition, temperature, and other unique signatures that are used to characterize an object, facility, or event. It is closely tied to GEOINT, because the same sensors often provide both imagery and signatures.

All objects emit electromagnetic energy both naturally and as a result of human actions. All matter (solids, liquids, and gases) at temperatures above absolute zero emits energy, mostly in the thermal (infrared) regions of the spectrum, as shown in Figure 6.5. Of primary intelligence importance are the emissive signatures created by explosions (especially nuclear explosions), facilities, and vehicles, as the figure shows. This emitted energy may be used to obtain a signature that is unique to a particular material object, or class of objects.

To illustrate the use of signatures, let's start with various classes of battlefield explosions. An easily understood example of a *temporal signature* (radiometric intensity vs. time) might be that collected by an EO radiometer of intensity (or brightness) of the *radiant emittance* from a series of battlefield weapons being employed—detonations, rocket exhaust plumes, and gun muzzle flashes. Figure 6.6 shows an example of this. If a MASINT analyst obtained a new data set from an unidentified target and compared it to these "known" signatures, he could readily classify the data set as an explosion and type or classify the *signature data* to a known temporal signature of certain classes of explosive devices.

If one desires to know what size weapon generated the signature data, Figure 6.7, which shows the temporal signatures of flashes from differing guns, would allow an even finer grain characterization of the EO sensor observation. Therefore, careful inspection of the magnitude, duration, and shape of the gun flash signature in Figure 6.6, given knowledge of the finer grain signatures in Figure 6.7, would lead a MASINT analyst to conclude that the gun muzzle flash is indeed from medium caliber gun.

Figure 6-5   MASINT Use of the Electro-optical Spectrum

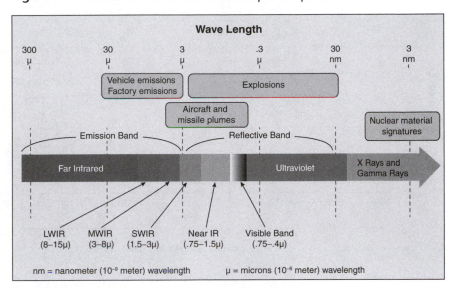

Source: Created by authors from an original figure (Figure 1-5) in Clark's *The Technical Collection of Intelligence.*

Figure 6-6   Temporal Signatures of Battlefield Events

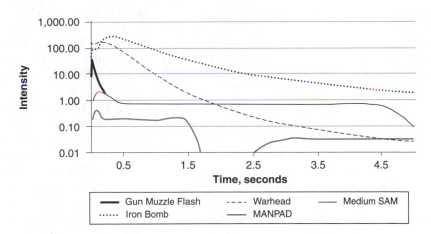

Source: Dr. James Lisowski, "Signatures," Memorandum for John Morris, April 5, 2014.

Note that the rapid rise time, the total intensity, the duration of the intensity, and more gradual decay time when taken together can literally "fingerprint" the explosive device as well as provide specific information about the explosive performance of this particular device.

Figure 6-7   Temporal Signatures of Differing Guns

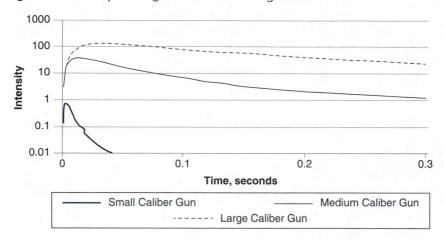

Source: Dr. James Lisowski, "Signatures," Memorandum for John Morris, April 5, 2014.

Many other signatures of intelligence importance in the optical band are *spectral signatures*. The interaction of EO energy or heat with matter can cause the emission of energy in specific parts of the spectrum. This can be observed during daylight hours due to sunlight stimulation or as the release of emissions at night after heating during the day. The resulting signature will be unique to the matter that emits the energy. A rule of thumb as to where in the spectrum to look for these signatures is as follows: solids—visible/near-visible infrared/short wave infrared; liquids—short wave/midwave infrared; gases—midwave/longwave infrared. Spectral signatures, therefore, can be used to identify individual solids, liquids, or gases—alone or in mixtures.

Once one has addressed radiometric intensity and spectral content of signatures, another key component of an EO signature of an object is its polarization of the electromagnetic wave. All electromagnetic waves, RF or optical, are polarized, meaning that the electric field vibrates in a specific direction. *Polarimetry* is the measurement of the polarization of electro-magnetic energy, and a polarimeter is used to make these measurements. Optical polarimetry is often called *ellipsometry*. EO energy emitted by the sun is randomly polarized, meaning that the polarization changes constantly in random fashion. But when sunlight is reflected from a man-made object, the reflection will likely be polarized linearly in a preferential direction cre-ating a specular or glint. One might think of polarization as a measure of roughness or smoothness of the observed object. For example, although EO energy emitted by the sun is randomly polarized, when it shines upon a pol-ished surface it might reflect in a preferential direction thus exhibiting linear polarization and giving rise to a specular or glint. On the other hand, a bead-blasted or uniformly rough surface would diffuse even polarized light, such as from a laser source, and scatter it from the bead-blasted surface in a lambertian manner, uniformly in all directions, with no evidence of a specular or glint.

The EO spectrum in Figure 6-5 also indicates that radioactive substances emit signatures in the form of gamma rays. These are discussed in the section on nuclear MASINT.

One of the early operational applications of EO MASINT was in the DSP, which collected what are now described as OPIR signatures. For many years, the DSP satellite was the primary sensor for OPIR collection. It has been replaced by the Space Based Infrared System (SBIRS). These satellites were designed to provide early warning of missile launches based on detecting and tracking the intense heat of the missile exhaust. These satellites measure energy wavelengths and strength in the infrared band and determine target locations and movements.

The U.S. Vela satellites dating from the 1960s carried a device called the bhangmeter designed to detect the dual flash from an atmospheric nuclear explosion. The bhangmeter technique was operationally tested in 1961 aboard a modified U.S. KC-135B aircraft monitoring the Soviet test of a hydrogen bomb nicknamed Tsar Bomba, the most powerful nuclear weapon ever detonated.

One of the rapidly expanding areas of EO MASINT is spectral sensing, which was introduced in the GEOINT chapter. Spectral sensing provides a graphic of energy versus frequency or wavelength. This graphic represents radiant intensity versus wavelength at an instant in time. The number of spectral bands in a sensor system determines the amount of detail that can be obtained about the source of the object being viewed. Sensor systems, both radiometers and spectrometers, derive their names from the following simplified definitions:

- multispectral (2 to 99 bands)
- hyperspectral (100 to 1,000 bands)
- ultraspectral (1,000+ bands)

The characteristic emission and absorption spectra in each wavelength of the spectral band serve to fingerprint or define the makeup of the feature that was observed. The intensity of emissions from an object is a function of several conditions including its temperature, surface properties or material, and how fast it is moving.

More bands provide more discrete information, or greater resolution, but not necessarily more intelligence. For many intelligence applications, only the signature from a few bands is enough, and a multispectral scanner is adequate. In the case of most lasers, for example, ultraspectral wavelength detection is required; however, that can be done by monitoring one specific spectral line that is characteristic of the laser.

Radar MASINT

Often called RADINT, radar MASINT requires that we illuminate targets with electromagnetic energy and analyze the reflected energy. Radar can produce several types of signatures that have MASINT value. At the macro level, radar can provide location, velocity, and acceleration signatures that allow assessments of the performance of missiles and aircraft. At the micro level, radars can obtain signatures that indicate the configuration and composition of targets and even can produce images of targets such as aircraft, missile warheads, and satellites. Figure 6.8 shows the parts of the RF spectrum in which some important MASINT radars operate.

RADINT collection provides information on radar cross sections and radar reflectance and absorption characteristics. It also is used for tracking targets of intelligence interest, obtaining precise spatial measurements of components, and observing motion of dynamic targets. In these roles, radars are an important contributor to air and space situational awareness.

Several different types of radars collect specialized types of RADINT, as indicated in Figure 6-8.

OTH radars have for decades been used to monitor air traffic and ballistic missile launches in denied areas for intelligence. OTH radar operates in or near the high frequency band, where radio waves are reflected from the ionosphere—the phenomenon that allows international radio broadcasts to be received from stations thousands of miles away.

Figure 6-8   MASINT Use of the Radio Frequency Spectrum

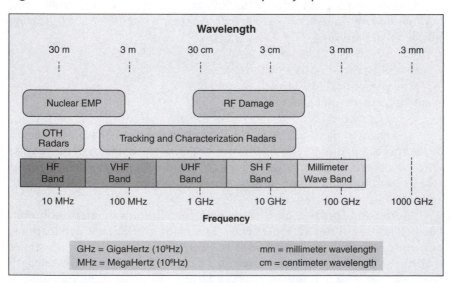

Source: Created by authors from an original figure (Figure 1-4) in Clark's *The Technical Collection of Intelligence.*

A historical example of OTH radar for U.S. MASINT collection was the 440L. The Air Force developed an OTH forward scatter radar called 440L during the 1960s to detect missile launches from Chinese or Soviet territory. A series of high-frequency radio transmitters and receivers on either side of the Sino-Soviet landmass produced continuous signals that bounced between the ionosphere and the surface of the earth until reaching the receiving stations. Any disturbances in the pattern indicated missiles penetrating the ionosphere. Atmospheric nuclear tests also disrupted the signals produced by 440L transmitters, so the radars also were used to monitor nuclear weapons testing.[4]

Most radars can be used for target detection and tracking. Some, though, are built explicitly to conduct MASINT, due to either their placement or their design and calibration. The AN/FPS-17 was deployed to satisfy S&TI collection requirements during the Cold War. It allowed the derivation of missile trajectories on launches from the USSR test range at Kapustin Yar. It also allowed the identification of Earth satellite launches from Kapustin Yar, the calculation of a satellite's ephemeris (position and orbit), and the synthesis of booster rocket performance. A tracking radar called the AN/FPS-79 was subsequently co-located with the AN/FPS-17 and provided an additional capability for estimating the configuration and dimensions of satellites or missiles and observing the reentry of manned or unmanned vehicles.[5] Figure 6.9 shows the coverage of missile trajectories that the radar obtained.

Figure 6-9 Missile Trajectory Coverage of the AN/FPS-17 Radar

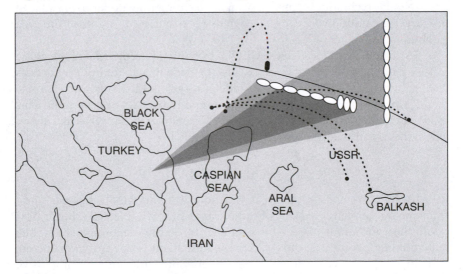

Source: Central Intelligence Agency, "The Diyarbkir Radar," *Studies in Intelligence,* v.8 no.4, https://www .cia.gov/library/center-for-the-study-of-intelligence/kent-csi/vol8no4/html/v08i4a05p_0001.htm

Long-range imaging radars, mostly operating in the microwave band, obtain a unique signature that is used to identify and characterize a target. That signature also is used to identify the target's mission or purpose. These RADINT targets include satellites, missiles, ships, aircraft, and battlefield vehicles.

- The ARPA Lincoln C-band Observable Radar (ALCOR) is located on the Kwajalein Atoll in the western Pacific. It has two missions: monitoring ABM testing by tracking reentry vehicles launched from the United States, and imaging of satellites.
- The Haystack radar, located in Massachusetts, uses its 120-foot diameter X band radar to produce images of satellites.

Laser radars were introduced in the EO MASINT section, in the context of collecting and analyzing the signal from an opponent's laser radars. But laser radars also are used for collection of the reflected signal from a target, and the product is used to identify materials at a distance. Many chemical and biological agents, and spoil from excavations, have characteristic fluorescence spectra when exposed to UV and visible light, so UV or visible lasers are used for fluorescence sensing. One might think of this as a very specialized form of spectroscopy.

Bistatic and multistatic radars have the transmitter and receiver(s) widely separated. Multistatic radars have more than one receiver. The geometry allows MASINT specialists to obtain more information about targets than is possible with a collocated transmitter and receiver. The 440L radar, discussed earlier, was multistatic as well as being an OTH radar. It is also possible create a bistatic or multistatic radar using what are called passive radar techniques—that is, using an existing noncooperative radar in the target area and processing the signals received from targets in the area to obtain intelligence.

SARs were introduced in the GEOINT chapter. Exploitation of the phase history data from these radars today also provide image quality products as well as help to provide evidence of hidden targets and changes detection— that is, what has happened in an area between radar views of the region. This usage of radars was discussed in the GEOINT chapter, but it relies heavily on techniques traditionally associated with MASINT.

Radio Frequency MASINT

RF MASINT, previously known as wideband RF and RINT, depends upon receiving the same frequencies of radio waves that SIGINT uses. But it processes them in unique ways—for example, to determine equipment status; if a computer is powered on; if electrical equipment is operating; or merely if energy is spread across a very broad bandwidth, indicating an impulsive signal in the time domain. RF MASINT concentrates not necessarily on finding a specific device but on characterizing the signatures of a class of devices, based on their intentional and unintentional radio emissions and in some cases determining their operational status or even fingerprinting them.

Unintentional Radiation

Man-made systems emit electromagnetic energy both intentionally and unintentionally. This component of RF MASINT involves the collection and analysis of RINT or spurious emissions from military and civil engines, power sources, weapons systems, electronic systems, machinery, equipment, instruments, or "leaky" electronic containers. One can, for example, determine the frequency to which a receiver is tuned by detecting the frequency of an oscillator inside a superheterodyne receiver. Truck and tank engines radiate electromagnetic energy from spark plugs. Electrical generators emit a strong signal associated with the generator's rotor movement. These emissions create a signature that can have intelligence use for locating a vehicle, identifying it, and tracking it as it moves. Leaving an opening in an electronic system, such as an open access door in a radar van, can give rise to an unintentional signal with a signal strength and frequency that relate to the size and shape of the opening and the intermediate frequency of the radar, even in standby mode.

Electromagnetic Pulses and Other Energetic Explosions

Another important category of RF MASINT concerns signatures that are obtained from explosions (especially nuclear explosions) and explosive power supplies for DEW. The parts of the RF spectrum where such signatures are obtained are shown in Fgure 6-8. Nuclear and large conventional explosions produce RF energy. The characteristics of the EMP will vary with altitude and burst size. Controlled explosions for generating the power that drives certain classes of pulsed high energy lasers and rail guns is of particular intelligence interest. These energetic explosions can give rise to both EO and RF observables.

Radio Frequency Weapons and Charged Particle Beams

RF weapons, based on the fact that a powerful burst of electromagnetic energy can damage sensitive electronics, have been deployed by a number of military organizations. They are particularly useful for causing missiles to miss their target as well as for such mundane tasks as clearing minefields for advancing troop and armor movements. These directed energy weapons are usually considered tactical in nature, and detecting their testing or use in combat is a mission of RF MASINT. Charged particle beams (CPBs), on the other hand, are considered to be strategic weapons, usually considered for countering ballistic missiles, and would be considered as a technological surprise. Think of a CPB as a controlled superbolt of lightning, following an ionized path directly to its target. The only way to avoid destruction is not to be in its path. Even the RF signature is somewhat similar to that of a superbolt of lightning. This discussion probably raises the question of neutral particle beams (NPBs), whose use would also constitute technological surprise in a missile defense system. Due to the physics of propagation of a neutral particle beam, their operation must occur in the electromagnetically neutral vacuum of outer space, once a missile rises above the ionosphere of planet Earth. Observations of such a test are more reliable using UV detection rather than RF.

Geophysical MASINT

This subdiscipline exploits both the audible and the very low frequency portion of the acoustic spectrum—that portion below what humans can hear—in order to detect vibrations from operating machinery, underground explosions, or even pressure differences created by opening and closing vault doors.

Geophysical MASINT depends on obtaining one of two signature types:

- Magnetic signatures are obtained by measuring slight variations in the earth's magnetic field, produced either by the presence of ferromagnetic materials such as steel or the presence of a large underground cavity such as a tunnel.
- Acoustic signatures are collected in the air, in the water, and underground, to allow the characterization of air and ground vehicle traffic, ship and submarine movements, and underground explosions. The collection spectrum for these signatures includes audible sound (above 20 Hz) and infrasound (below 20 Hz and usually not detectable by the human ear).

Geophysical MASINT has been defined as involving "phenomena transmitted through the earth (ground, water, atmosphere) and manmade structures including emitted or reflected sounds, pressure waves, vibrations, and magnetic field or ionosphere disturbances."[6]

This is a very broad definition, and it includes several distinct subdisciplines, discussed next.

Underwater Acoustics

ACOUSTINT derived from underwater sound is usually called *ACINT*. ACINT relies on a class of acoustic sensors that detect sound in water. Sound travels much better in water than in air. Underwater sound created by ships and submarines can be detected at distances of several hundred kilometers.

Underwater acoustics depend on the hydrophone, a type of microphone designed to operate underwater. Hydrophones convert sound to electrical energy, which then can undergo additional signal processing, or can be transmitted to a receiving station for more sophisticated signal processing.

Navies use a variety of passive acoustic sensors in antisubmarine warfare, both tactical and strategic. For tactical use, passive hydrophones, both on ships and airdropped sonobuoys, are used extensively in undersea warfare. They can detect targets even farther away than detection with active sonar but generally will not have the precision location of active sonar. However, passive sonar does have the advantage of not revealing the position of the sensor.

The United States has an elaborate network of such sensors, called the Integrated Undersea Surveillance System (IUSS). It comprises a mix of hydrophone arrays deployed on the ocean floor called the sound surveillance system (SOSUS) and arrays towed behind naval vessels called the surveillance towed array sensor system (SURTASS).

Acoustics in Air

Some acoustic sensors detect sound traveling through the atmosphere or in the ground near the surface and therefore function only at comparatively short ranges (a few meters to a few kilometers). The sounds of powerful vehicular engines can be detected and used to classify if not fingerprint the vehicles and their movements. The intelligence product of such collection is usually called ACOUSTINT.

Seismic and Teleseismic Sensing

The term *seismic sensing* is usually applied to detecting sound that travels through the earth. Seismic intelligence is defined as "the passive collection and measurement of seismic waves or vibrations in the earth's surface."[7]

At short ranges, seismic sensors called *geophones* (microphones emplaced in the earth or in a structure) can obtain a number of signatures of intelligence value. When emplaced in the earth, geophones can detect and often identify specific types of foot or vehicle traffic. The challenge for these seismic sensors often is not so much in detecting people and trucks as it is in separating out the false alarms generated by wind, thunder, rain, earth tremors, and animals. The greatest intelligence value from this specialized microphone typically occurs when the geophone can be placed directly in a building structure; it then can monitor activity in the building or in an underground facility.

One strategic application of seismic intelligence makes use of the science of seismology to locate and characterize nuclear testing, especially underground testing. This special category of seismic sensing is called *teleseismic sensing*. Teleseismic sensing involves the collection, processing, and exploitation of infrasound that travels deep in the earth. Depending on the strength of the source, such infrasound can be detected at distances of thousands of kilometers.

Teleseismic sensors also can characterize large conventional explosions that are used in testing the high-explosive components of nuclear weapons. Teleseismic intelligence also can help locate such things as large underground construction projects.

Since many areas of the world have a great deal of natural seismic activity, teleseismic MASINT requires a continuous measurement process so that the signatures associated with natural seismic behavior are well known and variations from naturally occurring signatures can be identified.

Magnetometry

A magnetometer is a specialized type of sensor used to measure variations in the strength and direction of the magnetic field in the vicinity of the sensor. The measurements from a magnetometer can be used to identify the signatures of vehicles on land and submarines underwater.

Combining Signatures

Many operational MASINT devices make use of different MASINT technologies to obtain a more complete picture of the target. This is especially true for the combination of RF MASINT and geophysical MASINT. An unattended vehicle sensing device, deployed near a roadway, might combine geophysical and radiofrequency MASINT. Acoustic or seismic sensing might allow the sensor to identify the presence of the vehicle, and the RF MASINT signature would allow identifying the vehicle type (such as tank, truck, or automobile) or even the specific vehicle.

Materials Science

Materials MASINT relies on signatures produced by the processing and analysis of gas, liquid, or solid samples. This enables analysts to determine chemical or biological composition of a substance and is critical in defense against CBR threats. The unique signature data of effluents and debris from explosives (such as those used in improvised explosive devices [IEDs]) allows determination of the origin of the explosives. Signatures produced by sampling effluents from missile propellants allow for typing the missile propellant and thus assessing the missile performance.

This subdiscipline divides generally into the two subfields of materials sensing and materials sampling.

- *Materials sensing* makes use of devices that sense chemical or physical changes in the environment immediately surrounding the sensor. These sensors measure phenomena within an object or at short ranges and typically detect such things as temperature, contaminants, nuclear radiation, or electric or magnetic fields.

- *Materials sampling* involves acquiring small quantities or traces of a material and using forensic processes to determine its nature. So materials sampling includes the collection and analysis of trace elements, particulates, effluents, and debris. Such materials are released into the atmosphere, water, or Earth by a wide range of industrial processes, tests, and military activities. Air sampling equipment, carried aloft by reconnaissance aircraft to detect the debris from atmospheric nuclear tests, is an example of such a sampling activity.

Materials sensing and sampling are important for many areas of intelligence interest. They support military planning and operations. They are used to identify nuclear testing, nuclear materials production and movement, and chemical warfare production. In that role, They are critical in defense against chemical, biological, and radiological threats (CBR) or nuclear, biological, and chemical (NBC) as well as more general safety and public health activities. Economic intelligence uses materials sampling to assess factory production. Materials collection can also include sensing or sampling for environmental monitoring, which increasingly is an intelligence concern because some governments and industrial enterprises attempt to conceal their pollution activities.

In intelligence applications, chemical signatures are used mostly to identify effluents from factories to determine what processes are being used in the factory. The most common requirement is to characterize facilities that are suspected of producing WMDs. Such characterization relies heavily on the ability to identify the signatures of chemical effluents from these facilities.

The sensors that detect chemical and biological materials of interest are developed by a number of companies in the United States, but the U.S. Department of Energy (DOE) national laboratories are leaders in this arena. Lawrence Livermore National Laboratory and Sandia National Laboratory, for example, have developed a range of sensors to detect explosives, chemicals, and biological agents.

Nuclear Intelligence

This MASINT specialty covers measurement and characterization of information derived from the nuclear radiation and physical phenomena associated with nuclear weapons, processes, materials, devices, or facilities. These measurements can help to locate storage sites and movements of nuclear materials. They can also glean intelligence from the signatures produced by nuclear testing.

Nuclear signatures are the physical, chemical, and isotopic characteristics that distinguish one nuclear or radiological material from another. Radiological signatures are created by emissions from radioactive material, in the form of alpha and beta particles and gamma rays. The specific combination of particles and rays emitted, along with the intensity of each type, constitutes a signature that allows for identification of the radioactive source material. The measurements that produce these signatures can be made only at very short ranges.

Nuclear monitoring can be done remotely or during onsite inspections of nuclear facilities. Data exploitation results in characterization of nuclear weapons, reactors, and materials. A number of systems detect and monitor the world for nuclear materials production and nuclear weapons testing.

A definite overlap exists between NUCINT and the nuclear analysis techniques in materials science, discussed earlier. The basic difference is that nuclear MASINT deals with the characteristics of real-time nuclear events, such as nuclear explosions, radioactive clouds from accidents or terrorism, and other types of radiation events. A materials scientist looking at the same phenomenon, however, will have a more microscopic view, doing such things as analyzing fallout particles from air sampling, ground contamination, or radioactive gases released into the atmosphere. So NUCINT divides into two broad categories: remote sensing of nuclear detonations, from the geophysical MASINT subdiscipline discussed earlier, or sensing either at very short ranges or by sampling.

Remote Sensing

Since the 1960s, the United States has operated satellites that are designed to detect nuclear weapons detonations. The sensors on these satellites detect the characteristic optical signature of a detonation, the EMP from a nuclear detonation, the X-rays and gamma rays emitted by the explosion, or all three. As discussed in the section on EO MASINT, beginning in 1963, the United States launched a series of Vela satellites that carried all three sensor types in orbits at approximately 73,000 miles altitude. Project Vela was developed and deployed by the United States to monitor compliance with the 1963 Partial Test Ban Treaty with the Soviet Union.

The DSP satellites replaced the Vela satellites during the 1970s and carried optical, X-ray, neutron, and gamma ray detectors to monitor nuclear events from within the atmosphere and out to deep space. The replacement for the DSP is the SBIRS, which carries sensors for detecting exoatmospheric detonations.

Airborne and Ground-Based Sampling

Above-ground testing produces an abundant amount of radioactive isotopes (called *radionuclides*) that can be detected. But underground testing also releases radioactive substances into the atmosphere. It is very difficult to contain the gases released in a nuclear explosion. If a nuclear test occurs, radioactive particles and gases might be vented at the time of the test or radioactive gases might subsequently seep out through the cracks in the rocks above the explosion.

A number of systems monitor the earth to detect nuclear explosions. In the U.S., this monitoring program dates back to August 1948, when the

U.S. Air Force created the Office of Atomic Energy-1 (AFOAT-1) and gave it responsibility for managing the Atomic Energy Detection System (AEDS). AFOAT-1 identified the first Soviet weapons test in 1949. It also tracked the production of fissile materials such as plutonium, based on atmospheric measurements of krypton-85 gas.[8]

AFOAT-1, subsequently renamed, did extensive acoustic, seismic, and radiological collection with the informed consent of host governments. Sometimes, the host governments could not be apprised of the collection effort, and the Air Force unit conducted unilateral operations. In 1961, it proposed to monitor secretly, from Libyan territory, French nuclear tests in Algeria.[9] Such operations from U.S. embassies and consulates could be conducted without host government approval. For example, a compact air monitoring unit called the B/20-4 was installed in embassies and consulates to measure the levels of gases such as krypton-85, allowing the U.S. to refine estimates of world-wide plutonium production.[10]

After the U.S ratified the 1963 limited nuclear test ban treaty, the AEDS was expanded with the deployment of ground filter units at a number of U.S. embassies, sometimes without the permission of host governments. These units collected airborne particulates that resulted from nuclear tests, and allowed assessments to be made of weapons design, yield, and composition.[11]

The Air Force has conducted airborne sampling missions. In an effort to measure plutonium production by the USSR and China, high altitude air sampling flights were staged by RB-57F aircraft from an Argentine air base in the mid-1960s. Called project CROWFLIGHT, these missions used an Air Weather Service cover. The purpose of the flight was kept secret from the Argentine government.[12]

Another airborne sampling effort by the U.S. Air Force followed the reactor meltdown and explosion at Chernobyl, USSR, on April 25, 1986. A WC-135 departed McClellan Air Force Base in California for RAF Mildenhall Air Base, England, on April 29 and encountered debris from the event north of Scandinavia. It was the first of forty-two air sampling sorties that would be flown all over the globe with WC-135, WC-130, and B-52 aircraft. The first mission encountered a visible cloud of debris about seven miles in diameter and more than 500 feet thick. The cloud gave the flight crew inflight positive readings that normally are encountered only after atmospheric nuclear explosions. Over the next ten days, mission aircraft encountered Chernobyl debris over the Pacific Ocean, Europe, and the Mediterranean.[13]

How MASINT Is Managed

During the past few decades, as discussed elsewhere in this book, the U.S. IC evolved into a functional management structure for the INTs. NSA was designated the functional manager for SIGINT, CIA for HUMINT, DIA for MASINT, and NGA for GEOINT.

For most of the collection INTs, this posed no serious problems because the process—from requirements to dissemination—was structurally within the purview of the functional manager. As discussed in the HUMINT chapter, collection of HUMINT is done by many agencies, but this is a manageable problem.

MASINT, though, had a serious management issue, even with a designated functional manager. Major MASINT subdisciplines always have had to rely on other INTs for collection. So a continuing issue is how to divide management responsibility for the MASINT process. Political and budgetary considerations, rather than technical ones, can therefore shape the definition of MASINT.

There is a natural tendency of any functional manager to define its collection programs so that they do not fall into another manager's realm of responsibility. For example, a HUMINT functional manager responsible for collecting material samples would undoubtedly prefer to have that effort defined as something other than "MASINT." And the Armed Forces Medical Intelligence Center does not treat its medical sampling efforts as MASINT. Yet both efforts fall within the MASINT definition. Not only oversight but also budgets will be affected by such definitions.

This is exactly what happened with the redefinition of GEOINT in 2005, as discussed in the section on the history of MASINT. Traditional MASINT programs that involved imaging radar and imaging EO collection were redefined to be GEOINT if they were currently spaceborne or could be satellite based at some point in the future. Thus, those imagery-derived programs that were not specifically hosted in space—that is, airborne- and surface-based—remained with the MASINT discipline and were usually "owned" by the U.S. military service that operated them. However, this was not a well-known fact.

Nonetheless, the practicality of transferring all space-based responsibility of imagery-derived MASINT was dictated by the need to assign one specific agent as functional manager that could best serve the needs of the most customers. That agent was then given overall funding oversight authority for growing the capability and serving the customer base. NGA was well positioned to do that.

An additional management challenge comes from the tendency of some to describe MASINT as "everything else." Occasionally, IC leaders and former leaders attempting to simplify the explanation of MASINT will say, "If it isn't SIGINT, HUMINT, or GEOINT, then it's MASINT." This simplistic approach may be convenient in dealing with a complex topic, but it can come across as technically vague at best. Not only does it leave too much room for ambiguity but it ignores Open Source Intelligence (OSINT), which is a distinct INT by itself. By omission, it also implies that foreign materiel exploitation (FME) is a subdiscipline of MASINT, although FME is generally considered to be distinct and separate.

Structure

Within the United States, the director of DIA is the functional manager for MASINT. In that role, the director of DIA provides guidance to program managers, recommends a MASINT budget to the DNI, and directly responds to Congress in order to fully explain the utility of MASINT and the intent of the MASINT budget request. In addition, the director of DIA promotes common standards, education, and training; establishes security policy; manages current requirements of intelligence operations; and solicits or validates future community requirements for new capabilities and thus for MASINT plans and program development. MASINT management and oversight is handled by a combination of three organizations, discussed next.

The Board of Governors

This is a senior-level IC group, chaired by the director of DIA. The board is generally populated by the other defense and IC directors. It is charged to formulate guidance for the future direction of the MASINT enterprise, achieve unity of purpose, establish a common vision, and address issues of mutual concern to the MASINT enterprise and its stakeholders.

The National MASINT Office

This is another joint IC–DoD organization, subordinate to the director of DIA, who manages and executes—on behalf of the DoD and the IC— MASINT services of common concern and other MASINT-related activities. The chief of the National MASINT Office (NMO) is dual-hatted as the chairman, MASCOM, discussed next. NMO provides the means and mechanisms to assist the director of DIA in leading the decentralized MASINT community as a fully integrated enterprise. Specific functions executed by NMO include but are not limited to strategy, policy, and programs; mission integration, which encompasses requirements and asssessments; and architectures in its broadest sense.

The National MASINT Committee

This multiagency group serves as an IC sounding board on MASINT issues, and advises the USD(I) and DNI on the status and strategic direction for MASINT capabilities. The National MASINT Requirements Subcommittee of MASCOM validates and prioritizes MASINT collection requirements for the IC. The MASCOM staff is now fully integrated with the NMO, with the chief of NMO dual-hatted as the chairman of the MASINT Committee.

These three organizations manage what is called the U.S. MASINT System. The MASINT System comprises a combination of technology, policies, capabilities, doctrine, activities, people, data, and communities that are necessary to produce MASINT in an integrated multi-intelligence, multi-domain environment. MASINT System participants include the IC, the Joint Staff, the military departments (to include the Services), the Combatant Commands, and selected international and civil partners. The MASINT System provides the framework for tasking, collection, processing, exploitation, and dissemination (TCPED) and R & D activities that support varied intelligence solutions for national policymakers and the DoD community.

Collection

In the United States, MASINT collection is based on the guidance provided by the National MASINT Requirements System. This is an intranet-based collection management application that supports the creation and submission of MASINT requirements and tracking of user satisfaction. NMO assesses the needs for future collection capabilities based upon shortcomings in the current architecture.

MASINT is not collected by any single intelligence organization—quite the contrary. Collection is performed by military personnel and civilians in separate organizations that often have little or no ongoing relationships. Some MASINT disciplines—materials science and NUCINT, for example—require detailed laboratory equipment and analysis, often taking weeks to reach conclusions that are subsequently documented in lengthy technical reports. At the other extreme, MASINT sometimes relies on relatively unsophisticated sensors with on-board processing that provides immediate indication of an activity of interest—bhangmeters and EMP sensors, for example.

Some MASINT is collected using dedicated systems that are specifically designed to acquire the detailed measurements and signatures required for a particular mission area. In other cases, MASINT is collected by specialized processing of the sensor output from operational or commercial systems that do not have a primary MASINT mission. MASINT, in some cases, includes the specialized processing of sensor data from the SIGINT and GEOINT disciplines.[14] Many MASINT subdisciplines also depend on HUMINT for success—material collection and sensor emplacement being examples.

To summarize, MASINT collection is usually under the active management of organizations other than the functional manager—executive agents (direct tasking by the functional manager), other INT managers (negotiated tasking or serendipity collection), or operational forces (cooperative tasking). This is the most difficult to manage, but it clearly builds relationships based on value-added results.

Processing, Exploitation, and Analysis

Each of the six MASINT subdisciplines relies on specialized processing and exploitation technologies that are unique to that subdiscipline. And the expertise required for analyzing the signatures usually differs from one subdiscipline to another.

Even within subdisciplines, separate organizational structures, or "stovepipes," are created based on the specialized expertise and technologies that are needed. Following are two subdisciplines that are typical of this point:

Radar MASINT

Radar processing and exploitation depends heavily on digital signal processing and sophisticated algorithms for extracting signatures from the raw radar data, which may include heavy ground clutter.

- SARs illuminate targets while the radar is moving in a constant stable direction and maintain highly accurate measurements of both amplitude and phase of the returned signal relative to the transmitted signal. This allows for a long "synthetic" aperture the length of their flight path while illuminating the target. The larger the synthetic aperture, the higher the resolution of the image. A number of different advanced processing algorithms have been developed to extract signature data to identify many different characteristics to include the changes in a scene that have occurred since the last images of the scene were taken.
- Precision line-of-sight signature and tracking radars, such as Cobra Judy and its replacement Cobra King, provide a phase one interim product on board its mobile platform; however, the complete data set is dispatched to MIT Lincoln Lab as soon as possible after collection. Detailed processing and analysis can be a lengthy process; however, this in-depth analysis is needed in order to determine small but significant changes in a missile system that may constitute a treaty violation.[15]
- Long-range imaging radars, on the other hand, are usually focused exclusively on space objects and must track the target, usually from horizon to horizon in orbit above them, in order to obtain enough aspect angle change for a reasonable resolution image to be formed. In many respects, this is much like SAR image processing, except the target is moving rather than the SAR radar. These radars typically can transmit waveforms of much greater RF bandwidth than those of the precision LOS tracking radars, thus allowing better spatial resolution of their images. Processing just a single data set equates to "large data processing" in the modern language of advanced signal processing, sometimes requiring the use of supercomputers.
- Over-the-horizon (OTH) radars rely on complex algorithms and Doppler frequency processing to extract targets of interest from the ground clutter. As explained earlier in this chapter, OTH radars always use a portion of the high frequency (HF) spectrum with its longer wavelengths to reflect from the lower side of the ionosphere

and extend the radar's detection range to "over the horizon." This type of data processing and analysis is so uniquely different in appearance that it is often referred to as an art rather than a science by those who are not well schooled in radar signal processing theory.

- Bistatic or multistatic radars depend on special processing algorithms to deal with the complex geometries that are involved. For example, the bistatic radar cross section (RCS) is equivalent to that of a monostatic radar that is located along the bisector of the angle formed by the transmitter-to-target and target-to-receiver lines of sight. Expertise in one of these radar specialties does not readily transfer to another. These were the first types of radars invented and were operationally employed in Europe during World War II.

Geophysical MASINT

In this subdiscipline, the specialties of analyzing magnetic, acoustic, and seismic or teleseismic signatures are separated organizationally.

- Monitoring of seismic and teleseismic events relies on recognizing the physical signatures that are associated with nuclear explosions. These signatures are the basis for (1) concluding that an event has occurred (detection); (2) determining the location of the event (location); (3) discriminating the event from nonexplosive phenomena, such as earthquake activity (identification); and (4) in the case of a suspected explosion, evaluating the yield, its nuclear or nonnuclear nature, and the source of the event (characterization and attribution).
- For geophysical MASINT, natural geological events, such as seismic activity and earthquakes, can serve to increase the noise level in certain regions of the world and thus make it difficult to characterize an event.

Similar observations can be made involving processing of each of the MASINT subdisciplines to some extent.

Dissemination, Storage, and Access

Each subdiscipline, as noted previously, requires different scientific and engineering expertise and uses different technologies. Each also has a different customer base with different requirements, although there may be an overlap in a few cases. So separate management structures also are necessary for disseminating the finished product, storing it, and arranging for searches on the signature databases.

Next, we will continue the previous two examples.

Radar MASINT

Line-of-sight precision radars, OTH radars, long-range imaging radars, SAR radars, and bistatic and multistatic radars all have different targets and different customers. In general, NASIC retains the intelligence databases for all radar, EO/IR, and RF MASINT event collections. All raw data are kept for a relatively short period of time, while event data tends to be kept for a number of years depending upon available computer storage. DIA/NMO specifies the minimum standards for retention. Data and signature products are provided to some customers on a routine basis and to others on an as-requested basis.

Geophysical MASINT

Magnetic signatures and underwater acoustics typically are of interest to the Navy. Acoustic signatures in a battlefield environment have Army customers. Seismic and teleseismic signatures have treaty monitoring organizations as customers for potential nuclear explosions, civil emergency response teams as customers for earthquakes, and military commanders as customers for information about explosions in the battlefield. The Air Force plays a prominent role in this component of geophysical MASINT.

Managing the Transition to Operational Use

The need for talented professionals with technical expertise is a defining characteristic of MASINT. MASINT depends—for its effectiveness—on specialists with a scientific or technical background. It draws heavily on physical, chemical, and electrical expertise. Such scientists and technicians usually are not professionally developed within the IC. They often come from academia and have current scientific knowledge from experimentation and research.[16] This is yet one more reason why the NMO maintains a solid relationship with the two service graduate schools, AFIT and the NPS. It is also the reason why AFIT has offered a MASINT Certificate Program since 2001 for graduate college credit or for continuing educational units (CEUs) for analysts to maintain MASINT standards for their jobs. In fact, many of the signatures explaining the different subdisciplines (or radar MASINT and EO MASINT) are used as teaching aids for the MASINT Certificate Program usually offered in Dayton, Ohio, but occasionally traveling to the Washington, DC, area so as to be accessible to more students who need the education and training.

Because of this close connection to academic research, MASINT long had more of a laboratory science nature than that of an operational INT. In recent years, though, MASINT has evolved into a mature means of detecting, identifying, and characterizing different threats in an operational environment quickly and efficiently. Its mission areas include supporting military operations, missile warning, counterproliferation, weapons acquisition, treaty monitoring, environmental activities, counterdrug operations, and counterterrorism.

Challenges to making this transition occur more quickly continue to be both real and perceptual. Consider the following:

- *Budget.* The United States is entering another period of DoD and IC budget reductions and reprioritization toward domestic issues. This will probably remain as the single most concerning issue.
- *Roles and responsibilities.* Those MASINT players with the technical capability do not have the acquisition responsibility of supporting war fighter operations.
- *Title 10 vs. Title 50.* U.S. law often creates stovepipes due to the way funding is appropriated, managed, and overseen by Congress. In this case, Title 10 reflects the manner in which funds supporting military operations may be expended. Congressional oversight is carried out by the Armed Services Committees. Title 50 is the public law dealing with oversight of intelligence activities and resources, and thus congressional oversight is carried out by the Intelligence Committees of the House and the Senate.

During times of tight budgets, these items may present special challenges for funding tightly controlled activities within stovepipes. Since MASINT is particularly useful to COCOMs for support to military operations, this area may require constant attention by the functional manager to define roles and relationships carefully and to sponsor routine exchanges with Congress in order to maximize performance of the U.S. MASINT System.

International MASINT

MASINT collectors worldwide have been developed largely to support military planning and military operations. Most of the MASINT sensors deployed to support four of the MASINT subdisciplines—radar, RF, geophysical, and materials science—have clearly defined tactical military purposes. The EO MASINT and NUCINT collectors are more oriented to strategic intelligence applications.

Only the United States has a distinct MASINT organization. The Commonwealth countries tend to manage their MASINT capabilities via their DoD organizations, with some subtle exceptions. Most other nations who have a capability have combined MASINT with either their SIGINT organization in some cases and in other cases with their GEOINT organization. This usually depends upon whether they are radar centric or imagery centric in their collection capabilities. Since both Russia and China have strong S & T capabilities, it is likely they have organizational focus to fully leverage their

S & T expertise, but these matters are not openly discussed in detail by their news media or on the Internet or in international conferences.

Electro-optical MASINT

Several countries operate imaging satellites that have a spectral sensing capability, including Japan, Taiwan (FORMOSAT), and France (SPOT 5 and Pleiades). Germany's EnMAP satellite is designed to provide hyperspectral imagery.

One country other than the United States has an OPIR satellite capability. The Russian Prognoz satellite has infrared detection capabilities similar to those provided by the U.S. DSP satellite system.[17] The Prognoz program dates from the 1970s with their first generation US-KS (Oko) space-based early warning system. In 1970, the USSR began development of the second-generation early warning system, the US-KMO Prognoz. In contrast to the first-generation system, which was designed to detect only launches of ICBMs from bases in U.S. territory, the US-KMO system was designed to provide coverage of submarine-launched ballistic missles from oceans as well. These satellites are being deployed in geosynchronous orbits, from which they provide coverage of most of the oceans. The US-KMO #8 was launched in 2012.[18]

Radar MASINT

Almost all countries have radar stations that are used for operational purposes—primarily monitoring air traffic. Many of these radars also are capable of providing MASINT worldwide; there exists a wide variety of sophisticated ground-based and seaborne radar systems that can be used for RADINT. And a few countries have developed radars with specific MASINT missions—primarily OTH radars and object identification radars.

Over-the-Horizon Radars

China reportedly developed its first skywave OTH radar back in 1967. Since the 1980s, two further installations may have been added to the inventory, with at least one system looking out into the China Sea area reportedly to track U.S. Navy fleet movements. China also has deployed at least one surface-wave OTH radar, intended to detect surface ship movements and low-altitude air activity beyond the visible horizon, out to about 300 km.[19]

Beginning in about 1970, Australia has developed a network of skywave OTH radars called Jindalee, currently deployed as the Jindalee Operational Radar Network (JORN). JORN comprises two operational radars and a R & D radar located in the Australian interior, providing coverage of ocean areas to the north and west of the continent. The three radars monitor air and ocean traffic in the region.

Russia has a history of building and deploying skywave OTH radars dating back to 1970. The USSR deployed two such radars, called Duga-1, that were intended to provide ballistic missile early warning by detecting missiles launched from U.S. territory during the boost phase. The radars apparently did not succeed in that mission, and subsequently the sites were abandoned.

In recent years, Russia has begun to deploy a new generation of such radars with a more manageable mission: detecting and tracking small aerial vehicles (such as cruise missiles and unmanned aerial vehicles) around the Russian periphery. The first such radar began operational service in December 2013. Called the 29B6 or Podsolnukh-E ("container-E"), the new radar is bistatic (transmitter and receiver stations are separated), as was the Duga-1. The transmitter is located near Gorodets on the outskirts of Nizhny Novgorod, with a receiver located 250 km away at Kovylkino, aligned to monitor the airspace west of Russia. A second 29B6, currently under construction in Russia's Eastern Military District, is scheduled for service entry in 2018.[20]

Object Identification Radars

Russia has developed several generations of missile defense and space tracking radars that have a secondary mission of providing MASINT about these targets. The Dnepr radars, dating to the 1960s, provide orbital information on satellites. The more powerful Daryal radars supplemented the older Dnepr radars during the 1970s. Both radars operate in the VHF frequency band. The newest generation radars are the Voronezh-M (VHF) and Voronezh-DM (UHF) radars that are currently being deployed.

Germany has one of the world's most sophisticated radars for obtaining MASINT on satellites. The tracking and imaging radar (TIRA) is located at the FGAN Research Institute for High Frequency Physics and Radar Techniques, near Bonn. It functions in many ways like the Haystack wideband long-range imaging radar discussed earlier. TIRA obtains radar data at 22.5 cm (L-band) and 1.8 cm (Ku-band) wavelengths and uses the data to produce radar images and perform feature based classification and identification. Features that are measured include orbital elements, satellite motion and maneuvers and orbital lifetimes. TIRA has produced numerous radar images of satellites, of the international space station, and of U.S. space shuttles.

Airborne and Spaceborne Radar MASINT

Airborne and spaceborne SARs primarily are intended to produce imagery, but many of them can produce MASINT. They are capable, for example, of providing change detection and polarization measurements. Germany's SAR-Lupe, TerraSAR-X, and TanDEM-X; India's RISAT; China's Yaogan Weixing SAR; Israel's TecSAR; and Italy's COSMO-SkyMed are all spaceborne SARs that are capable of obtaining MASINT signatures.

Radio Frequency MASINT

Since this subdiscipline is closely aligned with SIGINT collection for military applications, few acknowledge their capability in this area. However, one would assume that all countries with a sophisticated SIGINT capability also have an RF MASINT capability. The principal nonmilitary application is for detection and characterization of lightning. Since many universities around the world are actively engaged in research of this nature and since lightning is the largest natural cause of wildfires in large nations with remote regions, many countries have at least a rudimentary capability to collect wideband radio frequency.

Geophysical MASINT

Acoustic Sensing in Water

The sensing of underwater sound is widely used by naval forces of many countries, primarily for detecting, identifying, and tracking submerged submarines—though it also is used to identify surface ships. Russia, China, and India all have well-developed ACOUSTINT programs for anti-submarine warfare.[22] The British have developed towed sonar arrays that are sold commercially.

Magnetic Field Sensing

Russia, Australia, India, the United Kingdom, China, and France, among others, have deployed magnetic anomaly detectors on antisubmarine patrol aircraft. Several countries also have employed magnetic field sensors for short-range detection of vehicles.

Seismic Sensing

Military forces long have recognized the value of sensing ground vibrations due to foot or vehicle traffic. Sensors that can be deployed to recognize and classify vehicle signatures are increasingly used by ground forces worldwide. A combination of geophysical sensors seems to be the trend; Germany's ground sensor equipment (BSA), for example, uses a combination of seismic (geophone), magnetic, and acoustic (microphone) MASINT sensors for target detection and identification.

Teleseismic Sensing

Under the Comprehensive Nuclear-Test-Ban Treaty, an international network (the International Monitoring System, or IMS) monitors seismic events to detect and geolocate underground nuclear tests. Identification and further analysis of the results is a responsibility of the member states.[21] Russia has had a capability for such monitoring that dates back to the 1960s. The Borovoye seismic station in Kazakhstan detected underground nuclear explosions at the Nevada Test Site in the United States over the course of three decades, down to a yield of 2 to 5 kilotons. Aided by information from other seismic stations to identify the geological conditions of tests, the Borovoye site could estimate the yield of U.S. explosions with about 20 percent uncertainty.[23]

Materials Science

Many countries worldwide have developed sensors and methodologies for point and standoff detection of chemical, biological, radiological, nuclear, and explosive (CBRNE) materials. The threat of using these materials in terrorist attacks has spurred much of this development. Also, treaties limiting the production, use, and proliferation of such materials have required the establishment of international monitoring regimes.

Nuclear Intelligence

Nuclear sensing at borders around the world is driven by a concern about movement of nuclear materials for proliferation or for terrorist purposes. Several countries have passive gamma and neutron sensors that are intended to detect nuclear materials at choke points (primarily border crossings and ports). Much of this equipment was provided by the United States under the Proliferation Security Initiative. The sensors are capable, at short ranges, of detecting special nuclear materials (the fissile materials Uranium-235, Uranium-233, and Plutonium-239).

Russia has a highly developed NUCINT program that collects samples from nuclear testing.[24]

Treaties such as the Comprehensive Nuclear-Test-Ban Treaty and the Treaty on the Non-Proliferation of Nuclear Weapons led to the deployment of international monitoring networks that operate MASINT sensors. For example, eighty stations worldwide form the IMS Radionuclide Network, and forty of them monitor for isotopes of xenon gas that are diagnostic of nuclear explosions.

The Types of Intelligence Targets Against Which MASINT Works Best

In general, the MASINT primary value is in characterizing objects and facilities. Like GEOINT, MASINT does not provide access to human thought processes. So it also can't usually provide intent or predictive intelligence.

Following are three general categories that describe the intelligence value of MASINT. It is a primary source for a number of important intelligence issues. For others, it usually is not a primary source but contributes to the intelligence picture and on occasion becomes a critical source. And for some issues, it is seldom a contributor but may occasionally provide insights.

MASINT as a Primary Source

Situational awareness and missile warning. MASINT provides situational awareness to support national policy decisions, military operations, and law enforcement operations. It is especially useful for providing battlespace situational awareness—that is, identifying the operational status of both friendly and hostile units, monitoring force movements, and for battle damage assessment. Fortuitous or planned collection from areas near underground facilities can provide information on the facility's activity. A particularly important category of situational awareness that MASINT provides is that of indications and warning (I&W), particularly that of missile attacks. OPIR and radar MASINT, for example, have long provided I&W intelligence since ballistic missiles were first developed as major weapon systems capable of carrying explosive warheads. Unattended sensors have long provided situational awareness concerning movement of people and supplies for both military operations and nonmilitary applications, such as smuggling activities.

Arms control and treaty monitoring. MASINT has become increasingly important in arms control and treaty monitoring, particularly treaties meant to limit development of ballistic missiles capable of delivering WMDs. It allows monitoring of transportation of suspect materials from processing sites to disposal areas. It identifies materials that are crossing borders. It provides indications as to whether hazardous materials are being stored safely. It identifies excess production of suspect materials.

Environment and natural resources. MASINT, in conjunction with GEOINT, provides warning of environmental problems such as desertification, climate change, and industrial pollution. It may provide the first indication of natural or man-made water diversion, forest fires, volcanic activity, ash cloud formation, etc. During the 1990s, then senator Al Gore initiated an Environmental Task Force (ETF, later renamed Measurements of Earth Data for Environmental Analysis [MEDEA]) in cooperation with the U.S. IC to examine various intelligence sources using internationally acclaimed environmental experts from U.S. agencies and research institutes. Intelligence remote sensing sources, especially MASINT and IMINT, were found to be most useful. The U.S. Geological Survey (USGS) formed the unclassified Hazard Support Center on Maui along with a more robust classified center in Reston, Virginia. Unfortunately, the U.S. budget and security oversight processes had difficulties maintaining this forward-leaning cooperative relationship.

Humanitarian disaster and relief operations. MASINT provides information about on-the-ground conditions after natural and man-made disasters. It is especially important in identifying chemical spills and pollution subsequent to a disaster. Earthquakes are identified and the epicenter located in real time using geophysical MASINT. The formation of tsunamis can be predicted and monitored after earthquakes in or near large ocean areas. Forest fires, volcano eruptions, and the ash clouds from volcanoes are identified using EO MASINT.

MASINT as a Major Contributor

Agriculture and food security. MASINT, working with imagery, can support crop forecasts and so provide advance warning of food production shortfalls.[25]

Terrorism. Materials analysis is an important part of countering IEDs and the explosives used by suicide bombers. It enables identifying the design of these devices and the composition and source of the explosives used.

Transnational organized crime. MASINT has been a valuable source of intelligence in dealing with the narcotics trade by monitoring opium poppy and coca production using EO MASINT. On one occasion in the late 1990s, the CMTCO loaned a multispectral sensor to the U.S. Drug Enforcement Administration (DEA), who were mapping out coca growth in Colombia. Afterward, the DEA shared their results with the CMO. They had been ordered by the government of Colombia not to overfly government-maintained preserves any longer—since they were routinely finding coca plants flourishing throughout the country.

On another occasion, marijuana growers on the big island of Hawaii fired shotguns at a local helicopter being used by NASIC employees while conducting a MASINT-related ETF experiment in Volcano National Park.

In addition, MASINT sensors have helped to identify narcotics shipments, and materials analysis is used to determine the sources of narcotics. MASINT has demonstrated ship-tracking capabilities, making it very relevant to finding and tracking international smuggling operations.

Biological and chemical warfare development and proliferation. The manufacture, testing, movement, and storage of chemical and biological weaponry can often be identified by the unique signatures associated with such weaponry. MASINT can determine whether biological or chemical warfare weapons are appearing in alarmingly large numbers. It can determine when the materials necessary for the creation of biological or chemical warfare weapons are being manufactured or transported.

Infectious diseases and health. Biological material sampling is used to identify diseases. MASINT technical laboratories have a close relationship with the National Center for Infectious Diseases in Atlanta, Georgia, for the purpose of information sharing.

Missile development and proliferation. Ballistic missile tests are conducted from fixed sites that have unique imagery signatures. During these tests, the performance of the missile—characteristics such as range, accuracy, number, and design of warheads—can be determined by radar MASINT and EO MASINT systems. Cruise missile testing can be monitored by radar MASINT and EO MASINT systems to identify flight profiles as well. Rocket engine test stands can be monitored by several classes of MASINT sensors to reveal rocket engine developments for future ICBMs.

Nuclear weapons development and proliferation. The manufacture, movement, and storage of nuclear materials can often be identified by the unique signatures associated with the materials. Nuclear fuel reprocessing facilities are large complexes with distinct signatures, sometimes emplaced in underground facilities.

Human rights and war crimes. Materials science provides forensic evidence of war crimes, much as it does in law enforcement.

Energy security. Oil and gas drilling, and damage to or disruption of existing extraction or refining facilities, can usually be assessed using MASINT in conjunction with imagery.

Advanced conventional weapons development and proliferation. The production, deployment, testing, and proliferation of conventional weapons can be monitored using MASINT disciplines such as RADINT and EO MASINT. The MASINT products directly support defense acquisition programs, especially MASINT signatures that support the detection, classification, or identification of noncooperative targets beyond visual range. MASINT signatures, along with imagery, are critical to the development and successful operation of modern precision weapons.

Foreign military combat capabilities, operations, and intentions. MASINT can provide some specialized details about weaponry; radar MASINT and EO MASINT can identify artillery fire, direction of fire, and location of active artillery in addition to that of missiles. Increasingly, tactical weaponry relies on the existence of unique signatures for targeting. The F-22 Raptor fighter aircraft, for example, uses infrared signatures to target opposing aircraft and so must maintain a current signature library for rapid identification of both threats and friendly aircraft.

Emerging and disruptive technologies. These technologies generally are assessed using other INTs; however, exotic weapons, such as lasers and DEWs that have the potential to be "game changers" on the battlefield are indeed detectable by MASINT sources and methods. During the Cold War, many technologies and concepts of operations (CONOPs) were developed to remotely detect and characterize DEWs under development and testing in remote locations.

MASINT as an Ancillary Source

Military and civilian infrastructure. MASINT can provide some insights into foreign infrastructure. It finds use in assessing factory production.

Leadership intentions. MASINT sometimes can help in inferring leadership intentions. Clandestinely emplaced acoustic MASINT sensors, for example, can provide warning that combat units such as tanks and missile launchers have left a garrison and are deploying for offensive operations.

Counterintelligence. The primary contribution of MASINT here is in identifying an opponent's denial and deception efforts. Camouflage and dummy weaponry often can be identified using optical or radar MASINT.

Cyber threats. RF MASINT may have application here in special cases.

Political stability. MASINT generally cannot contribute other than to provide situational awareness of civil unrest and violence observable by widespread fires and explosions.

Foreign policy objectives and international relations. Foreign policy planning concerns intent, where MASINT usually does not contribute. However, continued testing of particular classes of weapons that MASINT easily can detect, characterize, and identify does provide inferential evidence that the leadership in a country has an intent to either use or sell those weapons.

International trade. Intelligence to support negotiations on trade typically makes little use of MASINT, although understanding the results of natural and man-made disasters can provide quantitative evidence of loss of capacity or stockpile in certain national industries, particularly agriculture.

Economic stability and threat to finance. Threats to economic stability, responses to sanctions, and similar assessments generally will not have a significant MASINT contribution, although MASINT ability to monitor widespread fires and explosions could provide indications of macro changes in closed societies or third world nations with little free press coverage.

Prisoners of war and missing in action. MASINT generally has not contributed in this area. To do so would require some active participation by the prisoners of war (POWs), such as starting large fires or setting off large explosions in order to draw attention of MASINT sensors that may already be actively engaged in support of search and rescue activities. Airborne SAR and thermal IR specialized processing could provide valuable insight as to whether holding facilities in remote areas are occupied or not. This would be a very specialized support activity that might occur in limited cases only.

References

1. John Morris, "MASINT," *American Intelligence Journal* 17, no. 1 & 2 (1996): 24–27.
2. DoD Instruction number 5105.58, April 22, 2009, http://www.dtic.mil/whs/directives/corres/pdf/510558p.pdf.
3. ODNI Memorandum, "Definition of Geospatial Intelligence (GEOINT)," DDNIC 2005–0111, December 1, 2005 (unclassified).
4. State Department Airgram to U.S. Embassy Rome, CA-6065, "Project Clear Sky," February 26, 1968 (retrieved from the National Archives, U.S. Department of State) http://www2.gwu.edu/~nsarchiv/NSAEBB/NSAEBB7/nsaebb7.htm.
5. Stanley G. Zabetakis & John F. Peterson, "The Dyarbakir Radar," *Studies in Intelligence,* https://www.cia.gov/library/center-for-the-study-of-intelligence/kent-csi/vol8no4/html/v08i4a05p_0001.htm.
6. U.S. Army FM 2–0, "Intelligence," March 2010.
7. Ibid.
8. Memorandum by R. C. Maude and D.L. Northrup, AFOAT/1, for Mr. Robert LeBaron, Deputy to the Secretary of Defense for Atomic Energy, "Notes on Technical Cooperation with British and Canadians in the Field of Atomic Energy Intelligence", 21 March 1951 (retrieved from the National Archives, U.S. Department of State)
9. Memorandum from Richard St. F. Post, U.S. State Department Bureau of African Affairs, Office of North African Affairs, to William Witman II, Director, Office of North African Affairs, "Coverage of French Underground Tests," 4 August 1961, and letter from Howard Furnas, Acting Special Assistant to the Secretary for Atomic Energy and Outer Space, to General J. F. Rosenhauser, Chief, Air Force Technical Applications Center, 15 August 1961 (retrieved from the National Archives, U.S. Department of State)
10. Memorandum from Col. Frank Griffith, Deputy Chief, Air Force Technical Applications Center, to Special Assistant for Atomic Energy and Outer Space, "20-4 System Expansion", 4 January 1962 (retrieved from the National Archives, U.S. Department of State)
11. State Department Circular Telegram 1444 to Various Embassies, "Project Clear Sky," 6 February 1964 (National Archives, U.S. Department of State)
12. State Department Airgram CA-3143 to U.S. Embassy, Buenos Aires, 17 September 1965 (retrieved from National Archives, U.S. Department of State), http://www2.gwu.edu/~nsarchiv/NSAEBB/NSAEBB7/nsaebb7.htm

13. Mary Welch, "AFTAC Celebrates 50 Years of Long Range Detection," *AFTAC Monitor* (October 1997): 8–32.
14. http://www.afit.edu/en/docs/CMSR/intelligence_What%20is%20MASINT.pdf
15. *Lincoln Laboratory Journal*, v. 12, no. 2, 2000, pp. 275-76, accessed at https://www.ll.mit.edu/publications/journal/pdf/vol12_no2/12_2widebandradar.pdf
16. U.S. House of Representatives, Permanent Select Committee on Intelligence Staff Study, "IC21: The Intelligence Community in the 21st Century," June 5, 1996.
17. William B. Scott, "Russian Pitches Common Early Warning Network," *Aviation Week and Space Technology,* January 9, 1995, 46–47.
18. Weebau Spaceflight Encyclopaedia, "Prognoz (US-KMO, 71KH6)," http://weebau.com/satcosmos/prognoz.htm.
19. "PLA Air Defence Radars," Technical Report APA-TR-2009–0103, January 27, 2014, http://www.ausairpower.net/APA-PLA-IADS-Radars.html#mozTocId663922.
20. "Russia Activates New Long-Range Radar," *IHS Jane's 360,* March 27, 2014, http://www.janes.com/article/31614/russia-activates-new-long-range-radar.
21. William B. Scott, "Russian Pitches Common Early Warning Network," *Aviation Week and Space Technology,* January 9, 1995, 46–47.
22. National Research Council, National Academies Press, "The Comprehensive Nuclear Test Ban Treaty—Technical Issues for the United States," Washington, DC: National Academies Press (2012): 36.
23. Vitaly V. Adushkin and Vadim A. An, "Teleseismic Monitoring of Underground Nuclear Explosions at the Nevada Test Site from Borovoye, Kazakhstan," *Science & Global Security* 3 (1993): 289–309.
24. Scott, "Russian Pitches Common Early Warning Network."
25. "USSR: A Third Consecutive Crop Failure," *CIA Intelligence Memorandum,* August 1981, http://www.foia.cia.gov/sites/default/files/document_conversions/89801/DOC_0000498196.pdf.

7

Managing Collection

As may be expected, managing intelligence collection can be a daunting task, on multiple levels. There are challenges not only in managing each individual intelligence collection discipline (INT) but also in managing the overall collection array so that it operates to maximum effectiveness and utility.

Each of the INTs is managed individually and yet they are also managed together, at the same time. Each of the INTs is considered a "stovepipe" (or, more comically and more cynically, "a cylinder of excellence"). Each stovepipe is overseen by a collection manager:

- Geospatial Intelligence (GEOINT): Director, National Geospatial-Intelligence Agency (NGA)
- Signals Intelligence (SIGINT): Director, National Security Agency (NSA)
- Human Intelligence (HUMINT): Director, Central Intelligence Agency (CIA)
- Open Source Intelligence (OSINT): Director, CIA
- Measurement and Signature Intelligence (MASINT): Director, Defense Intelligence Agency (DIA)

Several anomalies leap out. GEOINT and SIGINT are rather straightforward. Much of HUMINT comes from the CIA but not all of it. The Federal Bureau of Investigation (FBI), DIA, Drug Enforcement Administration (DEA), and State Department all conduct types of HUMINT. CIA is charged with overseeing all of it and with making decisions about who will collect HUMINT if there is more than one possibility. OSINT is largely located in the Open Source Center (OSC), which belongs to the director of National Intelligence (DNI) but comes under the Director of the Central Intelligence Agency (DCIA) as the executive agent. Moreover, many analysts also collect the OSINT they need on their own, which is unique among all of the INTs. MASINT comes under the director of the DIA, but a fair amount of MASINT is conducted by NGA in a very awkward arrangement.

This stovepipe approach is necessary at some level because each INT functions and behaves differently. For each to operate at maximum utility, knowledgeable people need to be in charge. But the stovepipe approach also increases the difficulty in managing collection on a broader basis or in trying to achieve the synergies between and among INTs that can be so vital to analysts. One must also remember that there are stovepipes within the stovepipes when one considers the various types of SIGINT or GEOINT or MASINT, further complicating the management picture. Similarly, HUMINT may be conducted for either foreign intelligence or law enforcement purposes, each of which has distinct operating rules.

Although functional management is a relatively recent term, it is not a new concept within the U.S. Intelligence Community (IC). Its origins date back to the establishment of the IC. To deal with the competing needs for the collection product, the director of Central Intelligence (DCI) established interagency committees soon after the CIA was established in 1947. For example, the SIGINT Committee, headed by a DCI official and with membership from all the IC agencies, reviewed, approved, and established the priority for all intelligence requirements that could be satisfied by the collection of SIGINT. The Committee on Imagery Requirements and Exploitation (COMIREX) did the same for satellite imagery.

Out of this system there evolved a new hybrid management model called "functional management." The Department of Defense (DoD) assigned to DIA the budget planning authority for general military intelligence in the mid-1970s. The director of DIA was named as the functional manager of the General Defense Intelligence Program (GDIP), which incorporated the non-SIGINT programs of DIA and the four services. The director of NSA became the functional manager for SIGINT, with oversight and influence over the allocation of funds and program priorities for SIGINT efforts in the services, the National Reconnaissance Office (NRO), and CIA.

The functional management structure has continued and expanded since the establishment of the DNI in 2004. Within the IC, there are now numerous functional managers for different collection disciplines. The director of NGA is the GEOINT functional manager and has cognizance over GEOINT activities that are conducted outside of NGA by all of the military services, DIA, CIA, the NRO, FBI, and a host of other government agencies—not all of whom are intelligence organizations (the U.S. Geological Survey [USGS], for example). The functional manager retains responsibility for satisfying collection requirements for that discipline. The director of NSA is invested with the responsibility to meet the requirements of all customers of SIGINT. NGA is responsible for managing imagery requirements. The National Clandestine Service (NCS), which reports to the DCIA, is responsible for clandestine human source requirements.

The functional management approach, again, is a hybrid model; it does not give the functional manager total management control. The functional manager must rely on persuasion and on cooperation by independent organizations. Functional management is a compromise between organizational management prerogatives and technical management of similar functions.

Design and Budget

One of the most difficult aspects of managing collection is designing new systems and budgeting for them. Among the issues to be considered are the state of current or expected technology and the issues that will likely be most important when the new system is put into place. With the exception of OSINT, there are significant time lags involved. Large overhead systems take on the order of ten to twelve years to be built. So determining what to build becomes much more difficult when you are asked to think about the likely set of intelligence priorities that will be most important ten years out. (If we just look at the past quarter century, we can see a series of changes, each of which had implications for intelligence collection: the fall of the Soviet Union, the rise of China, the rise of Jihadist terrorism, the Arab Spring, and Russian revanchism.) There is a certain amount of guesswork involved. Also, technologically, designs have to be frozen at some point and systems built. So it is likely that launched systems will usually lag behind the technology available at the time of launch, which cannot be included at that point. Therefore, policymakers in the executive branch and Congress are deciding to spend budget dollars on systems from which they will likely never see results.

HUMINT is somewhat different. Collectors need about five to seven years of training before they are fully capable. Much of the skills they need will be generic. But language skills are crucial and specific. Years may be spent gaining proficiency in a language that ceases to be important in terms of the intelligence target.

The Role of the Director of National Intelligence

The position of DNI was created by the Intelligence Reform and Terrorism Prevention Act of 2004 (IRTPA). The authorities of the DNI over IC organizations are defined by the IRTPA and by a series of executive orders. Executive Order (EO) 12333, issued in 1981, defined the authority of the IC head (then, the DCI). It was amended by EO 13355 in 2004 and by EO 13470 in 2008 to strengthen the role of the DNI. The IRTPA and subsequent executive orders give the DNI substantial powers within the national IC to manage and coordinate the production of finished intelligence. But DNI authorities in the realm of intelligence collection are less clear and arguably inadequate. Two reasons for this are the management structure of the collection organizations and the differing legal authorities under which these organizations operate.

The DNI was given some authority over the senior officials of the various departments comprising the IC. For example, EO 13470 provided that the DNI was responsible for ensuring the deconfliction, coordination, and integration of all intelligence activities conducted by an IC element or funded by the National Intelligence Program.[1] The provisions of EO 13470, though, expressly assign collection responsibilities to the various agencies. Except for the CIA, these agencies report to department heads (in most cases, to the secretary of Defense). The only intelligence agency head for whom the DNI has sole authority to recommend removal is the DCIA. For all others, the department head—again, usually the secretary of Defense— recommends removal, with DNI concurrence. For this reason, the secretary of Defense is often referred to within the IC as the "800-pound gorilla" in matters concerning intelligence writ large.

The legal authorities for collection add another layer of complexity. The CIA, the FBI, the U.S. Department of Homeland Security (DHS), and the U.S. military all collect intelligence. But their collection efforts are bounded by different laws. The CIA operates under Title 50 of the U.S. Code. The FBI collection is governed by U.S. Code Title 28. DHS collection is governed by U.S. Code Title 6. The military services—including NSA, NGA, DIA, and the armed forces branches—operate under U.S. Code Title 10. Each of these titles provides different guidance on how collection and other operations are to be conducted. Managing the conflicting legal guidance among these IC elements logically should be a responsibility of the DNI, but in practice, each agency follows its own rules as defined in the appropriate part of the U.S. Code.

Tasking, Processing, Exploitation, and Dissemination

As we have discussed in this book, each INT has its own variation on a process known as TPED (tasking, processing, exploitation, and dissemination):

- *Tasking:* Being told what needs to be collected
- *Processing:* Converting the raw intelligence into something that can be analyzed.
- *Exploitation:* Beginning to determine what the collected intelligence means
- *Dissemination:* Sending out the intelligence either to analysts or perhaps to a policymaker

Again, this all seems rather straightforward, but it is not.

Tasking

Tasking is of tremendous importance as everything else depends on this. The differences among collection systems matter a great deal at this point. For example, the capital city of a hostile state may be targeted for SIGINT collection that will capture intelligence across several issues: internal politics and economics, foreign policy decisions, military issues, and perhaps support for terrorism or weapons of mass destruction (WMD) programs. GEOINT targeted against that same nation will be less broadly cast but will look at specific areas or sites for the activity of interest. Finally, HUMINT must be more focused. You cannot drop a clandestine officer in the capital and say, "Get what you can on anything." They need to have "vectoring" by specific topics, issues, people, or institutions.

Tasking occurs at multiple levels. At the national level, collection tasking is determined on macro terms by the National Intelligence Priorities Framework (NIPF), which is managed by the DNI. Instituted in 2003 by DCI George Tenet under President George W. Bush, the NIPF is the mechanism by which the DNI receives intelligence priorities from the most senior policymakers, the members of the National Security Council (NSC), including the president. The NIPF is a list of issues that are grouped by priority (the president's issues go first) and by the degree to which these issues threaten U.S. national security. The NSC reviews the NIPF annually. The DNI staff makes adjustments each quarter as priorities and events change.

One of the major breakthroughs resulting from the NIPF was a means of addressing the "swarm ball" problem. Swarm ball refers to the tendency for each INT to volunteer eagerly to provide intelligence on a "hot" topic whether or not they have any relevant capability. For example, cyberspace is a topic of major concern, but little will likely be gotten from GEOINT. This behavior, which is driven largely by concerns about visibility and future budgets, is called swarm ball because it resembles how young children play soccer—everyone swarms on the ball regardless of their assigned position. When the NIPF was first instituted, the managing official, then the assistant director of Central Intelligence for Analysis and Production, assured each of the collection managers that they would not be penalized for not collecting on certain issues if their INT had little to offer. Each priority item was reviewed to determine which INTs would be expected to collect and which would not. One of the results of this agreement and review was the ability to collect on all of the issues in the NIPF to some degree, rather than having some issues go completely without collection support.

Responsibility for overseeing collection on each priority devolves to the national intelligence managers (NIMs). There are NIMs for regions and NIMs for functional areas, like WMD, terrorism, etc. The NIMs are responsible for ensuring that proper collection and analytic resources are brought to bear on their issue in an integrated manner. They are also tasked with creating Unified Intelligence Strategies for their portfolio.

The NIMs can be seen as a partial compromise between centralized management and decentralized operation of intelligence activities. They are the "go-to" officials on both collection and analysis for their specific subject, but they have no management authority to execute collection; their roles mostly involve conducting studies and analyses. Management of collection activities remains with the agency heads who are functional managers.

From 1997, there had been assistant directors of Central Intelligence for Collection and for Analysis and Production. After 2005 and the creation of the DNI, there were deputy DNIs for Collection and for Analysis.

DNI James Clapper abolished these positions as he believed they did not promote the intelligence integration that is the hallmark of his tenure. There is validity to this view, but it also means that there is no senior official dedicated to day-to-day oversight of all the collection. Much of the joint responsibilities for collection and analysis fall to the deputy director of National Intelligence for Intelligence Integration (DDII) but some question whether this is a manageable portfolio in and of itself and especially with the DDII's other duties.

Finally, it is important to understand that the NIPF is not a predictive document—that is, it is not attempting to forecast which issues will be of greatest concern over the next year or even next quarter. The NIPF is an effort to get guidance from the most senior policymakers on their concerns and then translate these into intelligence collection and analysis requirements. Inevitably, issues will arise that were not given high priority during the NIPF deliberations or will occur in regions that had been of little interest. This has been happening with some regularity recently in central Africa—Mali and Nigeria, for example. These "ad hocs," as they are sometimes called, will move to the top of the priority list for a while and will need to be addressed with collection assets that can only be taken from other issues or regions.

Again, the NIPF handles tasking at the national level. Collection tasking also takes place at other levels. For example, many collection assets are at the theater or tactical level and come under various COCOMs. Their J-2, or senior intelligence officer, will be tasking collection to meet the specific needs of that commander, which will be driven by the COCOMs' responsibilities and by events in that theater. For example, during the 1990s, parts of Europe were among the most violent places on Earth, thus demanding more collection. This arrangement can become problematic when there is a crisis in a regional COCOM. The commander will typically believe that his region is now the most important one of all and will seek not only all of his COCOM collectors to be working but will try to task national assets as well. However, what may seem like a raging regional issue may be seen as less crucial to policymakers in Washington, who may not wish to divert resources to that command. Depending on the nature of the issue and the collection platforms at stake, adjudication can take place either within the DoD or at the NSC level.

Below the COCOM level, there will be several military levels for tasking, going down to small units engaged in hostile areas.

Tasking decisions all take place within zero-sum games. There is no reserve collection capability on hand that can be rushed in during a crisis. The spaceborne array cannot suddenly be increased by launching more satellites (although this was Soviet practice, given their less capable satellites). HUMINT collectors are not easily shifted from one region to another given the requirements for language skills, cover stories, etc. Each decision to collect more here must deprive collection elsewhere. There are winners and losers, and the likely duration of a crisis can also become a factor in collection resource allocation.

Processing and Exploitation

Processing and exploitation (P&E) are two separate stages, but they are closely related and tend be treated as one. All collection needs to be processed, whether it is converting zeroes and ones into images or sounds or HUMINT collection into a report, or OSINT assessing the significance of news articles. Each of the chapters has discussed the peculiar processing issues for each INT. There is a tendency to think of processing only as it relates to the technical INTs, but it also relates to HUMINT and OSINT, as has been discussed.

The major issue for P&E is how much of it one can do against the vast amount of material that has been collected, especially for the technical INTs and for OSINT. There is no expectation that everything that is collected will be processed and exploited, but there has long been recognition that there is a strong imbalance in favor of collection at the expense of P&E. At some level, this makes little sense because the collected intelligence that is not processed and exploited has the same utility as the intelligence that was not collected in the first place—none.

The priorities for what gets processed and exploited should follow those for what gets collected. Key issues or targets should either be processed or exploited first or in greater volume than less important ones. This tends to be the case most of the time, using some of the techniques (such as keyword searches for communications intelligence, or COMINT, or specific imagery signatures for GEOINT) noted in the chapters. Again, one can differentiate between the three technical INTs that rely on technical means for processing and HUMINT and OSINT, which rely more on human beings.

Exploitation is a more iterative process as it is a series of refinements— first cut, second cut, etc. Again, this is more of an issue with the technical INTs. There has been a long debate within parts of the U.S. IC as to whether those individuals performing first-cut exploitation were analysts—a prejudice held by some all-source analysts. The view here is that of course they are analysts—in this case, single-source analysts. One can be doing analysis at the single-source, multi-INT, or all-source level.

One issue within the exploitation process is the tendency to do all of the refining possible and then send out the product for dissemination. Gen. Michael Hayden, when he was director of the NSA, used to say, "Get the intelligence out to the right as soon as it is useful to someone." What Hayden meant was that if the exploited intelligence was of use to some policymaker or consumer at the first cut of exploitation, it should be sent out, rather than wait until all exploitation had been completed. Still, this tendency to disseminate only at the end of all exploitation continues to some degree.

Dissemination

Again, this part of the process seems rather simple. Once the intelligence has been collected, processed, and exploited, send it out to those who need it—analysts, policymakers, or both. But dissemination raises the issues of clearances and compartments. Who is cleared for which intelligence? Who needs to see which intelligence and how quickly?

The entire security system of classification is based on the degree of harm that would be done if the material in question were leaked or lost. In other words, the protection of sources and methods, one of the crown jewels of intelligence, drives the security system. Everyone who is granted a clearance takes an oath to protect classified information. But only the DNI is responsible in law for the protection of sources and methods. (The president is not, at least not in law.)

For decades, this system operated on the principle of "need to know." This allowed intelligence to be restricted, which was both a good and bad thing as it also occasionally excluded some people whose need should have been established. But, by the late 1990s, many in U.S. intelligence recognized that important synergies were being lost and that some necessary intelligence was not being shared under "need to know." The IC progressed to "need to share" and, finally, under DNI Mike McConnell, "responsibility to provide." This last formulation was a significant change, as it placed a positive obligation on people to share their intelligence. However, in the aftermath of the Bradley Manning and Edward Snowden leaks where the two men had access to a great deal of intelligence on classified information technology (IT) systems, the emphasis on intelligence sharing is likely to be scaled back. The tension between sharing and security remains and can never be wholly resolved. Central to these issues is the following question: Whose intelligence is it? For many years, the agencies collecting and providing the intelligence asserted ownership and doled out the intelligence accordingly. Perhaps nothing underscored this view more than the classification marking "ORCON" or "originator control." ORCON means that any additional use of the intelligence, including in other documents, must be approved by the entity with which the intelligence originated. This designation has been used in the case of sensitive sources and methods, especially by NSA. The possibility of ORCON impeding intelligence sharing is obvious. So, the IC has also tried to get away from the concept of "data ownership" and to one of "data stewardship." As with many other issues in intelligence, this is a matter of continuing debate and modification.

Congress and Collection

This book is about each of the INTs, how they work, their strengths, and their weaknesses. We would be remiss, however, if we did not also discuss the role played by Congress in managing collection.

Ultimately, the size, shape, and capabilities of U.S. intelligence are determined by the Congress through the budget process. The president sends his budget to Congress in January or February, offering his preference on budget allocations for all executive branch activities, including intelligence. But the actual decisions are made by Congress through the budget authorization and appropriations process. Authorizing committees create programs, including those that encompass the collection capabilities discussed in this book. Appropriations committees fund these programs. This is a complex and time-consuming process created to safeguard various interests in Congress, not to create a streamlined and efficient budget system. The end result is that many different committees will have a hand in shaping collection capabilities, although the main ones are House and Senate Intelligence, House and Senate Armed Services, and House and Senate Appropriations. The following chart offers a slightly more refined breakdown by INT:

INT	Authorizing Committees	Appropriations Subcommittees
HUMINT	House and Senate Intelligence; House and Senate Armed Services; House and Senate Judiciary (FBI and DEA)	House and Senate Defense; House and Senate Justice
GEOINT	House and Senate Intelligence; House and Senate Armed Services	House and Senate Defense
SIGINT	House and Senate Intelligence; House and Senate Armed Services	House and Senate Defense
MASINT	House and Senate Intelligence; House and Senate Armed Services	House and Senate Defense
OSINT	House and Senate Intelligence	House and Senate Defense

It is important to remember that Congress does more than approve a certain amount of money for various programs. Congress can also play a role in shaping those programs in terms of capabilities. Here are some examples:

- In the late 1980s, as the United States and the Soviet Union neared the completion of two major arms control treaties, Intermediate-Range Nuclear Forces Treaty and the Strategic Arms Reduction Treaty (START), Senate Intelligence Committee chairman David Boren (D-OK) insisted that the United States purchase additional intelligence satellites to ensure sufficient monitoring capabilities for these treaties. Even though Reagan administration officials believed that these additional satellites were not necessary, they recognized that purchasing them was part of the price of Senate agreement to the treaties.

- In the mid-1990s, the House Intelligence Committee wanted to create a more diversified collection array with both the current big satellites and some smaller satellites ("small sats"). DCI John Deutch opposed the idea, even though a study that he had commissioned supported it. The initiative was not passed.
- In a reversal, a few years ago, the Senate Intelligence Committee became the small satellites advocates, with the House Intelligence Committee being less supportive. At one point, this difference prevented the passage of the intelligence authorization bill.
- In the aftermath of the 9/11 terrorist attacks, Congress passed the USA PATRIOT Act (Uniting and Strengthening America by Providing Appropriate Tools Required to Intercept and Obstruct Terrorism), which provided the legal basis for the signals collection programs later leaked (along with much else) by Edward Snowden. In 2014, the House passed legislation limiting the scope of those programs and sent the bill to the Senate.

In making these budget decisions, Congress faces the same uncertainties about future needs as do executive branch officials. Congress can also shape collection through its funding of the NRO, which will determine not only future collection platforms but the ability to launch them.

U.S. intelligence operates by license and permission from the American people. Congress is the expression of this license and permission. Intelligence officers and policymakers may not always like it or agree, but there is no alternative to operating all of intelligence in this manner in a democracy.

Looking Ahead

We have tried to give the reader a more detailed understanding of each INT and how it operates. We will close by pointing out some trends or issues that may shape intelligence collection over the next several years.

- The bulk collection program run by NSA and leaked by Edward Snowden will be revised not because they were found to be illegal but because the political support for them has changed.
- The Obama administration's "rebalance to the Pacific" and a more revanchist Russia will likely affect NGA more than other collectors. The heavy emphasis of NGA on unmanned aerial vehicles (UAVs) will come to an end because of the new targets. We operate UAVs with impunity in permissive areas in Southwest Asia and East Africa. The parts of China and Russia in which we are most interested are not accessible to UAV flights along coasts and borders and certainly are not permissive environments that will allow intrusion by airborne (as opposed to satellite) platforms. Therefore, there likely will have to be a shift back to relying more on space-based systems.

- Several factors will affect HUMINT cover. As noted, social media has created issues. Most people recruited into the NCS (or any other job anywhere) will likely have years of public profiles available on Facebook or similar platforms. This makes the creation of cover more difficult and may necessitate a second profile once the officer is in place. The widespread use of biometric data in passports will also make cover more difficult, until the officer gets to his or her destination.

- Other nations go to great lengths either to avoid being collected against or to transmit false intelligence. These two techniques are called denial and deception, or D&D. Obviously, such techniques benefit from leaks about U.S. intelligence capabilities. Finding D&D programs is also difficult as they are inevitably clandestine if not covert. There is a morbid joke among D&D analysts: "We have never discovered a successful D&D program." D&D will continue to be a challenge for intelligence collection.

In sum, intelligence collection must be an ongoing, dynamic activity if it is to keep abreast of new policymaker demands or interests, changing geopolitical issues, and the promise of new technologies. Management of collection is never at rest.

Reference

1. Executive Order 13470, Part IV, August 4, 2008, http://www.fas.org/irp/offdocs/eo/eo-13470.pdf.

Index

NOTE: Pages with boxes, figures, and tables are identified as (box), (fig.), and (table).